Physical Education for Children With Moderate to Severe Disabilities

Michelle Grenier, PhD
University of New Hampshire

Lauren J. Lieberman, PhD
The College at Brockport, State University of New York

Editors

HUMAN KINETICS

Library of Congress Cataloging-in-Publication Data

Names: Grenier, Michelle, 1956- author. | Lieberman, Lauren J., 1965- author.
Title: Physical education for children with moderate to severe disabilities /
  Michelle Grenier, PhD, University of New Hampshire, Lauren J. Lieberman,
  PhD, The College at Brockport, State University of New York.
Description: Champaign, IL : Human Kinetics, [2018] | Includes
  bibliographical references and index.
Identifiers: LCCN 2017016103 (print) | LCCN 2017038545 (ebook) | ISBN
  9781492544982 (ebook) | ISBN 9781492544975 (print)
Subjects: LCSH: Physical education for children with disabilities--United
  States.
Classification: LCC GV445 (ebook) | LCC GV445 .G736 2018 (print) | DDC
  371.9/04486--dc23
LC record available at https://lccn.loc.gov/2017016103

ISBN: 978-1-4925-4497-5 (print)

Copyright © 2018 by Michelle Grenier and Lauren J. Lieberman

All rights reserved. Except for use in a review, the reproduction or utilization of this work in any form or by any electronic, mechanical, or other means, now known or hereafter invented, including xerography, photocopying, and recording, and in any information storage and retrieval system, is forbidden without the written permission of the publisher.

The web addresses cited in this text were current as of May 2017, unless otherwise noted.

Acquisitions Editor: Ray Vallese; **Senior Developmental Editor:** Bethany J. Bentley; **Managing Editor:** Anna Lan Seaman; **Copyeditor:** Patsy Fortney; **Indexer:** Dan Connolly; **Permissions Manager:** Dalene Reeder; **Graphic Designer:** Dawn Sills; **Cover Designer:** Keri Evans; **Photograph (cover):** ©Lauren Lieberman and Maleda Funk.; **Photographs (interior):** Human Kinetics, unless otherwise noted; **Photo Production Manager:** Jason Allen; **Senior Art Manager:** Kelly Hendren; **Illustrations:** © Human Kinetics; **Printer:** McNaughton & Gunn

Printed in the United States of America   10 9 8 7 6 5 4 3 2 1

The paper in this book is certified under a sustainable forestry program.

Human Kinetics
P.O. Box 5076
Champaign, IL 61825-5076
Website: www.HumanKinetics.com

In the United States, e-mail info@hkusa.com or call 800-747-4457.

In Canada, e-mail info@hkcanada.com.

In Europe, e-mail hk@hkeurope.com.

For information about Human Kinetics' coverage in other areas of the world,
please visit our website: **www.HumanKinetics.com**

E6968

Michelle would like to dedicate this book to David, who is always there to provide support and encouragement. This book is also dedicated to her mother, Micheline, who at 87, continues to persist!

Michelle would also like to thank Dr. Lauren J. Lieberman for her contributions, positive energy, and mentorship.

Lauren would like to dedicate this book to Dr. Monica Lepore. Monica has been a teacher, mentor, and dear friend for many, many years, and this book would not have been possible without her.

Lauren would also like to thank Dr. Michelle Grenier for her unwavering passion, dedication, and commitment to all children. This book would not have been possible without her efforts and vision.

Contents

Foreword

Eli A. Wolff
Brown University

Mary A. Hums
University of Louisville

Students with moderate to severe disabilities are often the most marginalized, stigmatized, and invisible children in the school setting, particularly within physical education. They may experience separation from their classmates because their teachers are unsure about how to fully include them and because other students may feel uncomfortable or fearful around them. However, the walls created by these perceptions are illusory and need not stand for long, once a common ground of understanding is reached. This insightful and necessary book will help instructors bring students with moderate to severe disabilities into the fold, creating greater visibility and improved educational opportunities.

The pages of this book open the discourse on fostering more inclusive physical education environments for all students. With increased awareness and practical tools and strategies for teaching students with moderate to severe disabilities in physical education, instructors can proactively and intentionally create inclusive communities for students with and without disabilities, in and out of the gym, the classroom, and the school.

The authors who contributed to this textbook are global leaders in advancing inclusion for students with disabilities in physical education, and their work has inspired numerous scholars and students worldwide. They have been at the forefront of putting inclusive physical education, physical activity, and sport into action through research and education. The UNESCO Charter of Physical Education, Physical Activity and Sport and the United Nations Convention on the Rights of Persons with Disabilities come to life through the knowledge shared in the pages that follow.

This book is essential reading for all educators, including physical education and adapted physical education teachers, as well as parents and students in training to teach physical education. The authors are tearing down the walls of segregation and ignorance that have kept students with moderate to severe disabilities on the sidelines. The terms *sport* and *moderate to severe disabilities* may appear to be polar opposites at first glance. Viewing the issue of who is included in physical education through the transformational lens of this book, however, can forever change perceptions. Removing the walls of separation leads to fostering fully inclusive physical education, physical activity, and sporting environments.

Preface

With the implementation of Public Law 94-142 (the Education for all Handicapped Children Act, now called the Individuals with Disabilities Education Act, or IDEA) and the subsequent Individuals with Disabilities Education Improvement Act of 2004 (IDEA 2004) in the United States, public schools are expected to provide equitable experiences, accountability, and excellence in education to students with disabilities. There are approximately 6.7 million children and youth with disabilities in public schools across the United States, and many of them have severe disabilities. We estimate the percentage to be somewhere in the vicinity of 5.8 percent of the student population. Despite the positive outcomes of inclusion, research indicates that there is still much to be done when it comes to teaching students with disabilities (Haegele & Sutherland, 2015). Many teachers feel ill prepared and lacking in the skills and content knowledge needed for providing effective programming (Block & Obrusnikova, 2007; Hodge, Ammah, Casebolt, LaMaster, & O'Sullivan, 2004). As a result, students with disabilities are not receiving appropriate and meaningful physical education experiences that include a variety of physical and social opportunities.

Students with moderate to severe disabilities are often characterized by deficits in communication skills, physical and motor development, and self-help skills. As a result, physical education teachers face many challenges when working with students with disabilities. A curriculum focused on sports, large class sizes, and a lack of support can also make it difficult for teachers to assess students with disabilities and create appropriate goals (Ryndak, Jackson, & White, 2013).

What many educators do not know is that physical education services, specially designed if necessary, must be made available to every child with a disability to ensure a free, appropriate public education (IDEA, 2004, 121a.307). Access to the curriculum is also a requirement of the Individuals with Disabilities Education Act (IDEA). IDEA states that students, no matter how severe their disabilities, must be given assistance to make the most of the curriculum (Hodge, Lieberman, & Murata, 2012). All students have the right to a free and appropriate education with opportunities to learn across a range of domains including academic, social, and physical (Seymour, Reid, & Bloom, 2009). This book gives teachers, adapted and general physical educators, parents, paraeducators, and special educators the tools they need to teach students with disabilities in all settings.

The editors of this book, Michelle Grenier and Lauren J. Lieberman, solicited the input of experts in the field of general and adapted physical education. Some are practitioners, and others are faculty members in institutions of higher education. The purpose was to ensure that the material could be applied across a number of settings by faculty members as well as preservice and in-service teachers.

This book is divided into three parts. In part I, Michelle Grenier and Lauren J. Lieberman begin chapter 1, Understanding Disabilities and Universal Design for Learning, with an overview of what it means to have a moderate to severe disability, as well as some of the issues and concerns teachers face. In chapter 2, Collaborative Processes in Physical Education, Michelle Grenier and Nancy Miller discuss the need for collaborative teaming and personnel who can create the best possible educational program using a multidisciplinary approach. In chapter 3, Assessment Strategies, Cathy Houston-Wilson and Martin Block outline motivational strategies that provide optimal conditions for assessing student's functional abilities. In chapter 4, Communication Practices That Enhance Participation, Justin A. Haegele, Matthew Mescall, and James Gunther provide a variety of communication practices for enhancing students' participation levels. In chapter 5, Peer Tutoring, Aija Klavina and Lauren J. Lieberman share strategies that promote positive relationships between students with disabilities and their peers. In chapter 6, Paraeducators in Physical Education, Rocco Aiello and Lauren J. Lieberman outline steps for using paraeducators, who we believe are essential for effective instruction. In chapter 7, Creating Accessible Equipment, Sean Healy and Nancy Miller provide a framework for creating equipment that enables students to access the physical education curriculum while working on their individual skills.

Part II provides knowledge for grasping the skills needed to teach students with disabilities. In chapter 8, Foundational Skills and Sensory Integration, Thomas E. Moran and Brad M. Weiner lay the groundwork for identifying skills and skill development related to sensory motor integration through functional analysis. In chapter 9, Disability Sport in Physical Education, Wesley J. Wilson describes the importance of disability sport for students with disabilities. In chapter 10, Modified Programming in Physical Education, Michelle Grenier, Catherine Clermont, and Eilleen Cuell describe a modified physical education program that enables students with and without disabilities to participate in disability sport programming. In chapter 11, Transitioning to Recreational Opportunities Beyond School, Amaury Samalot-Rivera and Rocco Aiello provide ideas on how to ensure that youth with disabilities

transition into the community and actively participate in physical activity with friends and family members. In chapter 12, Aquatics for Students With Disabilities, Pamela Arnhold and David G. Lorenzi outline a comprehensive approach to teaching aquatics.

Part III utilizes the principles of Universal Design to describe activities that can be used in an educational setting. Resources enable educators to become advocates for their students while including transition services and opportunities for continued participation in physical activity.

Lauren and Michelle hope this text connects knowledge, planning, and implementation of educational opportunities. The intent of this text is to inspire professionals to consider the unlimited avenues for participation in sport and physical activity for all students, including those with moderate and severe disabilities. Through the collaborative process and the support of peers and paraeducators, students with disabilities can be a part of educational communities that have not always been available to them.

eBook
available at
HumanKinetics.com

Acknowledgments

Michelle and Lauren would like to thank the very talented and dedicated authors who contributed to this book:

Rocco Aiello, Pamela Arnhold, Martin Block, Catherine Clermont, Eilleen Cuell, James Gunther, Justin A. Haegele, Sean Healy, Cathy Houston-Wilson, Aija Klavina, David G. Lorenzi, Matthew Mescall, Nancy Miller, Thomas E. Moran, Amaury Samalot-Rivera, Brad M. Weiner, and Wesley J. Wilson.

In addition, we would like to thank the teachers who contributed lessons and games:

Toni Bader, Ken Black, Ann Griffin, Sheyla G. Martinez-Rivera, Matthew Mescall, Nancy Miller, Debbie Phillips, Joy Rose, Brad M. Weiner, and Morgan Wescliff.

PART I

Best Practices for Engaging All Students

This book is divided into three parts. Part I (chapters 1 through 7) provides an overview of the moderate to *severe disabilities*. Strategies for working collaboratively and assessing students' functional abilities are discussed. Also addressed are communication, peer tutoring, paraeducator support, and creating accessible equipment.

Understanding Disabilities and Universal Design for Learning

Michelle Grenier
University of New Hampshire

Lauren J. Lieberman
The College at Brockport, State University of New York

Chapter Objectives

By reading this chapter, you will:

▶ Gain an understanding of the term *severe disabilities*.
▶ Identify a variety of adapted physical education options within the least restrictive environment.
▶ Understand the benefits of universal design for learning.

Jaseena is an 11-year-old girl in fifth grade diagnosed with Aicardi syndrome. She is also legally blind. Her new adapted physical education (APE) teacher, Ms. Moore, is experimenting with a number of new activities in an attempt to expand on Jaseena's previous physical education experience, which involved swinging from a suspended swing during each 30-minute session.

Jaseena's fine motor skills are limited; however, there are activities she enjoys. She seems to like using the bowling ramp, although she does not react or look up when the pins crash. Ms. Moore has also learned that Jaseena does not like anything touching her face; nor does she like hand-over-hand assistance when gripping a racket. Jaseena's occupational therapist has recommended continued work on gripping skills despite her lack of enthusiasm for the task. Ms. Moore has also tried a variety of sensory equipment with different textures and sounds, including bells, buttons, scarves, and beanbags. She had limited success with these auditory stimulation strategies.

Ms. Moore would like to increase Jaseena's social interactions by bringing a few other students into the gym when she has her self-contained class, but she is unsure of the steps needed to implement the program. As a new APE teacher, Ms. Moore is seeking activity options and strategies for engaging Jaseena in her APE class.

The term *severe disabilities* refers to extensive difficulties that result in the requirement of significant levels of support for participation in educational settings (Westling & Fox, 2009). Severe disabilities, as defined by the Individuals with Disabilities Education Act (IDEA), typically include the following categories: vision impairments, hearing impairments, dual-sensory impairments, severe autism, significant cognitive impairment, and multiple disabilities (IDEA, 2004).

The term also implies a severe chronic condition attributed to a mental or physical impairment that is likely to continue indefinitely. People considered to have severe disabilities include those with moderate to profound levels of intellectual impairment; difficulties communicating their needs to others; and other concomitant physical, behavioral, sensory, or health impairments (Westling & Fox, 2009).

Those with severe disabilities typically have substantial functional limitations in three or more major life activities that may include self-care, receptive and expressive language, learning, mobility, self-direction, and capacity for independent living. The disability can be acquired or originate at birth (Hodge, Lieberman, & Murata, 2012).

Severe Disabilities

Some of the most common etiologies of severe disabilities are genetic and chromosomal defects, prematurity, complications of pregnancy, and acquired causes. Because the term *severe disabilities* is not one of the 13 special education categories defined under IDEA, it has no specific definition. However, it encompasses the categories of multiple disabilities and deafblindness. A child with severe disabilities is often diagnosed at birth or shortly thereafter. Many children have more than one disability, all of which may stem from a single cause. For example, a child who is born prematurely may have cerebral palsy, a visual impairment, and an intellectual disability, along with a severe seizure disorder. The following are a few of the disabilities seen in children with moderate, severe, or multiple disabilities:

- Angelman syndrome
- Autism
- Cerebral palsy

- CHARGE syndrome
- Chromosomal abnormalities
- Deafness
- Deafblindness
- Intellectual disability
- Prematurity
- Shaken baby syndrome
- Trisomy 18
- Visual impairment

Please note that many of the disabilities previously mentioned may cause a moderate disability, and the child will have more functional ability yet will still have significant needs. In this text, we will refer to children with moderate to severe disabilities as "students with disabilities."

The following descriptions of two disabilities present a picture of the extensiveness of students with severe disabilities.

Chromosomal Abnormalities

Chromosomal abnormalities are rare chromosome disorders resulting from extra, missing, or rearranged chromosome material. Because many genetic abnormalities are rare, parents often experience confusion, limited support, and little information that addresses their concerns (Batshaw, 2002). For example, CHARGE syndrome presents at birth as a collection of physical irregularities. This syndrome is an extremely complex disorder, typically involving extensive medical as well as physical challenges. The following is an explanation of the acronym:

C: Coloboma, a congenital condition resulting from an unusually shaped (teardrop) pupil or other abnormalities of the eye, which contributes to difficulty with vision

H: Heart defects that can range from minor to life-threatening

A: Atresia (Choanal atresia) is a congenital disorder where the back of the nasal passage (choana) is blocked.

R: Delayed physical growth (combined with intellectual impairment in some instances)

G: Genital abnormalities—incomplete or underdeveloped genitals

E: Ear defects—structural deformities that result in hearing loss

Multiple Disabilities

Multiple disabilities are combinations of disabilities, such as intellectual, visual, and orthopedic impairments, that result in extensive educational needs. The National Dissemination Center for Children with Disabilities (usually referred to as NICHCY) lists several common characteristics, including hampered speech and communication skills, challenges with mobility, and a need for assistance in performing everyday activities (Nakken & Vlaskamp, 2007).

Medical problems that can accompany severe disabilities include seizures, eating disorders requiring a feeding tube, breathing issues requiring a tracheotomy, hydrocephalus requiring a shunt, and scoliosis requiring rods in the spine. A close look at the categories of a student's disability can offer ideas for overcoming educational challenges and establishing school services. In addition to the preceding causes, children identified with severe disabilities often have the following characteristics:

- *Varying levels of awareness.* Students with low levels of awareness as a result of hearing, vision, processing, muscular, or expressive issues may not be able to respond well to prompts or instruction. Carpenter and colleagues (2015) described responses as either passive or active. Passive responses are those that are difficult to understand. Active responses include initiation, responsiveness, curiosity, anticipation, and persistence.

- *Limited response repertoires.* A child who understands what someone is asking may not be able to express his or her responses in an understandable way.

- *No coherent system of communication.* Some children have not developed a system of communication that enables them to receive information or express their feelings and needs clearly. Related service providers can contribute to the child's learning profile and assist in identifying communicable behaviors.

Students with severe disabilities often have several medical issues associated with the primary disability. Make sure to read the individual education plan (IEP) to get a complete picture of the child.

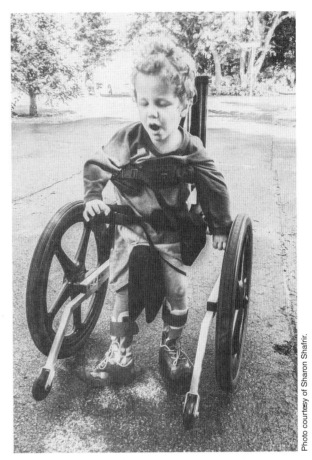

Photo courtesy of Sharon Shafrir.

This student has his own unique way of walking and communicating, and it is important for his team to learn exactly what he needs in order to be successful.

As illustrated in the opening scenario, students with severe disabilities have their own unique characteristics and learning styles. Getting to know them is essential. The next section describes relevant laws and concepts related to students with severe disabilities.

Individuals with Disabilities Education Act

Prior to the passing of legislation in the mid-1970s, students with severe disabilities were routinely excluded from public schools in the United States. The Education for All Handicapped Children Act (EHA) was passed in 1975 and reauthorized as IDEA in 1990, 1997, and 2004. The law outlined the need for an individualized plan of instruction, inclusion in the general education classroom, and parental input.

Every child identified with a disability is required by law to have physical education or adapted physical education services.

Individuals with Disabilities Education Act provided guidelines for identifying and educating students with disabilities while also articulating school systems' responsibility for physically educating children with disabilities. By definition, students with disabilities, as specifically named in the EHA, are required to have physical education.

The term *special education* means specially designed instruction, at no cost to the parents, to meet the unique needs of children with disabilities including classroom instruction, *instruction in physical education* [emphasis added], home instruction, and instruction in hospitals and institutions. (Federal Register, August 23, 1977, p. 42480)

Lawmakers further articulated the importance of physical education:

The Committee is concerned that although these services are available to and required of all children in our school systems, they are often viewed as a luxury for handicapped children. (Federal Register, August 23, 1977, p. 42489)

According to the Individuals with Disabilities Education Act (IDEA, 2004), physical education is defined as the development of physical and motor fitness, fundamental motor skills, and patterns and skills in aquatics, dance, and individual and group games and sports. IDEA also states that students with disabilities must have access to the general curriculum, be involved in the general curriculum, and progress in the general curriculum. When this is accomplished, the outcomes can be academic, social, physical, or a combination of these (Seymour, Reid, & Bloom, 2009).

How and where students with severe disabilities should spend their school days is the subject of policy and practice discussions (McLeskey, Landers, Williamson, & Hoppey, 2012). However, the percentage of students with severe disabilities being educated in general education settings has steadily increased (U.S. Department of Education, 2009). Although a primary purpose of inclusive practices for students with severe disabilities has been the promotion of social skills, active engagement with the curriculum is also a require-

ment. **Individual education plans (IEPs)** often emphasize progress in social and communication skills as a result of opportunities to engage with peers (Kwon, Elicker, & Kontos, 2011).

In recent years, there has been a strong push for students to access the general education curriculum. Although the ability to pay attention to the activities and complete learning tasks may be compromised for students with severe disabilities, without educators (in particular, physical educators and adapted physical educators who can help them build bridges within their communities of learning), they risk continued marginalization and exclusion from mainstream practices (Block & Obrusnikova, 2007). We believe that teachers should create lessons for all students that address SHAPE America's National Standards & Grade-Level Outcomes (2014) for physical education (Couturier, Chepko, & Holt/Hale, 2014). With proper support, students with severe disabilities can work toward achieving appropriate outcomes commensurate with their abilities. For example, if you are teaching basketball to a seventh-grade class, you may reference the following learning outcomes based on the SHAPE America's National Standards & Grade-Level Outcomes: *Dribbles with dominant and nondominant hands* using a change of speed and direction in *a variety of practice tasks* (S1.M8.7). An alternative outcome for a child with severe disabilities, based on assessments, might be to propel an object with appropriate hand release toward a target as independently as possible. Students should not be prevented from accessing content taught to their peers because of an inability to perform age-appropriate skills. Identify the student's functional skills that connect with the curriculum, differentiate practice, and personalize learning. Adopting new teaching strategies and modifying the curriculum to meet the learning needs of the child is essential.

To optimize learning for students with severe disabilities, provide APE services in the Least Restrictive Environment (LRE). LRE typically is described as the most appropriate placement for the students given their skills and abilities. Figure 1.1 identifies some of the educational placements

SHAPE America's National Standards & Grade-Level Outcomes are categorized by numbers that relate to the standard, school level, and grade level (e.g., S1.M8.7).

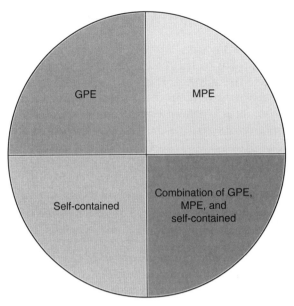

Figure 1.1 Instructional placement options for students with disabilities.

for students with severe disabilities in physical education. These placements are described here:

- General physical education (GPE) class: A class in which appropriate activities are delivered to all students with a range of abilities. Natural proportions within the GPE environment are identified as classes with approximately 10 to 15 percent of students identified with a disability.

- Modified physical education (MPE) class: A mixed-ability inclusive class of 10 to 20 students. Students both with and without disabilities follow the GPE curriculum (Lieberman, Cavanagh, Haegele, Aiello, & Wilson, 2017).

- Self-contained class: This is typically a small group of students with disabilities. The class is designed to support students' particular needs.

- Combination of GPE, modified physical education, and self-contained classes: Instruction can be delivered in any of the preceding settings.

Universal Design for Learning

As educators, we adopt the philosophy that all students are capable of learning, and we advocate for

instructional approaches that consider a range of skills and abilities. **Universal Design for Learning (UDL)** emerged from the field of architectural design when federal legislation began requiring universal access to buildings and other structures for people with disabilities (Rose & Meyer, 2006). Architects began to design accessibility into buildings during their initial design stages rather than retrofitting standard structures. Building on this architectural principle, UDL is a strategy for eliminating barriers to learning that includes Universally Designed Instruction (UDI), Universally Designed Curriculum (UDC), and Universally Designed Assessment (UDA) (Rapp, 2014; Rose & Meyer, 2006). For example, a curb cut enables a student who uses a wheelchair to access a sidewalk while moving outside the school area. Other examples are talking pedometers for people who are visually impaired and task cards for students who are hard of hearing or deaf. Lastly, universal symbols that communicate function, such as restroom signage and sign language, help both those who have trouble reading and those who do not speak the local language (Spooner, Baker, Harris, Ahlgrim-Delzell, & Browder, 2007).

Universally Designed for Learning in GPE means that the physical, social, and learning environments are designed to support diverse learners (Perez, 2014). Universally Designed for Learning is a concept, a set of principles, a framework, and a mindset that supports accessibility for the variety of students in classrooms today. It is achieved by varying lessons to meet the needs of every child. UDL provides alternative methods of instruction (in the broad sense), instruction delivery, materials (equipment), and assessment methods all within the general curriculum while addressing the needs of every student, regardless of ability or disability. To accomplish this, planning is essential (Odom, Brantlinger, Gersten, Horner, Thompson, & Harris, 2005; Rapp, 2014). For example, instructional strategies, such as small groups and peer support, can encourage students to work together. A variety of equipment options can ensure that all students have opportunities for success. Finally, students with severe disabilities can be given the opportunity to achieve age-appropriate outcomes within the physical education setting, such as playing hockey on scooters or practicing gymnastics in stations, addressing a variety of functional levels when teachers consider the learning needs of all their students.

Using UDL effectively occurs during the development of a lesson, not as an afterthought. Keep in mind that you are designing lessons with all possible students in mind. For example, a volleyball unit might include balls of different sizes and textures, a variety of ways to project balls over the net, different service areas, and rule variations. Offer these choices to everyone before the lesson starts, to create a culture of inclusion throughout the school year.

Universal Design for Learning is an efficient way to provide students with access to the physical education curriculum (Lieberman, Lytle, & Clarcq, 2008). It considers the range of students' abilities at the curriculum design stage. This built-in access for a wide range of users—with and without disabilities—is the underlying principle of UDL (Rapp & Arndt, 2012). Part III of this book provides lesson plans that adhere to the principles of UDL.

Summary

Our recommended approach has been to make the physical education curriculum accessible to all. In advocating for this position, we have to ask ourselves how inclusion intersects with access to create a learning environment in which all children can learn best. For some students, the physical education class is a highly stimulating and engaging environment. For others, it may be an overstimulating environment. Additionally, you must weigh the learning needs of the child with a disability against the overall goals of the class. There is no easy way to do this. Fundamental principles such as learning context, teaching skills, and individual needs should guide program development when considering the educational outcomes of students with severe disabilities. The remaining chapters present many useful tools for planning and delivering instruction.

▶ ▶

As the school year progressed, Ms. Moore began attending IEP meetings and working with other team members on a program that addressed Jaseena's learning needs. Eventually, she invited a few of Jaseena's classmates to come into her self-contained class so Jaseena could engage in age-appropriate activities that encouraged communication and friendships with her peers.

Over time, Ms. Moore built a repertoire of activities aligned with Jaseena's IEP goals that transferred to activities beyond the gymnasium. She rented a bike with an attached carriage from a local disability sport organization, which she began using in the spring during the bicycle unit. Ms. Moore taught Jaseena's **para-educator** how to use the bike, so that Jaseena could participate with her peers in general physical education. Jaseena's parents were so happy with her progress that they too rented such a bike for occasional family outings.

Review Questions

1. What is the definition of severe disabilities?
2. What are some of the primary concerns when working with students who have severe disabilities?
3. What are three optional settings for providing APE services?
4. What are some necessary considerations when universally designing a lesson?

Collaborative Processes in Physical Education

Michelle Grenier
University of New Hampshire

Nancy Miller
Newmarket Elementary School, New Hampshire

Chapter Objectives

By reading this chapter, you will:

► Understand the benefits of the collaborative process.
► Identify characteristics that make collaboration successful.
► Describe the use of shared goals in the development of adapted physical education goals.

Ms. Coe is a veteran teacher of 25 years. Throughout her teaching career, she has confidently taught students with various disabilities so that they became active, engaged learners in general physical education (GPE). Her general philosophy has been to provide inclusive physical education with the support of peers and paraeducators.

In preparation for her upcoming school year, Ms. Coe learns that a new second-grade student is entering her program. Natalia has severe and multiple disabilities.

From Natalia's individual education plan (IEP), Ms. Coe learns that she uses a wheelchair, requires the assistance of a full-time paraeducator, and is nonverbal. Ms. Coe also learns that Natalia generally acknowledges being addressed, is right handed, and can grasp with her right hand with assistance. Armed with this knowledge, Ms. Coe begins to write modifications in her GPE lesson for Natalia. Her plan is to share her modifications with Natalia's paraeducator at the start of the school year.

What Ms. Coe fails to understand is that she is setting Natalia up for what she later will call the floating island scenario. The term refers to the isolation a student experiences when working solely with a paraeducator. Although Ms. Coe understands that Natalia is nonverbal, she does not fully comprehend Natalia's mode of communication. This makes it difficult to create meaningful activities that will enable her to engage with her peers. Consequently, Natalia becomes a floating island, roaming about the class without engaging with other class members.

Ms. Coe's limited knowledge of Natalia's communication ability prevented her from understanding, for example, that Natalia could use a noodle to be a tagger in a class game. She also did not realize that Natalia communicates her intentions by looking at either an object or a person. Had Ms. Coe known this, she would have recognized that Natalia has a "voice" and can make decisions for herself. Knowing Natalia's communication style would have enabled Ms. Coe to model appropriate behaviors and skills to the paraeducator and to avoid the "floating island scenario."

Ms. Coe decides to reach out to the IEP team to learn more about her students with disabilities—Natalia, in particular. She believes this is the first step in becoming a more informed teacher.

The Practice of Collaboration

Most general physical education teachers know the developmental process of typically developing children and can plan and teach lessons that support their physical, cognitive, social, and emotional development. However, students with disabilities are distinctly different from their peers. Collaboration on **interdisciplinary teams** helps teachers learn about these students' unique skills and abilities. **Collaboration** refers to the practice of professionals working together to share ideas (Seaman, DePauw, Morton, & Omoto, 2007).

Students with disabilities often have functional, physical, communicative, and cognitive skills that are very different from those of their peers. Collaboration enables you to learn about these students' foundational and functional skills, develop shared goals, and create inclusive learning opportunities.

Every student identified with a disability has a special education team. Team members can include a general education classroom teacher, a GPE teacher, an adapted physical education (APE) teacher, a case manager, an occupational therapist (OT), a physical therapist (PT), a speech therapist (ST), and a teacher of visually impaired (TVI). Parents and administrations are also a part of the team. Collaboration with a special education team provides a holistic perspective of the student because each provider has unique knowledge that contributes to the student's education and well-being. Figure 2.1 provides guidelines for a positive collaborative process.

FIGURE 2.1

Guidelines for Making Collaborative Practice a Positive Experience

- *Build trust with the team.* Ask the educational team if you, as the GPE or APE teacher, can start attending meetings. Let members know that your goal is to better understand the student's abilities and skills to promote learning.

- *Be invested.* Be knowledgeable and ask questions about the student's IEP. Service providers want their students to be successful and are supportive of GPE or APE teachers. One important question to ask is how to reinforce the therapists' goals in GPE.

- *Share goals.* Describe how you will connect what therapists are teaching to your GPE lessons. Explain that the student will have opportunities to make connections, transfer skills, and achieve goals in a variety of settings.

Reach out to the educational team to get the support you need to educate the student inclusively. All team members are invested in working together to ensure the student's success.

In many cases, team members meet weekly to share goals and discuss the student's progress. In this way, they reinforce what and how they teach across sessions. In addition, most providers work on teaching their students skills that can transfer to their lives in the larger community. By becoming part of the team, you have the opportunity to share your insights and practices, become an invested member, and add to the student's learning program.

The benefits of collaboration include the following:

- Gaining a holistic view of the student
- Learning the student's communicative abilities
- Having the opportunity to observe therapists' communication and instructional strategies

- Sharing learning goals with occupational, physical, and speech therapists
- Developing dictionaries of the student's communication behaviors
- Providing opportunities for therapists to co-teach within the GPE environment
- Educating and empowering paraeducators to address APE goals in GPE lessons

By collaborating with Natalia's education team, Ms. Coe learned about her foundational, functional, and communicative skills. She also learned ways to share goals across therapeutic and educational settings to build on Natalia's functional skills.

Becoming Part of the Education Team

Like most GPE teachers, Ms. Coe's primary strategy for including Natalia in her GPE class was to adapt and modify equipment, tasks, and activities. When Ms. Coe started collaborating with the

The physical education teacher works with the physical therapist to infuse physical therapy goals with the physical education goals.

team, one of the first things she wanted to know was how to help Natalia communicate and make choices. Answers to her questions helped her meet Natalia's programmatic needs in GPE. Here are some of the questions Ms. Coe asked the team:

- How does Natalia say hello?
- How does she communicate her wants and needs?
- What are her receptive and expressive communicative behaviors?

Ms. Coe quickly learned many things about Natalia, including the following:

- She has cortical visual impairment, and she sees and processes best in her diagonal field of vision.
- She is right handed.
- She uses her vision to make choices.
- She reaches out to make a choice.
- She moves her head back and forth when she is interested in something.
- She moves her arms and legs when she is really interested in something.
- She smiles when she is enjoying something.
- She puts her head down when she is disinterested or tired.

With this information, Ms. Coe created a **communicative dictionary** for Natalia (Calculator, 2009). The dictionary identified the visual skills, physical gestures, and movement language Natalia uses to communicate, which was instrumental in making her a part of the class. Ms. Coe embedded communicative scripts and cues into her lessons to promote motor development and communication skills (Cervantes, Lieberman, Magnesio, & Wood, 2013; Grenier & Miller, 2015). By becoming familiar with Natalia's communicative dictionary, Ms. Coe was able to make connections between Natalia and her peers.

The following are some elements from Natalia's communicative dictionary:

- Looking at someone or something = wants to engage them in conversation or play.
- Reaching out to touch someone or something = wants to engage them in conversation or play.
- Using her vision and touch = making choices for herself.

- Smiling = recognizes a face or voice; is happy.
- Placing head down = is disinterested or tired.
- Rocking head back and forth = is interested in someone or something.
- Moving arms and legs = is very interested in someone or something.

Physical education is an optimal setting in which students with disabilities can engage in learning with peers. This dynamic environment fosters relationships between peers that enable these students to become active members of the classroom community. As a result of strong advocacy and policy efforts, students with disabilities are now spending more time in inclusive settings to access the general education curriculum (U.S. Department of Education, 2009).

As a GPE teacher, Ms. Coe needed to be knowledgeable about Natalia's skills and abilities to develop goals, instructional strategies, and activity modifications. Evaluating Natalia's current level of development (including behavioral, social, and communicative characteristics) helped Ms. Coe determine which aspects of her curriculum would align with Natalia's learning goals (Kelly, 2011). As she considered her program of instruction, Ms. Coe worked with the collaborative team to identify grade-level outcomes that could be customized to meet the learning goals identified in Natalia's IEP.

Developing Adapted Physical Education Goals Through Shared Goals

Collaboration enabled Ms. Coe to better understand Natalia's skills and communication style while working on the shared IEP goals. **Shared goals** are ability, skill, and educational goals that can be taught and reinforced across a number of settings. To develop shared goals, teachers and therapists need to understand the student's communication style, sensory motor needs, physical skills, cognitive processes, and

Think about the essential skills the student is trying to accomplish, and identify relevant standards for those skills.

interaction patterns. Once Ms. Coe understood the shared goals, she was able to create appropriate and meaningful APE goals connected to SHAPE America's National Standards & Grade-Level Outcomes (2014).

Observing therapists offers Ms. Coe insight into strategies that address the student's needs in a one-on-one setting. In many cases, therapists' goals align with students' APE goals. Table 2.1 presents examples of shared physical education (PE), PT, OT, and speech therapy goals.

Shared goals become the building blocks for developing adapted physical education goals by helping the GPE teacher access the curriculum. In other words, knowing therapeutic and academic benchmarks helps the GPE teacher develop goals that target areas of development that can be reinforced across a number of settings. By aligning with the therapists' and general education teachers' goals, Ms. Coe created opportunities for Natalia to have *equal status relationships* with her peers in the classroom community (Sherrill, Heikinaro-Johansson, & Slininger, 1994).

For example, a speech goal for Natalia is to be able to turn and look at someone who is addressing her three out of five times. The goal is designed to encourage Natalia to listen and respond to her peers. This goal could be extended to an APE goal of initiating conversation and play with peers. For this to happen, Ms. Coe has to coach Natalia's peers in her communication patterns, including vision, body movements, and reaching to touch (see chapter 5, Peer Tutoring). Table 2.2 illustrates how Ms. Coe used shared goals to create APE goals for Natalia in GPE.

Guidelines in the Collaborative Process

The collaborative process improves both the teaching skills and instructional strategies needed to develop APE goals for students with disabilities. The following is a list of essential guidelines in becoming a collaborative team player:

- Make sure to be invited to team meetings.
- Create shared goals with team members to be reinforced throughout the school setting. This enables the student with disabilities to draw on their team members background, knowledge, practice, and abilities.
- Empower and train paraeducators by reviewing and modeling APE goals and facilitating communication between students with disabilities and their peers.
- Debrief with the team about the appropriateness of the shard goals in the program.
- Create stand-alone APE goals—that is, goals that identify target behaviors that will help the student become physically active within GPE and community settings.
- Develop GPE lessons that align with the student's APE goals.
- Share GPE lessons with the educational team, parents, and paraeducator.
- Invite educational team members into the GPE classroom to team-teach or work on shared goals.

TABLE 2.1 Examples of Shared Goals

Therapy goals	Shared goals to access GPE curriculum
PT—Improve postural control, physical endurance, and core and extremity strength with verbal cues and adult manual assist as needed.	GPE—Use prescribed PT flexibility and strength exercises that are commensurate with GPE fitness and yoga activities with verbal cues and adult manual assist.
OT—Work on functional hand use to reach with the right hand to touch and grasp an object or activate a switch (with visual and verbal cues).	GPE—Work on using the right hand to reach and grasp a variety of manipulatives to engage in GPE activities (with visual and verbal cues).
Speech—Will look toward a speaker who is greeting him or her and reach to activate a Big Mack switch to say hello to the speaker (listening and responding, with visual and verbal cues).	GPE—The teacher will train peers who will greet and help students activate a Big Mack switch to say hello to the peer. She will look and reach to grasp a manipulative from a peer who is handing it to her using visual or verbal cues and hand-under-hand assist when needed.

TABLE 2.2   Example APE Goals Based on Shared Goals

Shared goals	Natalia's APE goals
PT/PE—Will be able to sit in a corner seat on the floor with peers, using verbal cues and occasional adult assist to sit upright. Will improve postural control, physical endurance, and core and extremity strength, with verbal cues and adult manual assist as needed.	APE—Will be able to sit in a corner seat on a scooter mat while pushing with her legs to propel herself (using verbal cues and adult assist to sit upright and push off with legs) while participating with peers in GPE scooter activities.
OT/PE—Will work on using her right hand to reach and grasp a variety of manipulatives to engage in GPE activities, with visual and verbal cues and adult hand-under-hand assist as needed.	APE—Will work on using her right hand to reach, grasp, and release a variety of manipulatives to engage in GPE activities. Examples of releasing or letting go: (1) letting go of a ball to have it travel down a ramp used for bowling; (2) letting go of a modified bowstring to shoot an arrow, with visual and verbal cues and adult hand-under-hand assist as needed.
OT/PE—Will look toward a peer who is greeting her and reach to activate a Big Mack switch to say hello to the peer. Will look and reach to grasp a manipulative from a peer who is handing or passing it to her, using visual and verbal cues and adult hand-under-hand assist as needed.	APE—Will initiate conversation and play with a peer in a variety of ways that include (1) making visual contact with a peer using her vision to communicate that she wants to say hello or engage in the activity with the peer, (2) reaching to touch a peer or using body movements or gestures to say hello or engage the peer in the activity, and (3) reaching and touching or grasping a piece of equipment to engage a peer in play. Peers may need adult help to recognize and interpret her initiating communicative behaviors.

Summary

Knowledge of the foundational skills of students with disabilities is essential for gaining a more complete picture of them. Collaboration is an integral part of this process. Remember that each member of the team has a unique skill set that complements the goals of most physical educa-tion or adapted physical education programs. Developing shared goals that cross disciplines is an effective way to bridge communication gaps and provide opportunities for team members to be a part of your program. Students' participation in the physical education program is enhanced by the diverse approach adopted by team members. It is simply a win-win situation.

▷ ▷

Ms. Coe was lucky to be one of those teachers who recognized the value of col-laboration. Her work with Natalia's team enabled her to better understand how Natalia communicated so that she could optimize her skills and abilities. Col-laboration with team members resulted in learning goals that were reinforced across a number of settings. By aligning her goals with those of other members of the IEP team, Ms. Coe created opportunities for Natalia to engage in mean-ingful interactions.

Review Questions

1. How does collaboration benefit a GPE teacher?
2. How does collaboration benefit members of the educational team?
3. What is the most important step for becoming a member of the IEP team?
4. What are shared goals?
5. How can the teacher implement shared goals in APE?

3

Assessment Strategies

Cathy Houston-Wilson
The College at Brockport, State University of New York

Martin Block
University of Virginia

Chapter Objectives

By reading this chapter, you will:

▶ Understand the role assessment plays in educating students with disabilities.
▶ Learn the types of alternative assessments that can be used with students with disabilities.
▶ Know how to use assessment data for program planning and implementation when teaching students with disabilities.

Marin is a nine-year-old girl with spastic cerebral palsy and mild cognitive delays. She uses a wheelchair to ambulate and has a paraeducator with her throughout day. Marin is in a special education class that includes five other students with disabilities part of the day but is included in the same general education class as her peers for music, art, library and technology, physical education, lunch, and recess. In addition to her general physical education (GPE) class, Marin receives adapted physical education (APE) because of her unique motor and learning needs.

Marin's participation in GPE presents unique challenges for her physical education teacher, Ms. Walsh. Ms. Walsh has been teaching general physical education for over 20 years and has received many accolades. However, this is the first year that her school district included students with severe disabilities in general education classes to the maximal extent possible. Ms. Walsh is excited about the prospect of teaching the students but will need some guidance to ensure that Marin receives the best possible educational experience. Ms. Walsh ponders, "Where do I start?"

Ms. Walsh's question is similar to those of many physical education teachers who have the responsibility of educating students such as Marin but have had minimal to no training in APE (Block & Obrusnikova, 2007). Relevant assessments would help Ms. Walsh identify Marin's capabilities and design a meaningful program for her.

Assessment is a process of measuring learning outcomes, which are then reported to students, parents, and administrators. As the cornerstone of effective teaching, appropriate assessments (a) determine the unique physical or motor needs of students with disabilities, (b) assist in the development of physical education goals, and (c) serve as a useful tool for monitoring student progress (Horvat, Block, Kelly, & Croce, 2018).

What determines the effectiveness of an assessment is how accurately it reflects the capabilities of the person being assessed. Traditional assessments such as the TGMD-3 (Test of Gross Motor Development; Ulrich, 2017) do not always accommodate students with disabilities. Even tests that have been developed for students with disabilities, such as the Brockport Physical Fitness Test (Winnick & Short, 2016), are not designed to accommodate students with severe disabilities. Therefore, **alternative assessments** must be considered when teaching students with disabilities. An array of alternative assessments are presented in this chapter. Before exploring them, however, we offer guidelines for testing students with disabilities.

The first step in assessing students with disabilities is collecting general information about primary and secondary disabilities, restrictions or **contraindications,** medications and surgeries that may affect movement and positioning, and any other general health or medical information that might influence how to work with them. For example, some children with severe cerebral palsy develop scoliosis (curvature of the spine), which may be corrected by surgically inserting rods along either side of the spine. These rods may restrict certain movements and may lead to contraindicated movements and positions. Similarly, some children with severe disabilities have feeding tubes that should be properly covered and padded when the children are prone on a mat or placed over a wedge. Students with multiple disabilities may have seizure disorders in addition to physical and cognitive disabilities. Those whose seizures are not well controlled with medication may have restrictions or need extra support in activities such as upright walking or swimming.

> *The first step in assessing students with disabilities is collecting general medical and health information.*

Parents, therapists, school nurses, doctors, and others can provide this information.

Once you have health and background information on your student, you are ready to begin the assessment process. If you have ever had to assess a student with a disability using a traditional assessment, you will agree that the process is frustrating and yields very little usable information. That is why professionals have created alternative assessments that can accommodate students with disabilities.

Alternative assessments reveal what students with disabilities can do and emphasize their strengths rather than their weaknesses. They focus heavily on authentic, or real-world, tasks; that is, those skills that students would do in a sport or recreational activity.

Authentic assessment is an ongoing feedback system that monitors and records student learning and outcomes under what are termed *authentic conditions* (Block, Lieberman, & Connor-Kuntz, 1998). Authentic assessment is conducted in real-life situations and gives students a chance to demonstrate skills, knowledge, and competencies in both age-appropriate and developmentally appropriate functional activities. **Functional activities** are those that occur in the everyday life of the learner. Authentic assessment is a **performance-based approach** to testing, which means that students are evaluated on skills directly related to the curricular content area, keeping in mind their unique needs, interests, and abilities. The results are used to develop appropriate goals as well as a method to evaluate progress and learning. The following section describes a number of ways to assess students with disabilities using an alternative assessment approach.

Functional Assessment of Students With Severe Disabilities

The **functional assessment of students with severe disabilities (FASSD)** is for students with severe disabilities and extremely limited mobility

It is important to assess the functional skills children use daily as well as their level of independence.

(Block, Lauer, & Jones, 2004). It assesses basic functional movement, positioning, mobility, physical fitness, and sensory abilities.

Positioning and Balance

To assess positioning and balance, place the student in these positions: lying face-up, lying face-down (with and without a wedge), sitting in a wheelchair, sitting on a mat, and standing in a stander or gait trainer. In each position, prompt the student to move the head, arms, and legs and to grasp and release objects. It is important to prompt the student to move when objects are presented to the left, to the right, and at midline. Record the results to determine which position promotes the best functional movement. Scoring ranges from 1 to 5: (1) *Cannot move*, (2) *Nonfunctional movement*, (3) *Limited functional movement*, (4) *Fair functional movement*, and (5) *Very good functional movement*.

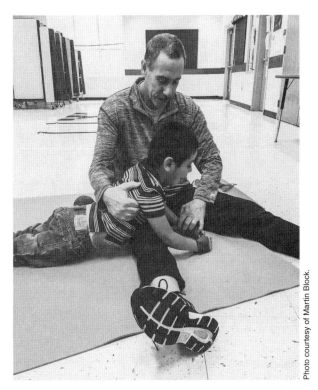

A teacher positions a child to work on grasping and reaching.

Photo courtesy of Martin Block.

Figure 3.1 provides an assessment to measure functional ability while standing in a stander.

Students should also be evaluated on their balance when placed in unsupported sitting or standing positions. Semi-independent sitting or standing (and perhaps walking with a walker) could be targeted goals for students who show some righting responses and the ability to maintain balance when sitting or standing. Score students based on how long they can sit or stand consistently in three to five trials of one to three minutes, noting how much support they need to sit or stand.

Information obtained from this assessment can be used to identify the limb the student can move most functionally and the position that promotes the most active and functional movements. For example, a student might be working on pushing a bowling ball down a ramp or using a switching device to activate a catapult that throws a ball to a peer. The functional positioning or balance analysis would reveal where to place the ramp and switch (to the left, to the right, or at midline) and what position is most functional for the student (e.g., in a wheelchair, in a stander, prone over a wedge).

Mobility

Functional mobility for students with severe disabilities refers to the ability to move from point A to point B using basic mobility skills such as rolling, walking (independently or with an assistive device), using a wheelchair (manual or electric), or crawling or creeping. Included in the analysis is preferred mobility methods (e.g., walking with a walker or pushing a wheelchair) and the distance the student can travel (e.g., walking independently for 10 or more steps, taking 2 or 3 reciprocal steps). The results can help you determine whether mobility is possible for the child, which type of mobility is most appropriate, and where to start teaching the student to improve mobility skills. The following is an example of measuring mobility using a gait trainer or walker.

The student can

- take 1 step,
- take 2 or 3 steps,
- take 4 to 7 steps,
- take 8 to 10 steps, or
- take 11 to 15 steps.

FIGURE 3.1

Assessment Criteria for Standing in a Stander

Record how far the hand moves toward objects or electronic switches. Switches are buttons or joysticks that trigger a response like a ball going down a ramp or lights going off.

LEFT ARM AND HAND MOVEMENT
- Objects or switches presented to the left
- Objects or switches presented to the right
- Objects or switches presented toward the midline

RIGHT ARM AND HAND MOVEMENT
- Objects or switches presented to the left
- Objects or switches presented to the right
- Objects or switches presented toward the midline

HEAD MOVEMENT
- Objects or switches presented to the left
- Objects or switches presented to the right
- Objects or switches presented toward the midline

The preceding can be measured with or without assistance. The level of assistance should be documented along with the distance walked. The goal, of course, is to increase the student's mobility and independence by providing opportunities to improve balance, strength, and coordination.

Physical Fitness

Most students with severe disabilities cannot perform traditional physical fitness test items such as push-ups, sit-ups, a mile run, or a sit and reach test. **Functional physical fitness** is a measure of basic strength, flexibility, and cardiorespiratory endurance with reference to daily activities. For example, strength is measured in terms of the ability to push their head off the mat when prone, bear weight when standing, hold a weighted object, or push a weighted object (e.g., push a ball down a ramp). **Functional cardiorespiratory endurance** is measured by how many steps a student can take in a gait trainer before needing to rest, how long a student can push a

wheelchair before needing to rest, or how long a student can participate in physical activities before getting tired. **Functional flexibility** is a measure of the general range of motion in arms and legs with reference to basic physical activities such as reaching to grasp an object or pushing a ball down a ramp.

Scoring functional fitness items can be relatively simple, such as the ability to reach the hand to the mouth or the top of the head. Adequate upper-body strength could be described as the ability to hold light objects in the hands for five seconds. Functional upper-body strength for bowling with a ramp could be described as having enough strength to push a regulation bowling ball down a ramp. In these examples, educators and therapists would target activities to improve the student's grasp and upper-body strength.

Sensory Processes

Assessing sensory processing is also important to learn the best sensory mode in which to present information (e.g., visual, auditory). Such an assessment also helps determine whether the student has any sensory sensitivity. This information can be obtained by talking to the student's parents, teacher, speech therapist, and vision specialist. In addition, sensory preferences (e.g., strength in understanding visual information), as well as sensory sensitivity to certain stimuli (e.g., the student might get upset in loud environments or be tactually defensive), can be tested systematically. For example, visual stimuli can be presented to determine whether the student can see and track the stimuli. Students who are not responsive to visual stimuli can have activities, objects, and instructions presented via sound or touch, or both. Similarly, students who consistently are frightened and easily agitated by touch should be respected; tactile stimulation should be limited until they build a tolerance. Assessing sensory stimuli can be accomplished in the following way:

Visual Abilities

Note whether the child wears glasses, the cause of vision loss (if known), the child's visual activity, and whether the child is nearsighted or farsighted.

- Excellent: Vision is the primary mode for gathering information; minimal deficits.
- Fair: Vision is used, but some information is missed; mild deficit.
- Poor: Residual vision is used but minimally; moderate deficit.
- Severe: Vision is not used at all.

Visual Sensitivity

- Enjoys visual stimulation
- Is mildly sensitive to visual stimulation
- Is severely sensitive to visual stimulation

Note that other members of the multidisciplinary team, as well as the parents, can help determine the student's visual abilities and visual sensitivity.

The FASSD provides useful information that can be used to create appropriate learning experiences for students with severe disabilities. Other forms of alternative assessment have also been useful for gathering information on student abilities and developing physical education programs. One of the most common and well-known is the rubric.

Rubrics

A **rubric** is a form of assessment used to measure the attainment of skills, knowledge, or performance against a consistent set of criteria. Rubrics are designed to be explicit, observable, and measurable. They are easily adapted for students with disabilities by adding a measure for levels of assistance, such as totally independent, partially independent or requiring partial physical assistance, and full physical assistance. This important component of the rubric can be used to determine progress that is hard to detect.

Rubrics can be developed based on the unit of instruction. The following are steps for creating a rubric for the skill of catching a ball. This system can be used for any discrete task or skill.

1. Task analyze the skill (breaking the skill down into its component parts).
2. Use the task analysis to create levels of difficulty.
3. Assign a point (1) or hierarchy score (1, 2, 3, . . .) to each level to determine the overall score.
4. Add levels of assistance (independent, partial physical assist, full physical assist), and note how much assistance the student needed to complete each component of the task.
5. Add measurable criteria to determine a criterion score.

Using this approach, figure 3.2 provides an example of a rubric for the skill of catching a ball. The rubric reveals how many of the components of the catch the student accomplished, how much assistance the student needed to complete the task, and how many times the student was able to perform the task. This information can then be used to determine whether the student has mastered the task and, if not, where the deficits occur.

Rubrics should be created with all students in mind—that is, they should be **universally designed** to consider as many variables as possible, such as equipment, rules, and environmental variations. Rubrics should also include a range of individual learning capabilities. The rubric in figure 3.2, for example, can be used to assess multiple learners on the catch. If independence is not a variable of concern, then that portion of the rubric can be ignored. For students who are

---

FIGURE 3.2

Rubric: Catching a Ball

Directions: For each task, score a point for an attempt or completion; check off the level of assistance needed; and score criteria based on the outcome.

Points	Task	Level of Assistance	Criteria
1	Hands are positioned in front of the body with elbows bent.	Full physical assistance Partial physical assistance Independent	1 out of 3 attempts 2 out of 3 attempts 3 out of 3 attempts
1	Arms extend to reach for the ball.	Full physical assistance Partial physical assistance Independent	1 out of 3 attempts 2 out of 3 attempts 3 out of 3 attempts
1	Ball is caught with hands only.	Full physical assistance Partial physical assistance Independent	1 out of 3 attempts 2 out of 3 attempts 3 out of 3 attempts

---

working toward independence, however, including the level of assistance needed to complete the task is crucial.

Task Analysis Assessment

Another form of assessment that relies heavily on measuring levels of independence is the **task analysis assessment (TAA)** developed by Houston-Wilson (1994). Like rubrics, the TAA analyzes each skill; unlike rubrics, however, it quantifies the levels of assistance and assigns a score of independence. Goals can then be developed for improving levels of independence in addition to improving performance. Often, minor changes in behavior can go unnoticed unless we carefully observe and monitor independence levels.

The unique aspect of the TAA is that it provides both a qualitative and quantitative way to measure skill. First, each skill is analyzed sequentially. Then levels of assistance are given a quantitative value: total physical assist (1), partial physical assist (2), and independent (3). A student who must physically be put through the full motion of the task would receive a score of 1. One who requires only guidance or touch cues would

receive a score of 2. Students who can complete the task without physical assistance receive a score of 3.

Figure 3.3 presents an example of the TAA using a weight training skill, the bench press. In this example, the learner completed two of the seven components independently, three with partial physical assistance, and two with total physical assistance. The sum of these scores is 14 points; the highest possible total score (if each component were completed independently) is 21 points. By dividing the score achieved by the total possible score, we find that this student was able to perform the bench press with 66 percent independence. The form also includes a space for product scores, and in this example, the student completed five bench presses. Goals can then be set for increasing the student's independence score.

Although many students with disabilities need physical assistance to complete tasks, others may be physically capable but possess other difficulties that require assessment modifications. One form of assessment that is helpful when working with students with disabilities is ecological task analysis (ETA).

FIGURE 3.3

Task Analysis Assessment for the Bench Press

Directions: Score the level of assistance needed to complete each task.

   IND = Independent—the person is able to perform the task without assistance (3 points).

   PPA = Partial physical assistance—the person needs some assistance to perform the task (2 points).

   TPA = Total physical assistance—the person needs assistance to perform the entire task (1 point).

Task	IND	PPA	TPA
1. Lie on back on bench.	3	2	1
2. Place each foot on proper side of bench with knees bent.	3	2	1
3. Extend arms to reach for bar.	3	2	1
4. Grasp bar with both hands directly above shoulders.	3	2	1
5. Raise bar to a straight-arm position.	3	2	1
6. Lower bar until it touches chest.	3	2	1
7. Raise bar to a straight-arm position.	3	2	1
Scoring sum (per column)	6	6	2
Total score achieved	14		
Total possible points	21		
% independent score	66%		
Product score	5		

Ecological Task Analysis

Ecological task analysis (ETA) provides students with choices for executing skills. Teachers set up the parameters or objectives, and students then choose the type of equipment, the rules, and the pace of the activity within which they are performing the skills. Teachers observe and record data about these behaviors and use the data to challenge students within their comfort levels. The following is an example of using ETA for the skill of striking a ball:

1. Present the task goal: striking or propelling a ball.

2. Provide options, such as the size, color, and weight of the ball; the size and weight of the bat; and a choice of batting tee, thrown pitch, or hanging ball to hit.

3. Document student choices (e.g., red ball off of a tee with a Wiffle bat).

4. Manipulate task variables to further challenge the student (e.g., decreasing the size of the ball or hitting implement).

This system offers several advantages: The teacher learns what movement form and equipment are most comfortable to the student, the student starts out with success, and the teacher knows that the student is being realistically challenged because the teacher has set the task goal. There are no right or wrong choices for equipment or performance execution; however, the equipment the teacher offers limits the student's choices (Carson, Bulger, & Townsend, 2007).

Ecological task analysis is used to determine preferences and skill levels and is a starting point for deciding how to further challenge the student (Mitchell & Oslin, 2007). Although, ideally, students would be in control of their own choices, some students with disabilities cannot independently perform the task or choose objects. In these cases, teachers must provide assistance, present a limited number of objects, and try to ascertain students' choices by facial expression, pointing, or other indicators. In many cases, the paraeducator or teaching assistant, who spends extensive time with the student, can help identify the student's preferences. Some students may be able to make choices by selecting from a picture board or using an app on an iPad. Maintain data as indicated above.

Basic Skills Assessment

Because adapted physical education is a service, not a placement, students such as Marin, whom we met at the beginning of this chapter,

are often included in the GPE class even though they have unique needs and IEPs for physical education. For this reason, assessments that can accommodate all learners are very useful for teachers. The **basic skills assessment (BSA)**, which was created by Kowalski, Houston-Wilson, and Daggett (in press), is ideal for use in inclusive physical education classes. The BSA was developed to assess a heterogeneous population of students—from those with severe disabilities to typically developing students—in a variety of curricular units. This **curriculum-based assessment** aligns with content areas taught in physical education programs.

The BSA example of softball in figure 3.4 is broken down into seven elements needed to participate in a game. Levels of performance are broken down into emerging, basic, competent, and proficient. Students are scored for each task; totals are matched to the scoring table to yield

---

FIGURE 3.4

Basic Skills Assessment for Softball

Directions: This test consists of seven elements, each comprising of several tasks. Begin by observing the student performing each task. Within each element, put a 1 in the box next to each task that the student can complete. If you are unsure whether the student can complete a task, require the students to perform it successfully in three out of five attempts. After the student has completed all of the elements, total the number of boxes marked, and apply the score to the following chart to determine the present level of ability (i.e., emerging, basic, competent, or proficient).

   Once you have a total for each component, use the scoring table at the bottom of the page to identify the student's ability level.

ELEMENT 1: THROWING

_____ Emerging:

- Throws the softball in any direction.

_____ Basic:

- Throws the softball in the desired direction.
- Throws the softball to the designated teammate.

_____ Competent:

- Throws a ball underhand to a target at a distance of 15 feet (4.6 m).
- Throws a ball overhand to a target at a distance of 45 feet (13.7 m).

_____ Proficient:
- Throws a ball to a teammate while on the move.
- Throws a ball overhand to a target at a distance of 60 feet (18.3 m).

ELEMENT 2: PITCHING

_____ Emerging:
- Attempts to pitch a softball.
- Pitches a softball in any direction.

_____ Basic:
- Pitches a softball underhand for a distance of 20 feet (6 m) over the plate.
- Pitches a softball underhand for a distance of 40 feet (12 m) over the plate.

_____ Competent:
- Pitches a softball underhand with good form and height.
- Pitches a softball into a regulation strike zone from 40 feet (12 m).

_____ Proficient:
- Able to adjust pitches for each batter.
- Demonstrates an understanding of defensive play and positioning for pitchers.

ELEMENT 3: CATCHING AND FIELDING

_____ Emerging:
- Attempts to catch a softball.
- Attempts to field a softball.

_____ Basic:
- Fields a rolled ball correctly.
- Makes an above-the-waist catch.
- Makes a below-the-waist catch.
- Catches an underhand throw.
- Catches an overhand throw.

_____ Competent:
- Fields a hit ball.
- Catches a hit ball.
- Moves into position (body in front of a hit ball) in a softball game.
- Catches or fields a hit ball and throws to an appropriate teammate.
- Catches or fields a hit ball cleanly in a softball game.

_____ Proficient:
- Adjusts position on the field in anticipation of batter.
- Positions for a relayed throw from a teammate who has caught or fielded a ball.
- Demonstrates an understanding of support and cover for teammates in order to make a play.

(continued)

Figure 3.4 *(continued)*

ELEMENT 4: BATTING

_____ Emerging:

- Assumes a proper batting stance.
- Attempts to hit a ball off a batting tee.
- Hits a ball off a tee in any direction.

_____ Basic:

- Hits a ball off a tee in the desired direction.
- Hits a ball off a tee into fair territory in a softball game.
- Hits a pitched ball.

_____ Competent:

- Demonstrates a proper bunt.
- Hits a pitched ball into fair territory.
- Hits a pitched ball in the desired direction.

_____ Proficient:

- Consistently controls the direction of a hit.
- Consistently selects a type of hit (e.g., bunt, grounder) appropriate for the situation.

ELEMENT 5: BASE RUNNING

_____ Emerging:

- Identifies the order of running bases.
- Walks to first base.
- Runs to first base.
- Runs to first base within the base path.

_____ Basic:

- Tags first base and runs beyond it.
- Attempts to run to first base after hitting a pitched ball.
- Runs safely to first base after hitting a pitched ball.

_____ Competent:

- Rounds first base when there is a chance for additional bases.
- When appropriate, tags up and runs on a caught fly ball.
- Follows base coach advice while on the bases.
- Demonstrates a correct slide into a base.

_____ Proficient:

- Uses the slide appropriately when running bases.
- Can execute stealing a base in an appropriate situation.
- Demonstrates the ability to be a base coach during a softball game.

ELEMENT 6: KNOWLEDGE OF SOFTBALL

_____ Emerging:

- Shows a basic understanding of softball (hitting, catching, throwing, running bases).
- Participates in softball skill activities and modified games with physical or verbal prompting, or both.

_____ Basic:

- Can describe an out.
- Can describe a foul ball, hit, strike, run, walk, and fly ball.
- Can locate the pitcher's mound, batter's box, bases, infield, and outfield.
- Recognizes playing positions on a team.

_____ Competent:

- Understands the rules and regulations of softball.
- Adapts to changes in game situations appropriately.
- Can assist in scoring for a softball game.
- Plays one or two positions on the field with confidence and consistency.

_____ Proficient:

- Plays multiple positions knowledgeably.
- Adapts game and drill activities to meet the needs of players.
- Keeps a box score sheet for a softball game.
- Plays softball regularly outside of school.

ELEMENT 7: PARTICIPATION, SAFETY, AND SOCIAL RESPONSIBILITY

_____ Emerging:

- Attempts to participate in a softball game.
- Participates a little; recognizes teammates and opponents.
- Practices individual softball skills.

_____ Basic:

- Understands the importance of safety and good sporting behavior while playing softball.
- Adapts various components of throwing, catching, and running such as throwing a bean bag, running with a walker, or catching a suspended swinging ball.
- Participates enthusiastically and with good effort.

_____ Competent:

- Exhibits safe and fair play while playing softball.
- Participates regularly on a softball team.
- Demonstrates an understanding of the fitness benefits associated with playing softball.
- Helps teammates with rules and play during a softball game.

_____ Proficient:

- Develops practice activities for others related to softball skill development.
- Coaches or officiates with confidence at the recreational or competitive level.
- Participates regularly in competitive or recreational softball outside of school.
- Understands the level of fitness required to play competitive softball.

SCORING TABLE

Level 1 emerging skills: Total of 1-36 tasks primarily in emerging and basic skills

Level 2 basic skills: Minimum of 14 emerging skill tasks and 16 basic skill tasks

Level 3 competent skills: Minimum of 18 basic skill tasks and 16 competent skill tasks

Level 4 proficient skills: Minimum of 18 competent skill tasks and 14 proficient skill tasks

an overall picture of development. The BSA uses an Excel platform so that scores can be tallied for each level by indicating a 1 for each task completed. Then total scores are compared to the scoring table to obtain an overall picture of the student's current level of performance (emerging, basic, competent, or proficient).

Although some students with disabilities may never progress to competent or proficient levels of performance, they can be included in the testing protocol and helped to reach their highest potential based on the sequential aspects of the assessment.

Summary

All of the assessments presented in this chapter have one thing in common: They provide data on the motor performance and learning abilities of students who have traditionally been difficult to assess. These alternative assessments yield information on students' present level of performance that can then be used to determine their strengths and weaknesses, set goals, and plan instruction. Additionally, these assessments can be used to provide formative (ongoing) as well as summative (year-end) data.

▷ ▷

Consider the student Marin presented at the start of the chapter. Her teacher, Ms. Walsh was able to appropriately assess her functional abilities to determine how best to include Marin within the class. She utilized the BSA because she felt it was easy to use and administer. The BSA was used as a pre- and posttest at the beginning and end of each unit to determine Marin's progress and skills development.

Review Questions

1. What are three outcomes of assessment?
2. Prior to assessing students with disabilities, you should learn as much as you can about them. What are three attributes you should find out about prior to testing?
3. What area of motor development does the FASSD measure?
4. What five steps can you take to create a physical education rubric?
5. Ecological task analysis uses a four-step process to obtain data on students' motor abilities. What are the four steps?
6. Which assessment presented in this chapter was created primarily to assess students' level of independence?
7. Which of the assessments presented in this chapter would be ideal to use in inclusive classes?

4

Communication Practices That Enhance Participation

Justin A. Haegele
Old Dominion University, Norfolk, Virginia

Matthew Mescall
Maryland School for the Blind

James Gunther
Norfolk Public Schools, Virginia

Chapter Objectives

By reading this chapter, you will:

▸ Gain an appreciation for the importance of communication for students with disabilities.
▸ Understand considerations for using communication practices.
▸ Learn about non-technology-dependent strategies and electronic communication devices for students with disabilities.

Mr. Casey is a first-year physical education teacher at Tuttle Elementary School in Lancaster School District, a large suburban district. He is an enthusiastic teacher who is excited about implementing programs that will teach his students about sport, health, fitness, and lifelong physical activity. During the first week of the school year, Mr. Casey learns that he will be teaching several children with disabilities. For the most part, this does not concern him, because he is philosophically oriented toward inclusion and had a very positive experience during his physical education teacher education program in an on-campus lab working one-on-one with a child with a mild intellectual disability.

Mr. Casey also learns that he will be teaching three students with severe disabilities in a separate physical education (SPE) class. Frances, a third-grader, has severe spastic cerebral palsy and seizures. She uses a manual wheelchair for mobility and can move short distances at a time. Sam, also in third grade, has level 3 autism spectrum disorder (ASD) and requires a great deal of support from teachers and paraeducators. He is nonverbal, demonstrates self-abusive behaviors, has an intellectual impairment, and has very limited receptive and expressive language. Riley, who is in first grade and is new to the school, has CHARGE syndrome, a complex genetic disorder that has resulted in both hearing and visual impairments.

Because he doesn't have experience teaching children with severe disabilities, Mr. Casey is anxious about this assignment. However, he is determined to provide the best educational experience possible for these students. When discussing this with his colleagues, he learns that among the most important considerations when teaching children with severe disabilities is communication. This prompts Mr. Casey to seek advice from the school's speech pathologist, special education teachers, and paraeducators about communication methods that can enhance his students' participation in physical education.

Communication is an essential consideration when teaching students with disabilities. No matter what the cause, people with disabilities tend to exhibit a **limited response repertoire** (Block, 1992; Hodge, Lieberman, & Murata, 2012). This means that they, like the students described in the opening scenario, may have a limited ability to respond to prompts because of hearing, vision, processing, muscular, or expressive issues. Furthermore, many people with disabilities do not develop a coherent system of communication, meaning that they do not receive information or express their feelings and needs clearly. Thus, you need to understand the communication needs of your students, be familiar with communication options, and use the best options available. This chapter presents considerations to take into account when making communication-based decisions, and it provides an overview of commonly used communication techniques.

Considerations for Communication Practices in Physical Education

Those who work with students with disabilities in physical education settings need to consider a number of issues prior to and during instruction. These students deserve the opportunity to participate with their teachers and peers to the greatest extent possible. The following sections provide guidelines for giving them that opportunity. To get started, figure 4.1 provides an at-a-glance list of dos and don'ts.

Select Appropriate Communication Techniques

Selecting appropriate communication techniques is key. First and foremost, keep in mind that each

Be sensitive to the needs of your students with disabilities and use techniques that best facilitate communication.

student is unique and should be taught using the communication method that is easiest for her or him, based on the individual education plan (IEP) (Best, Lieberman, & Arndt, 2002). A second consideration is making every effort to have students use the communication methods they use in other settings, such as in the classroom and at home. Consistency across settings creates easier transitions between environments and reinforces the skills classroom teachers, speech pathologists, and other therapists are also providing. Moreover, practicing communication in the same way in different settings can help with skill generalization.

Collaborate With the Team

Collaborating with other school personnel, including speech pathologists, paraeducators, interveners (specialists who work one-on-one with the children who are deafblind), and classroom teachers, can help you communicate with students with disabilities. These team members can provide information about the student's current level of communication skills and communication preferences, as well as simple actions that may improve the student's desire to communicate. They may also have up-to-date information about the strategies or devices the student uses, including whether their devices are appropriate for heavy use. For example, if a physical education activity requires a student to rapidly activate a switch or trigger on a communication device, you should discuss it with other school personnel. The device may not be able to handle such use, or the behaviors may be counterproductive to other academic or behavioral objectives.

FIGURE 4.1

Communication Dos and Don'ts in Physical Education

DO

- Expect and encourage students to communicate with you.
- Give students the time they need to respond to prompts.
- Facilitate social interactions with peers.
- Communicate with other school personnel about communication methods.
- Allow students to use techniques that work best for them.

DON'T

- Give instructions such as "Hit the switch;" rather, ask students to perform the task the switch is programmed to perform. For example, if using a switch to simulate batting, instruct the student to "Swing" rather than "Hit the switch."
- Take students communication devices away during activities.
- Allow peers to hit or play with communication devices.
- Expect all students with disabilities to communicate in the same way.
- Speak with paraeducators about students' needs rather than speaking with the students directly.

Set Clear Expectations for Communication

In addition to selecting the correct communication method, you must also set communication expectations for students with disabilities. These expectations include making choices during lessons and interacting appropriately with objects and classmates during activities. For example, when they enter their physical education classes, Sam and Riley are asked to decide which color ball they would like to use that day. In addition, during the culminating activity, they are expected to be actively engaged by cheering for classmates when it is not their turn to participate. These expectations require that students be cognitively aware of their options and be able to make selections. Some students with disabilities may not have mastered these skills.

The following are some strategies to promote choice making and social interactions during physical education. Ask students the following:

- What color piece of equipment do you want?
- What do you want to do?
- What team do you want to be on?
- Which activity do you prefer?
- Whom do you want to work with?
- Which movements do you want to perform in the game?

Here are ways to encourage students with disabilities to interact with objects or classmates:

- Have them cheer for classmates during activities.
- Reinforce learned concepts (e.g., in volleyball, "The ball is going over the net").
- Preprogram questions for peers and staff.
- Program responses to language games.
- Program responses that reinforce the rules of a game (e.g., as a referee, line judge, or coach).

Promote and Facilitate Peer Interaction

Communication is important not only for instructing students with disabilities but also for facilitating interactions with their peers. These interactions provide appropriately aged role models, natural supports, conversational partners, and motivators (Downing & Peckham-Hardin, 2007). Furthermore, successful communication with those with disabilities teaches typically developing peers what these students can do, rather than what they cannot do.

To elicit social communication, build opportunities into lessons. Students with disabilities attend to many activities each day, including activities of daily living (e.g., getting dressed), academic activities (e.g., going to class), and recreational activities (e.g., participating in sport and

Successful communication with those with disabilities teaches typically developing peers what these students can do, rather than what they cannot do.

leisure). Each presents important opportunities to communicate with others using preferred strategies or devices (Hodge et al., 2012). In physical education, you might encourage students with disabilities to respond to cues that motivate their participation with peers and staff, as well as with others. These responses can create an encouraging environment in which all students, both with and without disabilities, can get excited about activities together while providing purposeful communication that is in the control of students with disabilities. This may be especially important for elementary-aged students when playing games with their peers that require language. In games, such as What time is it, Mr. Fox?, a staff member could prerecord a message for a student to use.

Moving Toward Independence

The goal of communication in physical education should be for students to be as independent as possible. Facilitating independent communication during physical education can help students feel more engaged in activities while promoting a sense of self-determination. Even for students

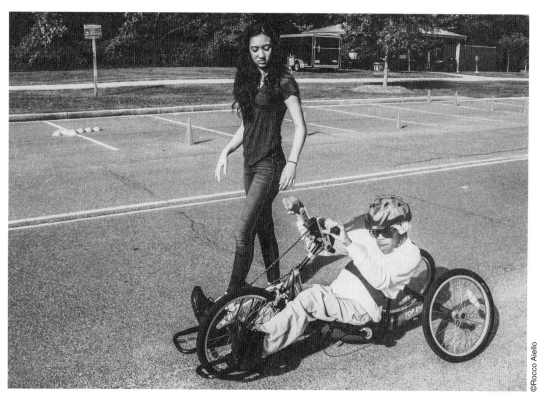

This student chose a bike as his reward by using his mode of communication on a tablet.

©Rocco Aiello

who require hand-over-hand instruction, independent communication gives them autonomy over some aspects of their educational experience. Promote independence early, and expect independent communication from students often. For example, initially, when Frances entered her physical education classes, her paraeducator prompted her communication with the physical education teacher. However, as the year went on, the paraeducator and physical education teacher developed strategies that required Frances to approach the teacher with requests. Because of this, she became more independent as a communicator and more self-confident.

Types of Communication Practices

A number of communication methods are available for students with disabilities, depending on personnel preference and other considerations. For the most part, they can be categorized into two groups; non-technology-dependent communication strategies and electronic communication devices. The two can also be combined (i.e., using a non-technology-dependent communication strategy with the assistance of an electronic communication device).

Non-Technology-Dependent Communication Strategies

Non-technology-dependent communication strategies allow those with disabilities to express themselves using little or no technology. Examples include the picture exchange communication system (PECS), scanning, direct selection, and gestural communication.

Picture Exchange Communication System. A **picture exchange communication system (PECS)** is a form of augmented communication that uses icons rather than words to help learners communicate. Primarily, PECS is used with children with ASD, including those with level 3 autism (those requiring very substantial support), like Sam, or those with ASD and other disabilities (e.g., visual impairment). In addition, children with other severe disabilities can use PECS icons along with other communication techniques, such as direct selection and scanning.

Direct Selection. **Direct selection** is a communication technique in which a learner points to a desired symbol on a communication board (Reichle, York, & Sigafoos, 1991). These boards may use PECS symbols or other icons or objects with particular meanings for individuals. Learners can point at the symbol with a body part (e.g., finger) or with a handheld or head-mounted pointing device. In addition to physically touching the symbol, students can use another form of direct selection called eye gaze. **Eye gaze** involves staring at a symbol to select it. The service provider sits directly in front of the learner and follows the gaze to determine the symbol (Reichle et al., 1991). Typically, eye gaze boards are made of a clear material to help the service provider see symbols clearly. Consult with a speech pathologist to determine whether an eye gaze board is available. They can also be made using Plexiglas, Velcro, and PECS symbols.

Scanning. **Scanning** is a process by which a learner is given a menu of choices; when the desired choice is presented, the learner produces a voluntary response to signal the listener (Reichle et al., 1991). Voluntary responses include blinking, dropping a hand off a table, and tilting the head to the side, depending on the student's capabilities. In addition to this manual version of scanning, a number of electronic scanning devices are available (see the section Electronic Communication Devices).

Gestural Communication. **Gestural communication** involves physical gestures that are commonly understood by members of a particular group or culture (Reichle et al., 1991). Gestures include a wave goodbye, a yes or no headshake, or a thumbs up. Gestural communication also includes types of sign language, such as **American Sign Language (ASL)**. American Sign Language is a communication technique commonly used by people who are deaf; it is a separate and distinct language consisting of manual signs, spelled-out language, gestures, facial expressions, and body movements (Lieberman, Ponchillia, & Ponchillia, 2013).

For people with deafblindness, like Riley, another gestural communication option is tactile sign language. **Tactile sign language** is based on a standard manual signing system in which the receiver's hand is placed lightly on the hand of the signer to receive signs. When using tactile sign language with a student, make sure the complexity and speed of the signs match the student's motor abilities, you don't use too many signs, and the student is ready to repeat signs if necessary. Also, make sure the signs match the skill and activity being taught (Lieberman et al., 2013).

Table 4.1 displays the pros and cons of each.

Electronic Communication Devices

Some children with severe disabilities who are nonverbal use electronic communication devices. These devices give them a voice and promote communication-based independence. With many devices, users can program specific information into the device. Electronic communication devices can be used along with non-technology-dependent strategies (e.g., scanning, direct selection) or independently.

Although there are many benefits to electronic communication devices, there are a few concerns. First, devices can be expensive, and because technology is constantly evolving, new devices may be needed to align with new software. Second, users (both students and teachers) typically need training, which can require patience. In many ways, these devices are not purchased by the physical education teacher, but are used by the student throughout the school day as part of their holistic educational program.

Electronic communication devices are categorized as either static or dynamic (Hodge et al., 2012). **Static communication devices** have fixed displays that represent needed or desired items. The student presses the display to make requests, which can trigger a stored audio message. Static devices typically have a set group of icons that are associated with requests. **Dynamic communication devices** include active displays that are typically accessed using touchscreen technology. These devices run on specially designed software and are customizable for users. Each cell can represent a word, phrase, or symbol that plays when items are selected. Unlike static devices, dynamic devices can include multiple display screens that can be changed easily.

Figure 4.2 displays several common static and dynamic electronic communication devices used in schools today. Table 4.2 weighs the pros and cons of each. In addition to considerations explained previously, things to consider when choosing a device are the cost of the device, the amount of time needed to train the students to use it, and the student's comfort level with it.

TABLE 4.1   Pros and Cons of Non-Technology-Dependent Communication Strategies

	Pros	Cons
PECS	• Provides a uniform communication method that is easy to learn and requires little training. • Can be updated regularly. • Can be cross-trained with other communication techniques, such as scanning and direct selection.	• If not planned well, it can create physical activity breaks. • Icons are needed for each word or phrase learners want to express. • Vocabulary can limited to available icons.
Scanning	• Selection option for people with less motoric capability than those using direct selection. • Can be a building block toward using automated scanning techniques.	• Blinks, or other behaviors that occur in high rates, can be misinterpreted. • Time-consuming process.
Direct selection	• Fast selection option. • Provides learners who are motorically capable to access targets. • Students can be active in communication.	• Photos or icons must be relevant to learners. • Spontaneous communication is limited. • Learners using eye gaze may not develop large vocabularies.
Gestural communication	• Basic gestures (thumbs up) are universal and understood by peers. • Complex and spontaneous conversations can occur between people who are well versed in sign or tactile sign language.	• Basic gestures allow for only rudimentary communication. • Teachers and peers must know sign language or tactile signs to communicate.

Based on Hodge et al. 2012; Reichle et al. 1991.

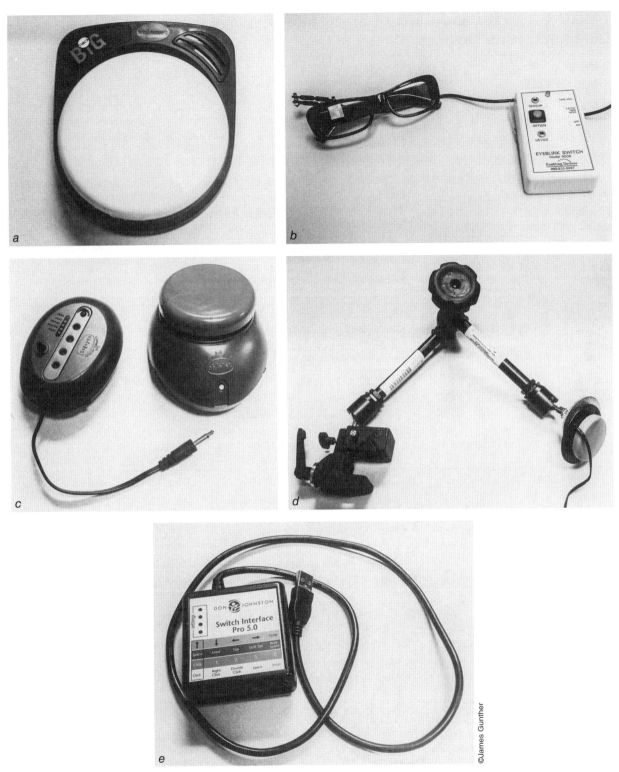

©James Gunther

Figure 4.2 Common electronic communication devices: (*a*) BIGmack, (*b*) Eyeblink switch, (*c*) Jelly Beamer and receiver, (*d*) Magic arm, and (*e*) Switch interface.

TABLE 4.2 Pros and Cons of Static and Dynamic Electronic Communication Devices

Example	Pros	Cons
STATIC DEVICES		
BIGmack: One-voice output that allows users to select from a single message.	• Message can be easily changed. • Easy to activate. • Large target. • Great beginner device. • Can attach image.	Limited to a single message; you need to change it frequently to promote authentic communication.
Rocking Say It Play It: Two-voice output that allows users to select from two choices (yes/no).	Easy to use when users need to respond to yes/no questions or choose between two items.	• Users need more gross motor control than they need for the BIGmack. • Limited to two choices.
Step-by-Step: Three-voice output that allows users to select from three options.	• Can record more messages than simpler devices. • Best used for sequenced responses.	• Complicated procedures for changing messages. • Not meant for spontaneous communication.
Cheap Talk: Allows users to select from four to eight displayed cells.	• Easy to change items. Uses voice commands. • Allows pictures to be associated with a word or message.	Users need fine motor control skills to hit the correct access point.
GoTalk: Allows users to select from 4, 9, 20, or 32 cells.	• A variety of boards can be created for users. • Allows picture to be associated with a word or message. • More durable than tablets and dynamic displays.	Users often need adults or staff to change overlays.
DYNAMIC DEVICES		
DynaVox: A variety of devices that use a tablet-style form with research-based communication software. Some, such as Tobii EyeMobile, allow users to select icons using eye gaze. Others can be used for automated scanning.	• Multiple cells and board allow users to create and form thought. • Provides preprogramed responses. • Has multiple ways for users to use device (eye gaze, scanning, touch). • Designed to adapt to user's needs.	• Expensive. • Often left in classroom so nothing happens during activity. • Learning curve can be large for the programmer and the user. • Can be bulky and can block vision when mounted to a wheelchair.
Commercial tablets: Several commercial tablets now have applications for communication for those with severe disabilities.	• Most adults and staff are familiar with use. • Multiple cells and boards allow the user to create and form thought. • Multiple protective cases support use. • May be less expensive than other dynamic displays.	• Because more people are familiar with the value of these items, the likelihood of their being stolen is higher. • Technology (e.g., firewalls) must meet school district standards. • No tactile feedback. • Size of screen may not be suitable depending on vision.

Summary

This chapter provides an overview of communication practices for students with severe disabilities and their application to physical education. Communication is among the most important aspects of education for those with severe disabilities in physical education. A number of considerations must be taken into account, such as expecting communication from students as well as using strategies in alignment with other school-based personnel. Non-technology-dependent communication strategies and electronic communication devices provide a variety of options for students to use during physical education. Importantly, the strategy or device must be one that gives the student with a disability the greatest chance for success.

▶ ▶

After consulting with his school's speech pathologist, special education teachers, and paraeducators, Mr. Casey feels far more prepared to teach Frances, Sam, and Riley in his upcoming physical education class. He now understands that he must be flexible in addressing the communication needs of his students, rather than preplanning communication methods to use with all three. He also knows the dos and don'ts of communicating with students with severe disabilities and will keep these in mind when teaching these students. Because of Mr. Casey's newfound knowledge, Frances, Sam, and Riley are having their best physical education experience yet. Currently, they are participating in a striking unit in which each of them is using an individualized communication method to ensure success. Although Mr. Casey, with assistance from a collaborative team, spends more time making sure that each activity is suitable for the preferred communication methods of these students, he is committed to providing a successful, independent, and meaningful physical education class.

Review Questions

1. Why is communication important for students with severe disabilities in physical education?
2. What do you need to consider when choosing communication strategies for students in physical education?
3. What are some dos and don'ts of using communication devices in physical education?
4. What is the difference between a static and dynamic communication device?
5. What are the pros and cons of non-technology-dependent communication strategies?
6. How should you decide which communication strategy a student should use?

5

Peer Tutoring

Aija Klavina
Latvian Academy of Sport Education

Lauren J. Lieberman
The College at Brockport, State University of New York

Chapter Objectives

By reading this chapter, you will:

- ▶ Gain an appreciation for the importance of peer tutoring for students with disabilities.
- ▶ Understand important considerations for using various types of peer tutoring.
- ▶ Learn how to train peers to work with students with disabilities.
- ▶ Know how to set up and implement a peer tutoring program for children with disabilities.
- ▶ Understand how to use assessments to evaluate a peer tutoring program.

Nick is a sixth-grader who has cerebral palsy and uses a wheelchair. He is nonverbal but uses facial expressions and a picture exchange communication system (PECS) board for expressive communication. He has a full-time paraeducator, Mrs. Zolwich, and his physical education teacher, Mrs. Meyers, who have both worked with him since the fourth grade. In his new school, he is in a self-contained, twice-a-week physical education class with six other students who are ambulatory and who have autism spectrum disorder. Nick has a peer buddy who comes as a guest to help him during one of his two physical education classes per week. His peer buddy's name is Cameron, and they have known each other since they were in second grade. Cameron went to the information session for the peer buddy program, and he enjoys working with Nick during physical education class because he also knows Mrs. Meyers from his grade-school days.

Children with moderate and severe disabilities benefit in their learning outcomes from increased ratios of students with disabilities to teachers and support staff (Orelove, Sobsey, & Gilles, 2017). For example, in New York, children with more severe disabilities may be in a 6:1:1 class ratio. This translates to six children to one teacher and one paraeducator. In general, the more severe the child's disability is, the lower the ratio. However, teachers should consider the age appropriate behaviors of peers without disabilities to support the learning needs of those with disabilities.

Peer support interventions have been demonstrated to be an effective alternative to traditional paraeducator models for helping students with disabilities access the physical education curriculum (Hodge, Lieberman, & Murata, 2012; Houston-Wilson, Lieberman, Horton, & Kasser, 1997; Klavina & Block, 2008; Klavina, Kristen, Hammar, Jerlinder, & Soulie, 2013; Lieberman, Newcomer, McCubbin, & Dalrymple, 1997; Lieberman, Dunn, Mars, & McCubbin, 2000). Peer tutors are taught to provide instructions related to individual education program (IEP) goals, provide frequent feedback, and promote communication between students with and without disabilities (Klavina & Block, 2008; Klavina & Rodionova, 2015). Moreover, the effectiveness of peer instructional assistance has been demonstrated across grade levels (i.e., elementary, middle, and high school) and disability categories (e.g., intellectual and physical disabilities, visual impairments, severe disabilities).

Peer tutoring students with disabilities may require additional training. These students are likely to be limited in their personal awareness, understanding of other people, and orientation to the environment. Moreover, the physical education environment can be especially stressful and distracting for someone with total blindness or severe autism. Peer tutors may need to learn how to use alternative or augmentative communication systems, manage inappropriate behavior, modify activities, or use adapted equipment (Downing, 2008). These issues are discussed later in this chapter.

Selecting Peer Tutors

Different forms of **peer tutoring programs** are likely to contribute in different ways to student outcomes. For example, the selection procedure and the number of peers assigned to work with a student with a disability (often called the **tutee**) can affect the degree of support the student receives during physical education. Klavina and Block (2008) followed the recommendations provided in the special education literature to outline criteria for selecting appropriate peer tutors:

©Nancy Miller

A peer tutor works with their tutee in a side-by-side hurdle program. The peer is modeling how to hurdle.

- Peer tutors are enrolled in the same class as the student requiring support (tutee).
- Peers are identified by the classroom teacher as being able to provide academic and social support to classmates with disabilities.
- Peers volunteer or agree to participate when asked by the teacher.
- Peers' parents' consent to their participation.

Also important in a potential peer tutor are characteristics such as sensitivity, responsibility, and a willingness to assist a peer with disabilities (Byrd, 1990; Peterson & Miller, 1990; Polloway, Patton, & Serna, 2000).

Research suggests advantages to selecting multiple peer tutors who take turns working with students with disabilities (Carter, Cushing, Clark, & Kennedy, 2005; Klavina & Block, 2008; Klavina & Rodionova, 2015). This enhances skill generalization, exposes students with disabilities to more students without disabilities, gives more students peer tutoring opportunities, and reduces fatigue and boredom in tutors (Giangreco, Halvorsen, Doyle, & Broer, 2004; Lieberman & Houston-Wilson, 2018).

When identifying potential peer tutors, consider the preferences, educational goals, and support needs of the students requiring tutoring (Carter & Kennedy, 2007). You will also need to consider the physical education activities in which students will engage in relation to their chronological age and skill level. Additionally, it is important to consider the grade level outcomes related to the state and national standards that the tutee will have to reach in order to ensure

they are engaging in those activities during the tutor program.

Training Peer Tutors

The peer tutor training program is based on the age of peer tutors, their experience interacting with students with disabilities, and their academic and social skill levels (table 5.1) (Cervantes, Lieberman, Magnesio, & Wood, 2013).

During the first training session, explain to prospective peer tutors the reason for their involvement in the peer tutoring program and your vision of their role in your class. Teach them about disability awareness concepts and person-first language, and about how their classmates with disabilities communicate and interact with others (Cervantes et al., 2013). Klavina and Block (2008) used the following five steps for peer tutoring prompting hierarchy:

1. Verbal Instruction: Tell your friend what to do and how to do it. If they don't respond correctly, then add a demonstration or model.
2. Demonstration: Show your friend how to do it. If they don't respond correctly, then use physical assistance.
3. Physical assistance: Help your friend do it. Physical assistance is the highest level of prompting.
4. Positive specific feedback: Give feedback that is both positive and related to the skill. ("Great job stepping with the opposite

TABLE 5.1 Examples of How to Implement Peer Tutoring

Peer tutor responsibility	Execution
Assessment	Evaluate present level of performance based on an authentic assessment. Peer tutors receive clear descriptions of what is expected during any activity—for example, Jake will grasp a beanbag and release it into a hula hoop that is 1 foot (30 cm) in front of his chair in five seconds with verbal assistance only.
Physical assistance	Peer tutors provide physical assistance with positioning or body parts (or both) during skill execution—for example, Ciara assists Jerome in parachute games by holding his hands onto the loops of the parachute during group activities.
Promoting social behavior	Peer tutors can promote healthy social behavior during class—for example, Justin helps Dean with a partner activity during a dance unit and ensures that all peers know how to work with him in each part of the dance unit.
Communication	Peer tutors facilitate communication—for example, Erika is taught how to use Proloquo2Go to help Shelley communicate.
IEP goal implementation	Peer tutors can help implement IEP goals that align with certain units—for example, Enrique helps Giovanni grasp a badminton racket and improve his arm and shoulder flexibility; he also documents Giovanni's level of skill and independence on the task.

foot!" "I like the way you bent your knees to jump!")

5. Error correction, if needed: Help your friend figure out the problem. ("Roll the ball forward, like this." "Next time extend your arms.")

Klavina and Block's (2008) study involved three students with severe and multiple disabilities and nine age-appropriate peer tutors. Training consisted of three 30-minute small-group training sessions within 1 week that occurred during free periods of the school day. The students with disabilities and their paraeducators participated in the second and third sessions, and they were part of small-group activities. Peer tutors were given peer tutor worksheets, like figure 5.1, to practice steps.

FIGURE 5.1

Peer Tutor Worksheet for the Overhand Throw

Name _____ Date _____

Equipment: three tennis balls

1. Tell your friend that you will do the overhand throw.
2. Watch your friend do the overhand throw steps described below.

Step number	Step description	Picture
1.	Stand with a ball in your hand and your opposite foot in front.	
2.	Bring your throwing arm back.	
3.	Step with the foot opposite your throwing arm.	
4.	Throw the ball.	
5.	Follow through and watch the ball.	

The peer tutor training sessions should include teaching instructions, error correction procedures, feedback, and skill assessment (see figure 5.2 for the peer tutor training evaluation form). During training, you and your paraeducator should praise peer tutors and students with disabilities on successful partnerships and performances. Teach tutors to pay attention and stay close to the students they are mentoring, as well as to use appropriate body language and verbal and nonverbal communication (see table 5.2). Klavina and Block (2008) suggested that teachers monitor activities and interactions from 10 to 16 feet (3 to 5 m) away. Intervene only if the peer tutor does not provide instructions correctly (e.g., fails to provide a cue before doing the activity), or if you witness unsafe conditions or lack of participation.

> Attention and positive feedback are very important to maintain the confidence and enjoyment of students tutoring peers with disabilities.

FIGURE 5.2

Peer Tutor Training Evaluation

Name _____ Date _____

Mark the correct answer.

1. What is the first step in peer tutoring instructions?
    a. Physical assistance
    b. Direct verbal prompt (instruction)
    c. Model (visual prompt)

2. When you say to the student "Good job!" or "You did great!" it is called
    a. Specific praise
    b. General praise
    c. Verbal feedback

3. When the student does not respond correctly to a verbal prompt, you should
    a. Provide physical assistance
    b. Model
    c. Ask the teacher for help

4. What is the highest, or most intrusive, level of prompting?
    a. Full physical
    b. Physical assistance
    c. Gesture

5. Which of the following statements is positive and specific?
    a. "Good job, but bend your knees more when you jump."
    b. "Good try, but you didn't lift your arm."
    c. "I like the way you are looking at the target."

TABLE 5.2 10 Steps for Setting Up a Peer Tutor Training Program

Steps	What to do	When to do it
PRIOR TO TRAINING		
1. Develop an application procedure.	Create an application and give it to eligible students. Accept into the program only students who want to be tutors and who exhibit the characteristics of a good tutor. Emphasize that peer tutoring is a privilege and an honor.	Prior to training—at the beginning of the school year.
2. Obtain permission from the parents of tutors and tutees, as well as administration.	Permission should be received from parents and administrators prior to training tutors and implementing the program.	Prior to training—at the beginning of the school year.
PEER TUTOR TRAINING		
3. Teach disability awareness.	The training should include a discussion of different types of disabilities to ensure that the tutor understands the disability of the tutee. Be sure to include the tutee in all of the training if possible.	At the beginning of the peer tutor training program.
4. Teach communication techniques.	Communication during a lesson or activity is extremely important. Teach terminology as well as how to communicate (e.g., sign language, PECS communication symbols, iPad).	This should be taught during the peer tutor training program and is disability specific.
5. Teach instructional techniques.	Teach tutors how to explain, demonstrate, and provide physical assistance. Explain positive general, positive specific, and corrective feedback and when to use each.	This should be embedded into the peer tutor training and practiced in scenarios. Include the tutee in the training whenever possible.
6. Use scenarios.	Present possible scenarios for upcoming units of instruction as well as real-life examples. For example: "You are tutoring for a swimming unit and your student shows signs of a seizure. What do you do?" "You are teaching volleyball and your student uses a wheelchair. What modifications will you make?"	This should be embedded into the peer tutor training and should be practiced in scenarios of upcoming lessons. Include the tutee in the training whenever possible.
7. Use behavior management programs (if necessary).	If a tutee requires behavior management, teach the peer tutor techniques that work for that child.	Embed these techniques throughout the training.
8. Test for understanding.	Assess tutor knowledge with a cognitive test, and require that they maintain a 90 percent average or higher.	This should be done at the end of training.
PEER TUTORING PROGRAM		
9. Ensure social interactions among students.	Use a system to ensure that the students with disabilities are having increased social interactions with their peers (e.g., verbal, eye contact, facial expressions, communication systems).	This should happen as soon as the program is implemented and throughout the program (see Klavina, 2011).
10. Monitor progress.	Establish a system to maintain tutors' performance and tutee and tutor interactions.	Provide ongoing feedback throughout each lesson on areas of strengths and areas that need improvement.

Adapted, by permission, from C.M. Cervantes et al., 2013, "Peer tutoring: Meeting the demands of inclusion in today's general physical education settings," *Journal of Physical Education, Recreation & Dance,* 84(3): 43-48

Evaluating the Tutoring Experience

In the case of Nick and Cameron from the opening scenario, a procedural fidelity checklist came in handy (see figure 5.3). Cameron used it to know when and how to communicate with Nick. The physical education teacher, Mrs. Meyers, continued to use this list to provide feedback as the communication between Nick and Cameron became more specific and clearer.

Questions can be asked to the peer tutors to learn the impact of tutoring on their participation in physical education. Klavina and Block (2008) used an eight-question survey (see figure 5.4) to learn about peer tutors' experiences of peer tutoring programs. Seven out of nine tutors reported that they did not know about peer tutoring before the program. All tutors indicated that their atti-

Provide continual feedback to peer tutors and tutees to ensure that tutees are refining their movements and skills and improving as much as possible.

tudes toward peers with disabilities improved. Although before the program some tutors anecdotally noted that their tutees were "unable to participate in activities," they realized that their classmates were capable "of doing many things together with other classmates." All peer tutors indicated that they would like to participate in peer tutoring activities in the future.

Summary

Peer tutoring is an instructional model that increases interactions between students with disabilities and their peers without disabilities in the general physical education (GPE) setting. Safety should be the first consideration when implementing peer tutoring, especially when physical contact between students is possible. You may want to set up safe areas where only students with disabilities can take part in activities with peer tutors. To be effective, tutoring should focus on goals commensurate with the student's IEP. In general, peer tutoring ensures that students with disabilities work on age-appropriate physical activities with their peers.

FIGURE 5.3

Procedural Fidelity Checklist

Tutor _____   Date _____

	Yes	Some of the time	No
Presented cue			
Use the prompting hierarchy			
Direct verbal prompt			
Model			
Physical prompt			
Full physical			
General praise			
Positive specific praise			
Error correction			
Reinforced student's attention			
Planned before asking for help			

FIGURE 5.4

Peer Tutor Survey

Answer as close as possible to how you feel after the program.

1. What was your main task when assisting the student in physical education?
   a. Tutoring
   b. Learning prompting hierarchy
   c. Improving my sport skills
   d. Talking to the student
2. How would you rate the physical skills of the student you assisted?
   __Very good   __ Good   __Moderate   __Low
3. Did you know something about peer tutoring before this program?
   __Yes   __No
4. How would you rate your performance in assisting the student?
   __Excellent   __Good   __Moderate   __Bad
5. How was your attitude toward the student you assisted after working with him or her?
   __Improved   __Did not change   __Made worse
6. What was your best experience in this program? What would you tell other people about your experience? _____

   _____

7. What was your worst experience during this program? What would have made this experience better for you? _____

   _____

8. If you had a chance to participate in a similar project in the future, would you do it? Why or why not? _____

   _____

▷ ▷

In the opening scenario, Nick was assisted in physical education by Cameron and several peers. With the training and support of his physical education teacher Mrs. Myers and his paraeducator, Mrs. Zolwich, Nick paired up with Cameron for many of his physical education classes. Cameron and several other peers were trained and then assessed, taught, provided feedback, and participated in class activities with Nick. Cameron and his peers worked on their goals and objectives necessary for their grade level while they took turns tutoring Nick. The result was more instruction and feedback for Nick while each peer tutor had a greater appreciation for the skills and abilities Nick could demonstrate.

Review Questions

1. What are the benefits of using peer tutors?
2. What are the benefits of peer tutoring for children with disabilities?
3. What are the criteria for selecting peer tutors?
4. What are the components of a peer tutor training program?
5. How can you measure the effectiveness of a peer tutoring program in terms of the tutors' experience?
6. How can you measure the effectiveness of a peer tutoring program in terms of the tutee's experience?

Paraeducators in Physical Education

Rocco Aiello
St. Mary's County Public Schools, Maryland

Lauren J. Lieberman
The College at Brockport, State University of New York

Chapter Objectives

By reading this chapter, you will:

- ▶ Gain an appreciation for the importance of paraeducators in physical education.
- ▶ Understand the roles and responsibilities of paraeducators.
- ▶ Learn strategies for preparing paraeducators to work with children with disabilities.

The local school district recently hired Ms. Conner as a full-time paraeducator to work in a separate special education classroom. During the hiring process, Ms. Conner received the school district's paraeducator handbook, which describes the roles and responsibilities of paraeducators who assist students with disabilities in general and special education classes. However, it does not mention their roles and responsibilities when assisting students with disabilities in physical education classes.

On the first day of orientation for new teachers, Ms. Conner was introduced to Ms. Baker, the special education teacher, and to Mr. Anderson, the adapted physical education (APE) teacher. In their initial meeting, Ms. Baker gave Ms. Conner her assignments, along with information about the two students she was assigned to work with: Morgan and Isaiah. Both students were diagnosed with severe autism. Ms. Conner also was told that she would assist Morgan and Isaiah in their third period, which is the separate placement APE class.

Because she was uncertain about her roles and responsibilities when assisting Morgan and Isaiah, Ms. Conner asked to meet with Mr. Anderson to find out more about APE. Mr. Anderson was impressed by Ms. Conner's initiative and put together a packet of information for her. He also gave her the book *Paraeducators in Physical Education: A Training Guide to Roles and Responsibilities* (Lieberman, 2007).

Mr. Anderson explained that in the weeks to come he and Ms. Conner would meet to discuss Morgan's and Isaiah's individual education plans (IEPs). They would also explore how best to facilitate instruction in physical education. In addition, he set up a team meeting with Ms. Baker and Ms. Conner to learn the instructional strategies that Ms. Baker uses in her self-contained special education classroom. Ms. Conner was thankful to have Mr. Anderson and Ms. Baker as mentors, who provided her with practical training and worked cooperatively with her to optimize Morgan's and Isaiah's learning.

A team approach creates a foundation of respect and unity, which contributed to Ms. Conner's feelings of self-worth as a valued, contributing team member.

A paraeducator, sometimes referred to as a teaching assistant or an educational assistant, supports the lead teacher in teaching children with disabilities. Some work one-on-one; others support all students in a classroom. Without question, paraeducators play a vital role in schools and make a difference in the lives of students with disabilities (Haegele & Kozub, 2010). Teachers and paraeducators who plan and work together develop a powerful bond and create classroom environments that provide the best possible education for their students with disabilities. This chapter outlines paraeducator roles and responsibilities in supporting students with disabilities in physical education.

The research literature reveals that paraeducators have a tremendous responsibility in teaching students with disabilities; however, they often lack appropriate training. In this chapter, we emphasize the importance of ongoing training, supervision, and support for paraeducators.

Understanding the Paraeducator's Role

Paraeducators are hired to work one-on-one or in small groups with children with moderate to severe disabilities. If a paraeducator is needed in the classroom to assist instruction of their students, it is very likely that they are needed in the gymnasium (Lieberman, 2007). According to Bryan, McCubbin, and van der Mars (2013), physical education teachers often do not know how to use paraeducators in the gymnasium. This may be the result of a lack of training in, and experience with, working with children with disabilities and paraeducators. Traditionally, classroom paraeducators have not always been expected to fulfill their responsibilities in the physical education setting for a number of reasons. It may not be in their contract as physical education may be seen as a "special" class similar to music and art from which they are excused. In other instances, paraeducators have used physical education as their break without consulting the physical educator ahead of time (Lieberman, 2007). However, many experts now assert that they should work in the physical education setting just as they do in the classroom (Piletic, Davis, & Aschemeier, 2005).

Paraeducators have an enormous responsibility for the well-being and safety of the students in their care during the school day. Teachers and paraeducators working as a team can ensure their well-being and safety while also significantly improving their learning outcomes (Sprick, Garrison, & Howard, 2005).

The physical educator should find ways to build a collaborative working relationship with the paraeducator for the benefit of increased physical education opportunities for students with disabilities (Lee & Haegele, 2016; Lieberman, & Houston-Wilson, 2018). Ultimately, this creates a healthy, trusting, and open relationship. Ideally, the team would include the entire **multidisciplinary team** and the paraeducator (see table 6.1).

Although scheduling team meetings with the paraeducator is not always easy given the limited amount of free time during the school day, doing so is important. Meetings can take place during professional days, during in-service workshops, before or after faculty meetings, or over breakfast prior to the school day. Such meetings can help the team clarify roles and responsibilities, which will ultimately benefit the students they teach. The result is a productive partnership that demonstrates open communication before, during,

The physical educator should find ways to build a collaborative working relationship with the paraeducator.

TABLE 6.1 Multidisciplinary Team Roles in Assisting the Paraeducator in Physical Education

Team member	Role	Ways to help the paraeducator in physical education
APE teacher	Create specialized programs, adaptations, and modifications to assist in the identification and remediation of physical education–related concerns for students with disabilities.	Provide instructional strategies and adaptive equipment along with training and supervision.
General physical education (GPE) teacher	Teach all children in the areas of fundamental motor skills, physical fitness, individual and team sports, and games and activities.	Provide daily lesson plans and classroom instructional strategies, and communicate on a daily basis.
Special education teacher	Design, implement, and monitor educational programs and services. Develop and implement students' IEPs and coordinate all student services with other special education team members.	Train and assist the paraeducator in carrying out instructional strategies and using assistive technology and adaptive equipment. Assist with data collection in special education classes.
Principal	Run a successful school, which includes an inclusive physical education program and other programs for students with disabilities.	Act as a resource to ensure effective instructional practices. Provide support, supervision, and appropriate evaluations. Provide opportunities to participate with other educators in professional development activities.
School nurse	Provide health care to students with disabilities, such as suctioning a tracheostomy or maintaining a feeding tube. Act as a liaison between parents, the paraeducator, and the special education team.	Support the paraeducator in acting as a liaison between the nurse's office, the GPE and APE teachers, and the special education team regarding students' medical needs and other concerns.
Recreational therapist	Provide support to the special education team and help students with disabilities participate in extracurricular activities with or without their peers without disabilities. Promote health and growth through recreational and leisure activities.	Advocate for extracurricular activities in an inclusive environment, and focus on helping students with disabilities move into adult life.
Physical therapist	Promote gross motor development along with activity of daily living skills such as accessing the school environment, dressing, toileting, and negotiating architectural barriers.	Promote the inclusion of students with disabilities in the GPE environment. Help them access the school environment, bathroom, and other places, as appropriate.
Occupational therapist	Act as a resource for the special education team regarding students' self-help and hygiene skills, fine motor skills, fundamental manipulative skills, sport-specific manipulative skills, and sensory integration.	Promote the inclusion of students with disabilities in the GPE environment. Assist with manipulative skills, sport-specific manipulative skills, and sensory integration.
Speech therapist	Assess, diagnose, treat, and help prevent speech, language, cognitive–communication, voice, swallowing, fluency, and other related disorders.	Consult with the paraeducator to understand the student's receptive and expressive language ability and how best to help the student communicate with others in physical education.
Audiologist	Work with students with hearing, balance, and other ear problems, and determine their degree of hearing loss and abilities.	Provide instructional strategies to communicate with students with hearing loss.
Vision specialist	Help students with visual impairments become as functional and independent as possible through the use of orientation and mobility techniques, Braille, magnifying glasses, canes, sighted guides, and large-print materials.	Create a classroom environment that encourages independence with gross motor skills, and prepare the student to be a productive member of the physical education class.
Orientation and mobility specialist	Teach students who are blind and visually impaired the skills they need regarding special awareness, body image, directionality, and traveling within the gymnasium and between rooms.	Provide in-service education activities in the areas of orientation and mobility (O&M) and explain the goals of the O&M program.
Assistive technology specialist	Help students with disabilities select and use technology such as computers, manual or electric wheelchairs, augmented communication devices, hearing aids, and tablets.	Help the paraeducator acquire assistive technology equipment and provide training in its use.
Parents	Collaborate with the special education team members. Advocate for the child by presenting management and training techniques that can be used in physical education.	Advocate for best practices in physical education.

Based on Block 2016.

> *It is the physical education teacher's responsibility to establish goals and expectations for the paraeducator.*

and after physical or APE class (Lee & Haegele, 2016). To further personalize this partnership, the teacher and paraeducator can work on lesson plans together to ensure consistency in goal attainment for the student (Malian, 2011). It is up to the physical education teacher to establish goals and expectations for the paraeducator when working with students with disabilities in the physical education setting. Table 6.2 offers some expectations of paraeducators when assisting all students with disabilities in physical education.

Working One-on-One and in Small Groups

Paraeducators work with individual students or small groups of students, but the ultimate respon-

sibility for the success of the lesson lays with the supervising teacher. Physical education teachers have a duty to give paraeducators clear instructions (Rouse, 2009) about student placement, the use of adaptive equipment, and strategies to meet students' educational objectives (Sprick, Garrison, & Howard, 2005). The paraeducator is responsible for helping the physical educator carry out those instructions. In many cases, students with disabilities require unique positioning or support during physical education class. Paraeducators must feel comfortable asking for help if needed.

Paraeducators may receive help from physical educators, adapted physical educators, physical therapists, or other special education team members when assisting students with motor activities (Haegele & Kozub, 2010). For example, a student with a severe disability who is participating in GPE and has a physical therapy goal of increased flexibility may need to perform a variety of stretches (see table 6.1). The APE teacher looking to improve the student's physical fitness

TABLE 6.2   Expectations of Paraeducators Working With Students With Disabilities in the Physical Education Setting

Responsibilities	General expectations
Have a good working knowledge of the student's movement.	Have a good working knowledge of the student in movement settings and outdoor environments. Students with disabilities may have reactions to and limitations in settings other than the classroom. In addition, physical education teachers may not remember information about the student. For example, when going outdoors, a friendly reminder to the teacher that the student is allergic to bee stings can be helpful. When the weather is warm, remind the teacher and the student with spina bifida about thermoregulation.
Learn technology.	Learn general technology relating to movement and physical activity (e.g., dynamic balance, flexibility, target heart rate). This increases confidence in active settings and facilitates communication with the teacher and therapists who work with the student.
Know the student's present level of performance (PLP) and goals and objectives.	Know the student's strengths and weaknesses as described in the PLP, along with goals and objectives for APE. Both can be found in the student's IEP.
Know the units and lesson plans for the class.	Find out units of instruction and lesson plans for the week before entering the gymnasium. This helps to maximize physical education time.
Keep the physical educator up-to-date.	Keep the physical educator posted with up-to-date information about the student, such as whether a student with cerebral palsy experiences seizures, if a student with autism has a behavioral intervention plan (BIP), or anything else that might impede physical education performance.
Dress appropriately.	Wear comfortable clothing and appropriate footwear for physical activity.
Instruct.	Follow the direction of the physical education teacher. Do not go beyond the teacher's directions or lessons without consulting with the teacher. Give positive and specific feedback as appropriate. Maintain a healthy and safe environment. Provide assistance retrieving and storing adaptive equipment.
Record data.	If requested by the physical education teacher, record data related to students behavior, cognitive assessments, and motor performance (Bechtel, Stevens, & Brett, 2012).

Adapted, by permission, from L.J. Lieberman, 2007, *Paraeducators in physical education: A training guide to roles and responsibilities* (Champaign, IL: Human Kinetics), 17.

in the area of flexibility or range of motion may share that goal.

Employing Differentiated Instruction

At the beginning of a school year, teachers and paraeducators get accustomed to each other's teaching styles, as well as with their students' strengths and areas in need of improvement. Both the teacher and the paraeducator should work together to establish a classroom environment that offers **differentiated instruction,** which is instruction that addresses students' specific learning styles and needs (Ellis, Lieberman, & LeRoux, 2009). For example, Tucker and Jamiah, two students in a third-grade class of 27 students, have very short attention spans for instructions and are predominantly visual learners. The teacher often sets up stations with short, clear directions on posters. During the jump rope unit, there were eight stations with various levels from jumping forward and backward over a line to jumping backward a substantial number of times. Tucker and Jamiah both spend two to three minutes at each station with a peer mentor who has task persistence.

> *Use a paraeducator to facilitate instruction through modeling, providing feedback, and demonstrating appropriate social behaviors.*

Training for Paraeducators

A major responsibility of physical education teachers is to provide direct instruction and guidance to all students and paraeducators under their supervision. Paraeducators should receive training and guidance throughout the school year. U.S. Public Law 94-142, or the Individuals with Disabilities Education Act (IDEA, 2004) requires that paraeducators be adequately and appropriately trained and supervised in accordance with state law. Most schools offer paraeducators professional development programs to enhance their professional growth and, in turn, increase their contributions to the quality of instruction offered to students with disabilities.

Ongoing training provided by physical educators can be incorporated into a school's professional development program (O'Connor & French, 1998). This can include creating a lending library that provides materials such as books, journals, and CDs, as well as sharing APE websites (Lytle, Lieberman, & Aiello, 2007). Additional training tips are presented in figure 6.1.

The physical education teacher should clearly define the paraeducator's roles and responsibility within the physical education setting, while offering ongoing and purposeful training. The physical education program runs more smoothly when the teacher makes time for training paraeducators, sets up regular meetings, and provides timely feedback and evaluation (Carroll, 2001).

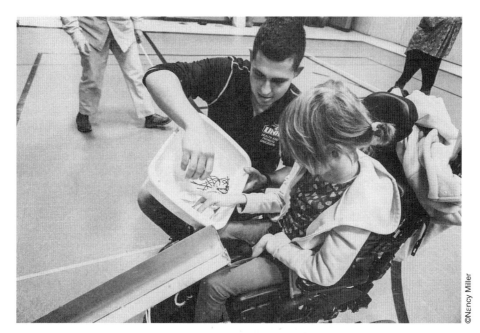

©Nancy Miller

A paraeducator helps a student choose an item to use for bowling.

FIGURE 6.1

Training Ideas for Paraeducators

- Provide a clear job description for their role in physical education.
- Review goals and objectives for students with disabilities in physical education.
- Provide a documentation log either electronically or written in which paraeducators can write daily notes.
- Supply rubrics or observation tools for each unit.
- Make appropriate modifications to equipment, rules, or activities to support student learning.
- Create guidelines for interacting with the student.
- Develop guidelines for how close to stand to the student.
- Review guidelines for social interactions with peers.
- Provide a description of the protocol for taking the student to physical education, supervising the student during physical education, and returning the student to the classroom.
- Encourage the paraeducator to assist all students in the class when possible.
- Provide feedback before, during, and after class.
- Hold in-service days.

Adapted, by permission, from R. Lytle, L.A. Lieberman., R. Aiello, 2007, "Motivating paraeducators to be actively involved in physical education," *Journal of Physical Education, Recreation & Dance,* 78(4): 26-30.

Paraeducators often wonder what their role is when the class is using trained peer tutors. The following are some ideas for paraeducator responsibilities during peer tutoring:

- Demonstrate the skills being taught.
- Provide feedback to peer tutors and students with disabilities.
- Provide continual encouragement for positive tutoring and skill development.
- Ensure safety consistently.
- Assess skill development for tutees and peer tutors.
- Ensure the proper use of equipment (modified if necessary).
- Ensure that activities are modified appropriately.
- Facilitate socialization with all students.

Ideas for Acknowledging Paraeducators' Contributions

Paraeducators who feel appreciated for their dedication and professionalism will continue to offer the best instruction to students with disabilities (Lytle et al., 2007). Many paraeducators make a lasting impact on students by improving their achievements and their educational experiences, and they deserve to be recognized. Although monetary compensation in the form of bonuses is not customary, teachers can express their gratitude, admiration, and appreciation to paraeducators in other ways.

Acknowledging paraeducators can take the form of recognition at staff or board of education meetings, at parent meetings, or in school newsletters (Giangreco, Edelman, & Broer, 2001). Such recognition brings awareness, credibility, and accountability to the incredible work paraeducators provide. Acknowledging them does not have to be a one-time event; it can be done periodically throughout the school year. The following are some suggestions:

- Send copies of commendations to principals or supervisors.
- Put letters of commendation in their professional folders.
- Provide tangible awards such as plaques and certificates.

- Recognize them during staff appreciation days or weeks.
- Mention their efforts and work with students with disabilities in school papers, newsletters, or local newspapers.
- Announce over the school's public address system, or place in the daily bulletin the important work paraeducators have been doing.
- Hang a bulletin board near the main entryway of the school and gymnasium to highlight paraeducators.
- Post success stories and pictures on bulletin boards.
- Highlight paraeducators' names on gymnasium or office doors.
- Establish a bulletin board to spotlight a different paraeducator each month.
- Include paraeducators in teacher appreciation week.

Adapted from The Presidential Youth Fitness Program 2013; Lytle, Lieberman, and Aiello, 2007.

As schools change, so have the roles of paraeducators, which has brought about significant improvements both for schools and for paraeducators (Twachtman-Cullen, 2008). Their commitment, dedication, and perseverance have been appreciated by teachers, administrators, and parents, as well as by the students they serve. As paraeducators become better prepared to work with all students, especially students with disabilities, their efforts should be valued and recognized. Those who demonstrate exceptional skills, dedication, and perseverance should be acknowledged.

Summary

Students with disabilities can learn and improve their skills and abilities in physical education. Paraeducators are key personnel in classes with students with disabilities. Physical education teachers must know what they need from paraeducators and communicate clearly with them to ensure that they know their roles and responsibilities. In ongoing training programs, paraeducators should learn, among other things, instruction techniques, how to work with the multidisciplinary team, positioning, and transfers. They also must be rewarded for their valuable contributions.

▷ ▷

During Ms. Conner's first year as a paraeducator, she learned an incredible amount about working with students with disabilities. Her on-the-job training was conducted by an exceptional team that included a physical therapist, an occupational therapist, the special education teachers, an APE teacher, nurses, and family members, among others. This support improved Ms. Conner's content knowledge, instruction skills, and collaborative skills, allowing her to meet the needs of the students with disabilities who were assigned to her.

In the years that followed, Ms. Conner continued to provide support and instruction to Morgan and Isaiah in all areas of their education. In the inclusive educational environment, she bridged the gap between teachers and students. As a result of her wealth of knowledge, Ms. Conner was viewed as the nucleus of the special education team.

Review Questions

1. What are some of the roles of paraeducators?
2. What topics should be covered in a paraeducator training program?
3. How can teachers show their appreciation for paraeducators?
4. How can paraeducators contribute during peer tutoring programs?

7

Creating Accessible Equipment

Sean Healy
Department of Behavioral Health and Nutrition, University of Delaware

Nancy Miller
Newmarket Elementary School, New Hampshire

Chapter Objectives

By reading this chapter, you will:

- ▶ Recognize the need for adapted equipment for providing individualized, effective physical education to students with disabilities.
- ▶ Use equipment that ensures the safe and successful participation of all students.
- ▶ Apply the six Ss model for equipment adaptation to ensure that all students can achieve SHAPE America's National Standards & Grade-Level Outcomes for K-12 physical education.

Abby is a friendly, bubbly third-grade student. She has spasticity in her arms and legs, has a cortical visual impairment, and requires an electric wheelchair for mobility. She uses vision, touch, and body movements to convey her intentions, and she has a full-time paraeducator who takes care of her daily and safety needs. Abby comes from an active family. Among their many hobbies, Abby's parents and two sisters enjoy participating in archery on weekends at a local sports facility. Abby would love to participate also, and her parents have requested that the adapted physical education (APE) teacher focus on archery skills with her.

Ms. Owens, Abby's APE teacher, gladly includes archery on Abby's individual education plan (IEP). Ms. Owens has taught archery before, and it is an IEP goal for other students on her caseload, but she now questions whether she can adapt the archery equipment to ensure that Abby achieves her goal. Ms. Owens also questions how she can ensure that Abby is meeting the grade 3 standards from SHAPE America's National Standards & Grade-Level Outcomes for K-12 physical education. In particular, she wonders how Abby could achieve the standards relating to the manipulative skills of catching, throwing, dribbling, volleying, and striking. Ms. Owens realizes that she will need to adapt equipment to ensure Abby's success.

Many physical education teachers and adapted physical education specialists find themselves in a situation similar to that of Ms. Owens. They have limited equipment to meet SHAPE America's National Standards & Grade-Level Outcomes for K-12 physical education for all students. This may be because specialized equipment is expensive; it is needed by only a small percentage of the student body; or it may not be high on the purchase list. Moreover, equipment for students with disabilities must be highly individualized; traditional equipment may not match their needs and abilities. Finally, equipment that could help particular students may not even be available commercially. For these reasons, being able to create or adapt equipment is an essential skill for physical educators.

Adapting Equipment With SENSE

Adapting equipment is a daily practice for physical educators teaching students with disabilities. **Adapted equipment** must contribute to the student's learning. To assess the value of an activity, ask the question, "Does it make **SENSE**?" This acronym stands for the following essential characteristics of a worthwhile activity:

- **S**afe: Does the activity and the equipment allow for safe participation? When creating or adapting equipment, consider the safety of the user and those in the vicinity.
- **E**ducational: Is the activity contributing to the attainment of the student's goals, as noted on the student's IEP. Does it align with SHAPE America's National Standards & Grade-Level Outcomes for K-12 physical education? Avoid using equipment simply because it is suitable for the student. It must contribute to the attainment of the student's goals or standards.
- **N**umber of practice trials: Does the activity and the equipment provide the student with maximal practice trials? Having a sufficient number of equipment pieces can contribute to this. Equipment can also reduce wait time, as discussed later in the chapter (e.g., reducing the time spent retrieving struck or thrown balls).
- **S**uccess: Does the equipment allow for success in the majority of the student's trials? Later in the chapter we discuss ways to adapt equipment to increase success.

> When observing a student using equipment in a physical education class, or when planning an activity, ask yourself, "Does it make SENSE?" If it fails to meet one of the criteria in this acronym, perhaps you can improve it.

- **E**njoyment: Is the student enjoying using the equipment? Does the equipment result in positive interactions with fellow classmates? Enjoyment increases the likelihood of transfer of skills to settings outside of physical education.

Six Ss for Adapting Equipment

Adapting equipment requires creativity and ingenuity. These four steps will help you adapt or create equipment:

1. Identify the skill you want to teach. It should contribute to the achievement of one of the student's or the class's goals aligned with SHAPE America's National Standards & Grade-Level Outcomes for K-12 physical education.
2. Identify the functional ability of the student and the student's current ability to perform the skill.
3. Apply the **six Ss model of equipment adaptation** to allow the student to use his or her functional ability to meet the goals of the skill. These include size, sound, support, surface, speed, and switches.
4. Assess the student's use of the equipment using the SENSE criteria.

For example, the process of adapting equipment for Abby may look as follows:

1. Identify the skill you want to teach. For Abby, this is shooting an arrow at a target.
2. Identify the functional ability of the student. Abby's upper-body strength allows her to lift light items; she finds it easiest to grip larger items; and she can see items that are brightly colored.
3. Apply the six Ss model of equipment adaptation to help Abby perform the skill.
4. Assess Abby's performance using the SENSE criteria.

To guide you in adapting equipment, the following sections outline the six Ss of size, sound, support, surface, speed, and switches. In many instances, you will need to apply several adaptations to a piece of equipment.

Size

With physical education equipment, one size does not fit all. All equipment should be adapted in terms of size to allow the child to perform optimal movement patterns. For example, when teaching throwing, kicking, or striking, use balls that are an appropriate size for the students.

For throwing, the ball should be of a suitable size and weight so the child can easily lift it and feels comfortable holding it. You may need to deflate the ball so a child can grasp it. For kicking and striking, a bigger ball helps children with coordination difficulties by providing a larger target area for making contact. When selecting equipment such as nets, basketball rings, bowling pins, goals, hula hoops, poly spots, and jump ropes, consider their size. Students may benefit from being allowed to choose from a variety of equipment sizes. Figures 7.1, 7.2, 7.3, and 7.4

Figure 7.1 Target sizes are adapted to ensure success for all students as they learn to throw at a target.

Figure 7.2 Small climbing wall grips can be made bigger to be easier to see and reach.

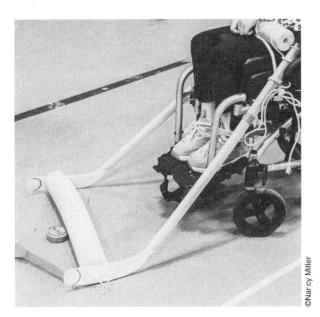

Figure 7.3 Noodles fastened to a wheelchair allow for easy striking of the puck.

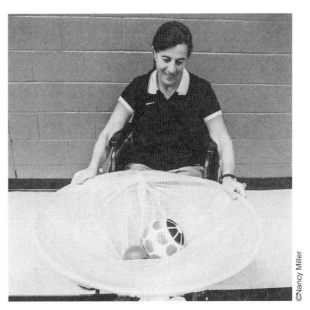

Figure 7.4 Instead of carrying the ball on a small racket, the student may use a larger net. A bag wrapped around a hoop is an easy solution.

show further examples of adapting the sizes of equipment to suit the children.

Sound

Particularly for children with vision loss, adding sound to sporting equipment can make previously inaccessible activities accessible. Devices such as battery-operated security beepers and bells can be added (see figure 7.5). For example, to insert security beepers into sponge balls, remove a piece of the outer plastic coating, scrape out some sponge, insert the beeper with the on/off switch showing, and re-stitch the outer plastic covering (or seal it with tape). Bells (such as those used in Christmas tree decorations) can also be inserted into hollow balls such as wiffle balls. To create a low-cost audible ball, place a soccer ball in a plastic bag; it will rustle as it rolls, helping the student practice a sport such as soccer or goalball.

You can add sound-emitting devices to targets and cones to help students with visual impairments locate them. Simply tape a beeper to the equipment. In some instances, sound does not have to be emitted constantly. A student holding a string attached to a bell can ring it when necessary. For example, a student practicing a basketball free throw may need help locating the hoop. Rather than placing a device that emits a constant sound from the hoop, you can fasten a doorbell to a string that the student can ring at will.

Support

Supported equipment is particularly useful when teaching ball activities. Suspending a ball from a rope, for example, makes a striking activity less dynamic and increases the child's chance of succeeding at striking. It also reduces the need to retrieve the ball. A hanging ball swung to a child travels in a more predictable trajectory than a tossed ball does.

Support may also include a platform to support equipment (e.g., a ball tee). For those with limited upper-body strength, a first step in practicing the strike may be sitting at a table and moving a bat along the tabletop to strike an oncoming rolling ball. To teach the overhand throw, you could string a ball, such as a Bendy Ball, which is available from most major equipment companies on a horizontal line (a plastic clothesline is best for this). The student grips the ball and uses an overhand throw pattern to slide the ball along the line. This adaptation helps the student hold up the ball and encourages correct arm movement.

In bowling, various types of ramps can be used for support. Figure 7.6 shows a straight ramp;

> Skills such as striking and catching a tossed ball require coordination and visual tracking skills. A ball swinging lightly from a suspended rope can greatly help students predict the trajectory of the ball.

Figure 7.5 Adding bells to a climbing wall provides auditory feedback.

Figure 7.6 A straight ramp provides support for bowling.

figure 7.7 shows an air conditioning tube; and figure 7.8 shows a plastic tube.

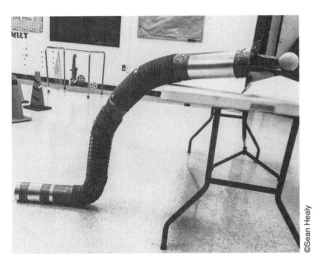

Figure 7.7 A ramp for bowling supported on a table.

Figure 7.8 A ramp for bowling created with a plastic tube.

Surface

Adapting the surface of equipment can also help students with disabilities. You might add texture to a ball or a bat handle to improve a student's grip. This can be done by wrapping thin rope or string around the equipment and covering it with tape. You can also sew Velcro into the palm of a glove and fasten it with tape. (*Note:* A tennis ball will stick to Velcro without adaptation.) For children with visual impairments, adapting equipment surfaces is particularly important

Figure 7.9 A variety of textures on the surface of this climbing wall gives the student greater feedback.

because it allows them to more efficiently use their proprioceptive skills (see figure 7.9). Adding color or lights to equipment can greatly help some children with visual impairments see it more clearly (e.g., fasten Christmas tree lights in a circle around a target frame).

Speed

Slowing down the speed of some equipment can be a great help to some children. Balls, in particular, often need to move slower for easier throwing, catching, kicking, and striking. To slow down the speed of a catching activity, consider using a scarf, a balloon, or a lightweight ball; these all travel much slower than a regular ball, giving students more time to prepare for the catch. A balloon wrapped in a stocking also makes for a cheap, durable lightweight ball. As the student's ability develops, progress to a faster-moving object. For students learning to dribble or trap a ball with the foot, simply use a slightly deflated ball. Weighted balls (also called slow-motion balls) are now available from most major equipment companies.

Switches

Switches in this context are low- or high-tech methods of activating equipment with less force than is normally needed, or with an alternative movement from the child. The power in the **switch-activated equipment** comes from a variety of sources ranging from battery-operated motors to elastic to grasp and release. Switches that activate equipment should encourage students to move as far as they can. For example, a student with limited use of one hand should be encouraged to activate the equipment using the hand's maximal range of motion. Switches may also be activated by using the foot, head, or mouth or an electric wheelchair. Figures 7.10, 7.11, and 7.12 present a variety of switches used to include children in physical education activities.

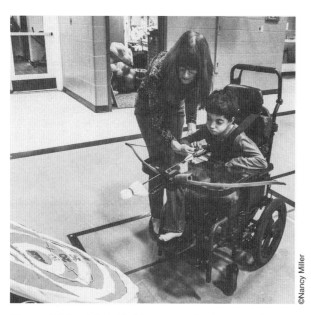

Figure 7.10   A handheld grasp and release on the arrow enables the student to release the arrow.

Figure 7.11   A rope is strung through a hockey stick and wound up. When the student releases the handheld rope, the stick swings to strike the ball.

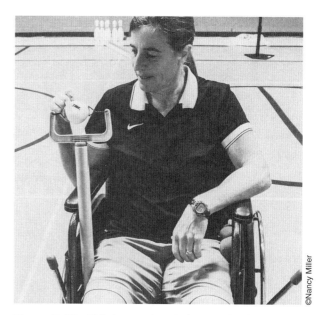

Figure 7.12   This low-tech switch uses elastic to launch a lightweight ball.

> *Switches should encourage students to use their maximal range of motion (e.g., place a switch in such a way that the child must fully extend an arm to press it).*

You can apply the six Ss of adaptation to existing equipment or use them to create new equipment to help students achieve their goals based on SHAPE America's National Standards & Grade-Level Outcomes for K-12 physical education. Table 7.1 provides practical examples of using the six Ss model of equipment adaptation to ensure that all students achieve the national standards relating to manipulative skills.

Summary

Students, like Abby, often require adapted equipment to achieve SHAPE America's National Standards & Grade-Level Outcomes for K-12 physical education. Using the six Ss model of equipment adaptation (size, sound, support, surface, speed, and switches), you can adapt equipment to ensure student success. Moreover, when using equipment, consider the SENSE criteria, and ensure that equipment is safe, is educational (relating to the SHAPE America's National Standards & Grade-Level Outcomes), affords a high number of practice trials, ensures success, and is enjoyable to use.

TABLE 7.1 Using the Six Ss to Meet SHAPE America's National Standards & Grade-Level Outcomes for K-12 Physical Education for Manipulative Skills

SHAPE America's National Standards & Grade-Level Outcomes for K-12 physical education	Using the six Ss to adapt equipment
Underhand throw (S1.E13)	• Vary the size and weight of the ball. • Suspend the ball from a rope and have the student swing or release it to strike the pins or target. • Vary the size of the target. • Allow the student to launch the ball using a switch. • Allow the student to roll the ball. • Allow the student to use a ramp to roll the ball. • Use a switch to help the student release the ball.
Overhand throw (S1.E14)	• Vary the size and weight of the ball. • Suspend the ball. • Allow the student to launch the ball using a switch.
Catching (S1.E16)	• Vary the size and weight of the ball. • Support the ball with a rope to create a more predictable trajectory. • Use a ball with a bright surface so it is easily seen. • Add sound to the ball using bells or a beeper. • Use a textured surface to increase the student's ability to grip the ball (consider replacing the ball with a scarf, or put the ball in a net).
Dribbling/ball control with hands (S1.E17)	• Choose a size that is comfortable for the student (a larger ball provides a larger surface area to hit). • Use a brightly colored ball to increase visibility. • Use a lighter ball that moves more slowly (e.g., have the student dribble a helium balloon secured to a weight on the ground).
Dribbling/ball control with feet (S1.E18)	• Adapt the speed of the ball by adding weight or deflating the ball. • Support the ball by tying it to the student's belt to facilitate retrieving. • Use a brightly colored ball to increase visibility.
Passing and receiving with feet (S1.E19)	• Use a larger ball to make kicking and receiving easier. • Make receiving easier by adding weight (sand or beans) or deflating the ball. • Add sound (with bells or by putting the ball in a plastic bag) so a student with vision loss can better predict its trajectory. • The student may strike the ball with switch-activated equipment instead of kicking.
Volley, underhand; volley, overhead (S1.E22 or S1.E23)	• Use a lighter ball, which moves more slowly. • Support the ball using a rope that is fixed to the ceiling, a basketball hoop, or a volleyball net to give the student time to volley. • Use a brightly colored ball, which is more easily seen and volleyed. • Allow the student to use a switch to launch the volleyball over the net.
Striking, short implement; striking, long implement (S1.E24 or S1.E25)	• Use a larger ball or bat (or both) to increase student success. • Support the ball using a tee or by hanging it on a rope to increase striking success. • Use a brightly colored ball, which is more easily seen. • Allow the student to use a switch-activated bat to strike the ball. • Place the ball on a table; student moves hand or bat across table to strike ball off table.

Reprinted from SHAPE America, 2014, *National standards & grade-level outcomes for K-12 physical education* (Champaign, IL: Human Kinetics), 28-31.

▷ ▷

Miss Owens used the six Ss model of equipment adaptation to help Abby achieve her archery goal. Five of the six Ss were used to adapt the equipment:

▶ Size: Abby used a smaller bow.
▶ Sound: Adding a bell to the bow string increased Abby's motivation to grab it.
▶ Support: The bow was mounted horizontally to a scooter using a clamp and was placed on Abby's lap.
▶ Surface: The bright yellow scooter, large colorful felt arrow tips, large colorful target, and big shiny bell on the bowstring all visually engaged Abby, who has a cortical visual impairment. A beeper was also added to the target so she knew where to shoot the arrow.
▶ Speed: Because the bow was supported, Abby could go at a slower pace because she did not have to hold the bow.

Review Questions

1. What are the SENSE criteria, and why are they used?
2. What are the six Ss of equipment adaptation?
3. What are three possible equipment adaptations for a student with a disability who wants to bowl?
4. What are two possible equipment adaptations for a student with a disability who is learning to catch a ball?
5. What are two possible equipment adaptations for a student with a disability who wants to practice hand dribbling a ball?

Participation for All in Sport Activities

Part II provides foundational knowledge for developing content through sensory integration and functional analysis. Because there is a need to provide physical activity opportunities beyond the school day, transitional services and extracurricular activities, including disability sports, are also discussed. The chapters in part II also describe modified programming and aquatics as part of the physical education experience.

Foundational Skills and Sensory Integration

Thomas E. Moran
James Madison University, Virginia

Brad M. Weiner
Montgomery County Public Schools, Maryland

Chapter Objectives

By reading this chapter, you will:

▶ Understand essential foundational skills.
▶ Learn how to align instruction and the curriculum to grade-level outcomes based on each student's ability level(s).
▶ Learn to create lessons that link the development of foundational skills to the student's ability to enjoy lifetime leisure.
▶ Understand sensorimotor instruction and how it affects student behaviors.
▶ Use sensory integration strategies to enhance or support instruction.

Seacoast United Area Public Schools has recently implemented a full-inclusion philosophy, and Mr. Richardson, a 12-year physical education veteran, is seeking professional development to help him include students with disabilities in his general physical education (GPE) classes. He would like to include Kathy, a 10-year-old fifth-grader, with her 27 classmates. At the age of three, Kathy was involved in an accident that significantly affected her learning and motor development. Kathy's individual education program (IEP) identifies her as having multiple disabilities that include an intellectual disability, an orthopedic impairment, a hearing impairment, and visual impairments. Kathy receives special education, adapted physical education, physical therapy, occupational therapy, audiology, and vision services. The IEP provides Kathy with a one-on-one paraeducator throughout the school day, who helps her with toileting, eating, and academic instruction.

Kathy accepts passive stretching exercises and, with physical assistance, demonstrates full range of motion at her shoulders. Independently, she can lift her arms to eye level. Kathy's biceps are contracted, keeping her arms in a flexed position. She has difficulty maintaining a grasp and releasing objects in a controlled way. Kathy's hamstrings are also contracted so that her legs are bent in a seated position. She can rotate her head left, right, up, and down with control.

The physical therapist primarily focuses on Kathy's posture, body positioning, and weight bearing with the support of a supine stander. She is working with Kathy to enhance independent mobility through the use of a motorized wheelchair with a joystick.

Kathy often smiles and bobs her head, especially when she hears music and familiar voices. She laughs when startled by quick, loud sounds. She performs best when red or shiny items are presented to her against a black background. Kathy is inconsistent with tracking slow-moving objects across her field of view and does not always turn her head toward sounds.

Mr. Richardson recognizes the importance of having a program that meets the needs of all his students, while addressing Kathy's particular and extensive needs.

According to the Society of Health and Physical Educators (SHAPE) America's National Standards & Grade-Level Outcomes, there are overarching benchmarks along "the road to a lifetime of physical activity" (see figure 8.1). These benchmarks guide teachers like Mr. Richardson as they review physical education curricula and determine how to implement their instructional plans. Regardless of an individual's ability level, the road to a lifetime of physical activity begins with learning fundamental skills, content, and values at the elementary level (Couturier, Chepko, & Holt/Hale, 2014). This chapter addresses sensory integration theory and foundational skills for aligning curricula with the Universal Design for Learning (UDL) framework for students with disabilities.

Understanding Sensory Integration Theory

Cheatum and Hammond (2000) described **sensory integration** as "the ability to receive, orga- nize, interpret, and use the vast amount of sensory information that enters the body and neurological system through both external and internal stimuli" (p. 132). The adequate processing and integration of sensory information is an important foundation for **adaptive behaviors**—that is, actions such as play and activities of daily living (Lane & Schaaf, 2010). Anna Jean Ayres, known by many as the founder of sensory integration theory, hypothesized that some deficits in sensory processing and integration result in limitations in the production of adaptive behaviors and, therefore, in participation. Table 8.1 describes the five sensory systems.

Mr. Richardson knows that Kathy has a visual impairment and that he can stimulate her visual perception with shiny materials against a black background. He also uses the strength of her tactile system to help her meet the curriculum goals. Even though Kathy has a limited range of motion in some joints, promoting some movement with resistance will provide proprioceptive input to help her understand where her limbs are in space. Mr. Richardson has Kathy do a fitness warm-up along with her peers. Her peers do jumping jacks,

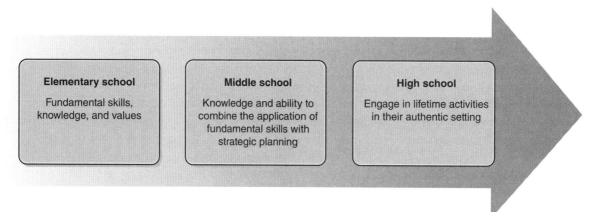

Figure 8.1   The road to a lifetime of physical activity.

TABLE 8.1   Five Sensory Systems Commonly Affected in Physical Education

Sensory system	Definition	Examples
Auditory system (sense of hearing)	The system through which we receive and process sound; a stimulation is received through the peripheral receptors and then transmitted to the central auditory nervous system.	• Recognizing sounds and rhythms • Signals for attention • Stop-and-go games • Simon says • Pacer test
Proprioceptive system (sense of body awareness)	The system that receives sensations from receptors in the muscles, joints, skin, tendons, and underlying tissue. It is through this system that a person can sense a static position within dynamic movement.	• Animal walks • Body balances • Planks and push-ups • Yoga poses
Tactile system (sense of touch)	The system that receives information when something comes in contact with the skin. Seven types of skin receptors are stimulated by pressure, temperature, and pain.	• Using objects with different textures • Teaching outside versus inside • Using objects that vibrate or have different temperatures
Vestibular system (sense of balance and motion)	The system that informs the nervous system where the body is in relationship to the pull of gravity so that the person can maintain equilibrium.	• Body balances • Balance beam • Walking a line • Playground swings • Scooters (spinning) • Swaying and rocking
Visual system (sense of sight)	The system that, through a learned process, changes images gained through acuity into useful information.	• Teaching outside on a sunny day versus inside with low light • Using brightly colored equipment • Using a flashlight or glow stick • Tracking slow-moving objects • Suspending objects • Scarf catching

Note: Educators need to be aware of the olfactory and gustatory systems, but these are predominantly stimulated in the classroom.

> *Sensory experiences are for developing foundational skills and organizing and producing appropriate responses.*

push-ups, and mountain climbers. Meanwhile, Kathy has light weights and bells strapped to her arms so that when she lifts or extends them, she feels the resistance of the weights and receives auditory feedback from the bells.

Developing Foundational Skills

Foundational skills are the skills that support and make up more complex movements and higher-order concepts (see figure 8.2). A 16-week-old infant grasps the finger of a parent as it is placed in the palm. What begins as a reflexive movement becomes voluntary and supports the child's discovery of the surrounding environment. Similarly, a professional baseball player grasps a baseball with a specialized technique to throw a knuckleball to strike out a batter. Both are examples of using foundational skill(s) and body coordination to perform a task or meet task demands. The infant and the baseball player are at different points along the same spectrum; their coordinated movements, performed to grasp the object, seem different, but they stem from the same rudimentary skill. The infant is developing foundational skills to use throughout life.

Mr. Richardson now understands that to help Kathy achieve educational success, he must focus

Psychomotor skills	Affective skills	Cognitive skills
Balance	Facial expression	Cause and effect
Visual perception	Attention span	Prior experiences
Range of motion	Social interaction	Follows one-step directions
Body coordination	Displayed behaviors	Expressive communication
Weight shifting	Sensory receptors	Receptive communication

Figure 8.2 Foundational skills.

on foundational skills. The U.S. Office of Special Education and Rehabilitative Services sent out a letter confirming that "the annual goals need not necessarily result in the child's reaching grade-level within the year covered by the IEP, but the goals should be sufficiently ambitious to help close the gap" (Special Education and Rehabilitative Services, 2015, p. 5). The purpose of special education services and supports is to work toward closing the educational gap. This can be related to overall curriculum programming and everyday lesson planning. Using foundational skills through traditional task analysis and ecological task analysis, which are discussed in the next section, helps move students in the direction of achieving grade-level outcomes.

Traditional Versus Ecological Task Analysis

A **traditional task analysis** involves breaking a motor skill down into its discrete and underlying parts (Davis & Burton, 1991). An ecological task analysis, in addition to breaking down the skill, takes into account the preferences of the students related to the task, the skill, and the learner (Davis & Burton, 1991). This is a very important additional step in addressing the needs of all students, especially when considering the unique needs of students with disabilities. The next section describes the process of analyzing foundational skills for students with disabilities.

Foundational Psychomotor Skills

The development of motor skills travels along a spectrum that starts with reflexes and ends

©Michelle Grenier

In this setup, students can work on the foundational skills of balance, posture, and coordination.

with coordinated specialized movements (Gallahue, Ozman, & Goodway, 2012). Foundational psychomotor skills support the development of controlled and coordinated movements known as purposeful movements. As a teacher, it is your task to determine the required foundational skills students need to perform motor skills. These foundational skills determine their level of success with a given movement. Although understanding each foundational skill is critical, the next step is realizing that a given motor skill may require a combination of foundational skills depending on its complexity.

Understand the demands of each task presented to your students. Tasks that require the integration of numerous foundational skills may not be developmentally appropriate for students at a given grade level, regardless of their ability or disability.

Table 8.2 shows a sample task analysis for fifth-graders.

Foundational Affective Skills

Emotional well-being affects students' engagement in leisure, recreation, and sport activities. Developing foundational affective skills results in emotionally self-confident individuals who are intrinsically motivated to participate in social activities. SHAPE America's Standard 4 focuses on personal and social behavior, as shown in table 8.3, which describes how the foundational skills apply to the affective domain.

Teachers can recognize students' emotional status and sense of well-being through eye, cheek, and mouth movements and by the way they hold their heads. Mr. Richardson has learned that when Kathy's eyes are open wide, she is excited; when her eyes are closed, her intrinsic motivation is low. Self-confidence and intrinsic motivation are developed through enjoyable and successful practice trials. Mr. Richardson learned about Kathy's by observing her facial expressions when her peers were interacting with her versus when she was in an isolated situation. Her multiple disabilities affect her ability to communicate with peers, which creates a social barrier to interaction.

TABLE 8.2 Sample Task Analysis for Fifth-Graders: Kicking and Punting

SHAPE America's National Standards & Grade-Level Outcome for fifth-graders: "Demonstrates mature patterns in kicking and punting in small-sided practice task environments" (S1.E21.5) (SHAPE America, 2014, p. 30).

	Kicking	Punting
Fifth-grade cues	• Continuous motion to the ball. • Nonkicking foot steps forward, placed next to ball. • Shoulders are square to target. • Contacts ball with laces, instep on shoe. • Follows through.	• Holds ball in front. • Takes three or four continuous steps forward. • Maintains balance on one foot. • Drops ball while bringing kicking foot up. • Follows through.
Foundational skills associated with the grade-level outcome skills	• Balance • Body coordination • Visual perception • Range of motion • Weight shift • Object control • Body awareness • Mobility	• Balance • Body coordination • Visual perception • Range of motion • Weight shift • Object control • Body awareness • Mobility
Foundational skills to focus on for Kathy	• Visual perception • Body awareness • Body coordination • Mobility	• Visual perception • Body awareness • Body coordination • Mobility
Kathy's developmental outcome aligned to the fifth-grade outcome	• Visual perception: Able to detect the location of the ball by moving her eyes or head in the appropriate direction. • Body awareness: Faces her chair in the appropriate direction in relationship to the ball while on defense in a small-sided game of power soccer. • Body coordination and mobility: Able to move her wheelchair's joystick in the appropriate direction to attempt to receive the ball.	

TABLE 8.3   Sample Task Analysis for Fifth-Graders: Responsible Personal Behavior

SHAPE America's National Standards & Grade-Level Outcome for fifth graders: "Participates with responsible personal behavior in a variety of physical activity contexts, environments and facilities" (S4.E2.5a) (SHAPE America, 2014, p. 36).

Fifth-grade cues	• Provides peers with positive feedback. • Promotes a positive environment. • Provides corrective feedback. • Follows the rules and expectations of the class and activities.
Foundational skills associated with the grade-level outcome skills	• Facial expression • Attention span • Social interaction • Displayed behaviors
Foundational skills to focus on for Kathy	• Attention span • Displayed behaviors
Kathy's developmental outcome aligned to the fifth-grade outcome	With the integration of motivational stimulation, Kathy keeps her eyes open and focused on a variety of activities, displaying responsible personal behavior through the acceptance of physical guidance.

Foundational Cognitive Skills

Students' comprehension of instructional content is measured by their ability to produce a response (Hourcade, Pilotte, West, & Parette, 2004). The response may be an eye gaze, turn of the head, cheek movement, or facial expression; the student may press an assistive communication device or verbalize a sound. Members of the multidisciplinary team can help you understand each student's mode and level of communication. The list is extensive, and each student with communication barriers communicates in a uniquely personalized way. Foundational cognitive skills support the development of students' abilities to communicate their understanding of the content.

Students with disabilities should to work on developmentally appropriate skills that align specifically with the age-appropriate grade-level outcomes. In table 8.4, Kathy's classmates are working toward mastery of an age-appropriate grade-level outcome. Mr. Richardson uses his knowledge of Kathy's current abilities to determine the developmentally appropriate skills to work on that support Kathy's growth toward the grade-level outcome. Standard 2 focuses on applying knowledge, which describes how

the foundational skills apply to the cognitive domain. Table 8.4 is an example of a knowledge assessment.

Putting Your Plan Into Action

Teachers must follow a clear curriculum that goes from basic to complex skills each year and for each grade level. This is referred to as the scope and sequence of the curriculum. Mr. Richardson notes that his curriculum includes tennis. Before he can develop an appropriate striking lesson for Kathy or any of his fifth-grade students, he must conduct an ecological task analysis of the skill of striking with a short-handled implement. As part of the analysis, Mr. Richardson should consider the individual, the task, and the environment. Racquet activities are very popular in the community and within the school district. Kathy will be surrounded by peers who likely engage in racquet activities, and she deserves the opportunity to engage alongside them. As part of his analysis, Mr. Richardson must take into account the skills students must possess to perform the task of striking such as gripping a striking implement, moving the arm back and forth, and watching the ball, balloon, or birdie. Next, he must break down the task itself. The technique of the skill, the rules associated with the skill, the equipment needed, and the environmental factors that will affect students' performances during the unit (table 8.5). Mr. Richardson now has the challenge of maxi-

Take the time to learn how your student communicates. This is the doorway to teaching and developing a relationship with the student.

mizing each student's functional abilities, including Kathy's, by manipulating the task and the environment. All of the objects Kathy will strike will be large and bright and have bells attached to them. Each will be suspended from a string and be at the level of her arm or implement so she can strike without having to lift or lower her arm or the implement. Mr. Richardson has decided to try two strategies: (1) Attach a large lightweight implement to Kathy's arm using a Velcro band to eliminate the issue of grip strength (all she needs to do is initiate extension), and (2) create a pull

TABLE 8.4   Sample Task Analysis: Strategic Movements in Game Environments

SHAPE America's National Standards & Grade-Level Outcome for fifth-graders: "Analyzes movement situations and applies movement concepts (e.g., force, direction, speed, pathways, extensions) in small-sided practice tasks in game environments, dance and gymnastics" (S2.E3.5c) (Couturier et al., 2014, p. 32).

Fifth-grade cues	• Demonstrates knowledge of the pathways of basic plays. • Demonstrates knowledge of when to change direction during basic plays. • Demonstrates knowledge of the appropriate time to apply force and to change speed during basic plays.
Foundational skills associated with the grade-level outcome skills	• Cause and effect • Prior experiences • Receptive communication (communicates with peers and reads body language of peers)
Foundational skills to focus on for Kathy	Cause and effect: For example, Kathy presses a voice output device that says "Fast," and she is pushed fast in her wheelchair. Kathy may also be given a choice of pressing one of two output devices that say "Left" and "Right." Her wheelchair is pushed in the direction of the button she presses.
Kathy's developmental outcome aligned to the fifth-grade outcome	Presented with a large obstacle in her pathway, Kathy will use the joystick to change the direction of her motorized wheelchair to maneuver around the obstacle without touching it.

TABLE 8.5   Sample Skill Breakdown: Striking With a Short-Handled Implement

Individual	Task: Technique (with or without assistance; with paraeducator or peer)	Task: Rules	Task: Equipment	Environment
Body orientation	Face or side orientation?	Strike a bounced versus a tossed ball?	Type and size of object to be struck?	Physical space?
Spatial orientation	Lift arm to start position.	Allow for one bounce or multiple bounces?	Type and size of implement?	Self, partner, or small group?
Tracking ability	Move eyes to match the path of the object.	Start with hitting a ball off a tee or on a string.	Height of net?	Activity is important in community.
Eye–hand coordination	Swing arm (overhead motion).		Pull cord to strike the ball with one pull.	
Grip strength	Grip implement.		Attach racket to hand with Velcro if necessary.	
Limb dexterity	Forehand motion with implement.			
Upper-body strength	Overhead motion with implement.			

cord lever that Kathy can pull to extend the implement toward the object to strike it. Most exciting for Mr. Richardson is that this approach to instruction has allowed him to seamlessly address the needs of all of his students, including Kathy.

Summary

This chapter explains foundational skills and sensory integration and the essential role each plays in student success. The breakdown of the foundational skills by domains ensures both age-appropriate and developmentally appropriate instruction for all students in a class. An understanding of the role of foundational skills and sensory integration reveals the relationship between students' sensory needs and their relationship to learning motor skills that meet the national standards. Finally, the actions steps of an ecological task analysis ensure that lessons are universally designed for all.

▷ ▷

Mr. Richardson's dedication to researching, collaborating, and planning throughout the year helped him provide a quality physical education program for Kathy. He understood the importance of knowing the benefits of the sensory integration to teach the foundational skills to meet grade-level standards. For Kathy, this meant focusing on mobility, body awareness, body coordination, and visual perception while her peers where focused on kicking and punting patterns. All students practiced their skills in the same activity or task, even though the lesson objectives were individualized.

Review Questions

1. What is sensory motor integration?
2. How can you measure the strengths and abilities of your students?
3. What skills can be used to demonstrate motor abilities?
4. What variations can be used to teach motor skills to children with severe disabilities?
5. What strategies could be used to universally design a badminton unit for a student with a severe disability in a fifth-grade GPE class?

Disability Sport in Physical Education

Wesley J. Wilson
University of Virginia

Chapter Objectives

By reading this chapter, you will:

▶ Understand the contribution of disability sport to the overall well-being of students with disabilities.

▶ Learn about types of disability sports and how they can be modified further to accommodate students even with the most severe disabilities.

▶ Recognize the important role of the physical educators and adapted physical educators in disability sport.

Muhammad is a 13-year-old boy who loves everything about sports. On weekends, he and his family watch his older brother play on the high school soccer team. Because of severe spastic cerebral palsy that affects all four of his limbs and a moderate intellectual disability, Muhammad often feels excluded from soccer and other sports offered in the local community leagues. His physical education teacher and his paraeducator work hard on modifying activities during his physical education class, but his community sports programs are ill-equipped to accommodate his unique needs. In many cases, the program coordinators worry about his safety as well as the safety of the other children. On the recommendation of a special education teacher, Muhammad's parents have begun to look at a variety of disability sport options that are available in neighboring townships. A small community power soccer program looks promising. His parents are anxious about how he might fit into this program and wonder whether the program can accommodate him. Would their past experience with sport programs be repeated?

Although elite disability sport competitions, such as the Paralympic Games and Special Olympic World Games exist, few youth with disabilities (especially those with severe disabilities) have the prerequisite skills and opportunities to achieve such high levels of participation (Paciorek, 2011). Many community- and school-based sport programs need extensive modifications to provide children with disabilities the greatest opportunity for participation. The unique characteristics of these children, including physical, intellectual, and behavioral issues, have historically limited organized sport opportunities outside of school (U.S. Government Accountability Office, 2010). Nonparticipation in sport has stemmed from a lack of transportation, lack of accessible facilities, funding, and the inability to effectively integrate children with disabilities (King, Law, King, Rosenbaum, Kertoy, & Young, 2003; Kleinert, Miracle, & Sheppard-Jones, 2007).

Several publications (e.g., Block, 2016; Davis, 2011; Hodge, Lieberman, & Murata, 2012; Murphy & Carbone, 2008; Paciorek, 2011; Ryan, Katsiyannis, Cadorette, Hodge, & Markham, 2014) have emphasized the need for sport opportunities for students with disabilities and have offered suggestions for accommodating them in sport environments. This chapter extends this work by focusing on students with severe disabilities. Common disability sports are described, along with suggested modifications to accommodate students. In addressing disability sports, two fundamental questions must be addressed: (1) What is disability sport, and (2) why are the sports important for students with severe disabilities?

Disability sports, also called adapted or adaptive sports, are sports designed for people with a wide range of disabilities and needs (DePauw & Gavron, 2005). These sports provide many benefits to children with severe disabilities. Perhaps the most notable is increased physical activity, which may reverse the deconditioning secondary to impaired mobility and enhance overall well-being (Murphy & Carbone, 2008). Sport participation can also foster inclusion in physical activity settings with other children with severe disabilities. Depending on the type and context of the disability, participation in disability sports may provide enough skill development (in psychomotor, cognitive, and affective domains) that children can be included in sports programs with typically developing children (with appropriate modifications, if necessary).

> *Much like their typically developing peers, students with severe disabilities reap many benefits from participating in sports and physical activities.*

Sport Opportunities for Students With Severe Disabilities

Although a number of disability sports exist, this chapter focuses on sport opportunities for children with severe disabilities. This nonexhaustive list includes modified activities such as para table tennis, power soccer, power hockey, table cricket, sitting volleyball, Little League Challenger baseball, and boccia. Further resources are provided in the appendix.

Para Table Tennis

According to the International Table Tennis Federation (ITTF) of North America (n.d.), **para table tennis** is "the form of table tennis for people with a disability." The ITTF describes para table tennis as aimed at people with acquired or congenital physical or intellectual disabilities (or both) who cannot play traditional table tennis. It debuted at the 1960 Rome Paralympic Games for wheelchair users. By the 1980 Paralympics, people with cerebral palsy participated, and now the sport is practiced in over 100 countries (International Paralympic Committee [IPC], 2012).

Rules.   Para table tennis rules are very similar to traditional table tennis rules. A major exception is the rule that a wheelchair athlete's service ball must leave the end of the table instead of the side, so that the ball is within the immediate reach of the receiving player. In addition, athletes with upper limb amputations or hand impairments do not have to toss the ball in the air on service (IPC, 2012).

Classification.   Per the ITTF, for general participation, no classification is necessary for this sport. Those who are interested in competing at any level must meet the minimal disability criteria in three classifications: provisional, national, and international. The provisional classification allows an athlete to generally participate at a club, at a school, or in a local competition. The national and international classifications include sport classes. The IPC (2012) states that sport classes 1 through 5 are for athletes in wheelchairs; classes 6 through 10 are for standing athletes. The lower the number in each set, the greater the athlete's needs. For example, class 1 would be for an athlete who has no sitting balance and a severely affected arm. Class 10, on the other hand, would be for an athlete with minimal physical constraints such as a stiff ankle or wrist. Class 11 is for athletes with intellectual impairments.

Modifications

- For students with visual impairments, use table tennis balls with high color contrast.
- For students with low functionality in the wrist and hands, attach Velcro straps to the handle of the paddle to secure it in their grip.
- For students with low motor control and coordination, stack some tissue boxes across a small desk to make a net, and have them strike a balloon back and forth across the desk.

Power Soccer

According to the United States Power Soccer Association (USPSA) (n.d.), **power soccer** is like soccer but is played on a basketball court using only power wheelchairs. Even though power soccer was created in France in the 1970s and introduced to the United States in the 1980s, it was not until 2005 in Paris that international rules were devised. A relatively new disability sport, power soccer is for people who use power chairs. Many of the athletes involved in the sport have disabilities including quadriplegia, multiple sclerosis, muscular dystrophy, cerebral palsy, head trauma, and spinal cord injuries.

Rules. According to the USPSA, power soccer is played on a regulation-size basketball court; four power chair athletes (three offensive players and one goalie) play on each team. Power chairs are used to perform a variety of moves such as attacking, defending, and spin-kicking a 13-inch (33 cm) soccer ball. The objective is to protect one's own goal line while attempting to get the soccer ball past the other team's goal line. The ball is maneuvered around ("kicked") using a guard placed on the front of the power chair. Like traditional soccer, corner and penalty kicks are used, as are red and yellow penalty cards. A

detailed and extensive rulebook can be accessed from the website provided in the appendix.

Classification. The USPSA has yet to officially adopt a classification system. Questions about future classification systems may be directed to the current USPSA president. Practically speaking, you can ensure a fair composition of teams by carefully considering each child's physical capabilities (e.g., range of motion, strength and dexterity of upper limbs) and cognitive capabilities (e.g., understanding of strategies).

Modifications

- Based on the number of students in power chairs, extend or shrink the playable area.
- If a soccer ball is too challenging to hit with the guards, use an exercise ball or physio ball. These would also move slower so they may be easier to control. Also, if the power chairs don't have guards on them, use a bigger ball.
- Adjust the speeds on the student's power chairs so that everyone can participate safely. As they become more skilled, increase the speed thresholds.
- Safety is paramount. Do not mix power chair users with wheelchair users; doing so is dangerous.

Power Hockey

According to the International Wheelchair and Amputee Sports Federation (IWAS) (n.d.), **power hockey**, also called electric wheelchair hockey, emerged in the 1970s for students who had low muscle tone and played using hockey sticks and light balls. Over time, with the use of wheelchairs and electric power wheelchairs, the sport spread across Europe. By the late 1970s, two tournaments were offered in the Netherlands. Although the International Committee for Wheelchair Hockey was composed mainly of European countries, the United States developed PowerHockey, which has some differences in rules and game play. Whatever version is played, power hockey is appropriate for children who have disabilities such as muscular dystrophy, cerebral palsy, and severe spinal injuries.

Rules. Power hockey borrows many rules from traditional ice hockey. For example, off-sides, interference, delay of game, and high sticking are considered penalties. Obviously, the objective remains to score the "puck" (a plastic ball) in the opponent's goal. Notable differences include the fact that power hockey, much like power soccer, is played on a basketball court with athletes driving power chairs. Another difference from ice hockey is that the goalie cannot reach down and "freeze" the puck if it rolls under the chair. In this case, the referee whistles to indicate a frozen puck. Finally, each team is composed of five athletes on the court at a time: two forwards, two defense players, and one goalie. The official rules dictate who can be on the floor at any given time based on the classification system (U.S. Electric Wheelchair Hockey Association [USEWHA]; n.d.). Detailed tournament and league play rules are available at the website link in the appendix.

Classification.   For tournament and league play, the USEWHA designed a three-tiered player classification system. Level 1 athletes have more upper-body strength and range of motion; they can make quick, forceful passes and shots. Level 2 athletes do not have the same level of strength and range of motion as level 1 athletes, and so they are not able to move the puck as quickly or forcefully. Level 3 athletes may have extremely limited strength in their arms and hands and may have to have their hockey sticks taped to their power chairs. How a coach organizes a roster on the court depends on whether the teams are playing under league or tournament rules.

Modifications

- Use plastic hockey sticks because they are lighter than wooden ones. This should help children with less upper-body strength and range of motion. Plastic hockey sticks with oversized foam blades may add extra safety for children who tend to high stick.
- If the small plastic ball is too difficult for children to hit, find a larger "puck," such as a volleyball-sized ball or even a Frisbee.
- For children who cannot hold a hockey stick, tape it to the power chair. Children having trouble striking the ball with an attached stick can still use the chair to propel the ball.
- Adjust the speeds on the children's power chairs so that everyone can participate safely. As they become more skilled, increase the speed thresholds.
- Safety is paramount. Do not mix power chair users with wheelchair users; doing so may be dangerous.

Table Cricket

Table cricket, also call tabletop cricket, is a derivation of the popular bat-and-ball English game of cricket. Doug Williamson created table cricket in 1990 for people with severe physical disabilities, especially cerebral palsy. Initially, the sport was piloted in Nottingham through Project Adapted, a research and development unit (Grant, 2016). As the name implies, table cricket is a microcosm of the traditional game of cricket and takes place on a table tennis table or equivalent surface (called the pitch). Ten-centimeter-high (4 in.) side panels are extended upward around three sides of the table, leaving a short side open (see figure 9.1). On the far-end, short side, a ball launcher (miniature ramp) is on the table; the near-end, short side (the side left open) is the batter's area. Along the three sides with panels are nine sliding fielders, which are hung from the panels on the inside of the playing area. Each sliding fielder has a picture of a catcher (30 cm, or 12 in., long) on it. A small plastic ball (35 mm, or 1.8 in., in diameter) and a small flat wooden bat are also needed to simulate an authentic cricket match (Black & Williamson, 2010; Lord's Taverners, 2015). Table cricket equipment can be either bought (see the website list in the appendix) or made.

Rules.   For the full-length rule handbook, see Lord's Taverners (2015). This section addresses only the rules integral to playing a functional game. The goal is to score as many runs as possible while preventing the opponent from doing so. Each team, constructed by a classification system discussed later, consists of six players who eventually rotate to assume the roles of batting, fielding, and bowling (these roles are described next). Team captains determine the batting order, the fielding positions, and defensive rotations (i.e., who the new bowler will be after each over) for their respective teams. The official determines the number of innings or overs that will be played. During innings each member of the batting team receives an over, which is six bowls. After each player from the batting side bats for an over, the batting and fielding teams switch roles. The team with the higher score at the end of the designated number of innings wins. The rules for batting, bowling, and fielding are outlined next.

Batting

- The batting team starts with 200 runs.
- The batter must strike the ball behind the batter's crease (see figure 9.1).

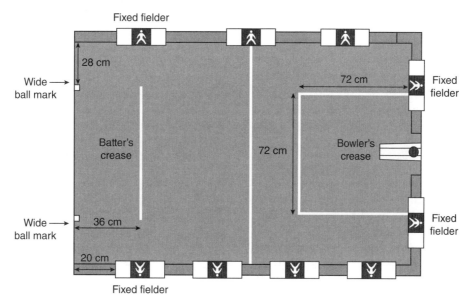

Figure 9.1   Setup for table cricket.

Acknowledgement to: Lord's Taverners (www.lordstaverners.org/table-cricket) and Doug Williamson; The inventor-Project Adapted. Nottingham, UK.

- The batter must aim the ball to scoring areas along the panels to score two, four, or six runs. Only first contacts count. One point is awarded for a struck ball that lands in the playing area but does not reach any of the panels.

- No runs are scored if the ball hits the white area on the sliding fielder or the side of the launcher.

- Five runs are deducted if the ball hits the red area on the sliding fielder or the side of the launcher, hits any part of the hand, or leaves the table (hitting the batter, going behind the batter, or going over the sides of the table). Excessive force also results in this penalty. These actions deem the batter out.

- Regardless of how many outs a batter has during the over, the batter still receives the full six bowls.

Bowling

- Bowling consists of pushing (not flicking) the ball down the launcher toward the batter.

- A wide bowl (outside the wide markers; see figure 9.1) results in four runs for the batter with an extra delivery allowed but only in the last innings.

- The bowler must use a swing ball (i.e., a ball that does not roll true) for the first over of every innings. The remaining bowlers for the

innings may choose between the swing ball and the nonbiased ball.

- The bowler may use ramp as a fielder in the bowling crease (see figure 9.1).

Fielding

- Sliding fielders can be moved by defensive players along the side panels of the pitch (except for the fixed fielders on either side of the launcher and the batter's crease; see figure 9.1).

- If two sliding fielders touch each other along the side panel, four runs are awarded to the batter.

- Positioning the fielders correctly can prevent the batter from scoring or even deduct points from the batting team.

Classification.   The new system, for competition purposes, sets the age range for players between 12 and 25 and is described as pan disability. To this end, all players with learning and physical disabilities play in mixed teams within the same competitions. This differs from the original classification system in which there is no limit for the number of players with a physical disability on a given team. Instead, team leaders determine the most appropriate composition of teams by carefully considering each player's disability severity. Ultimately, the classification system should ensure that all players can compete with independence and dignity (Lord's Taverners, 2015).

Modifications

- Use smaller teams with fewer fielders to create larger scoring zones.
- Use table tennis balls if the plastic ball is too heavy for a child to propel off the bat.
- Use a wider paddle instead of the wooden bat to increase the likelihood of hitting the ball.
- If the scoring rules become too much of a burden, simplify them.
- For children who cannot grip the bat or bowl the ball with their hands, attach a paint stirrer to a hat so they can use their heads to strike at the ball. Increase the ball size to increase the chances for a successful strike.
- For children with visual impairments, use a yellow or spotted ball or a ball containing bells. Place yellow Post-it notes on the sliding fielders.
- Attach grips to the sliding fielders so that children with limited hand dexterity and strength can slide them across the panels more easily.

Sitting Volleyball

Sitting volleyball is the most widely known version of ParaVolley because of its first appearance in the Paralympic Games in the Netherlands in 1980. It is now played by over 10,000 athletes in more than 55 countries. This form of volleyball dictates that participants play in a seated position on the floor or ground; players have a wide range of conditions such as impaired muscle power, impaired passive range of movement, amputations or other limb deficiencies, leg length differences, hypertonia, ataxia, and athetosis (ParaVolley, 2015, 2016).

Rules.   Although many of the rules for sitting volleyball are similar to those of its traditional counterpart (e.g., sets played to 25 points, best of 5 sets wins), several rule changes and modifications make the sport more appropriate for people with disabilities. A major change is that participants must have a portion of their torsos in contact with the floor or ground at all times. Sitting volleyball uses smaller court dimensions (10 by 6 m) and a lower net (1.15 and 1.05 m for men and women, respectively). Because of the smaller playing area, the game can be faster than standing volleyball (ParaVolley, 2016). The configuration of the six teammates on the court is determined by each player's sport class; a team is allowed a maximum of one player with a minimal disability on the court at a time. Sport classes are discussed in more detail next (ParaVolley, 2015).

Classification.   The two sport classes for sitting volleyball are (1) minimal disability, which designates the most physically able, and (2) disabled, which designates the least physically able. There are established criteria for what constitutes these two sport classes based on the potential impact of the impairment on the sitting volleyball functions. Classification considerations include the

Students in a modified physical education class learn how to play a modified version of sitting volleyball.

functionality of the joints of the ankle, hip, knee, elbow, shoulder, wrist, and finger joints as well as the trunk. Amputations and shortened extremities are also evaluated (ParaVolley, 2015). A website link to the classification handbook in the appendix provides more information on the nuances of the classification procedures.

Modifications

- Volleyballs may be too difficult for a child with a severe disability to strike. Beach balls, Finger light balls (see appendix for websites), or balloons move more slowly, giving children with limited mobility and reaction time increased opportunities for success.

- The game can be modified so that not all players are required to sit directly on the floor or ground. Moving some children from their wheelchairs or power chairs to the floor or ground may be unfeasible or unsafe. For these children, park (turn off or lock wheels) their chairs on the court and space them out on the court using poly spots. This allows both chair users and children sitting on the floor to participate in the game.

- Sitting volleyball is a great inclusion game because children without disabilities can play as well. In these circumstances, the rules may need to be modified to ensure that children with disabilities have opportunities to be successful. For example, you might dictate that a team has to volley the balloon to the child with a disability once before hitting it across the net. See chapter 10 for functional assessments.

Little League Challenger Baseball

Created in 1989, the Challenger Division of Little League Baseball is a special baseball league for children ages 4 to 18 with physical and intellectual disabilities that cannot be reasonably accommodated in the traditional Little League baseball or softball programs. Notably, this league makes use of a buddy system in which people help participants with batting, base running, and defense. **Challenger baseball** is not competitive; rather, the objective is for participants to learn about baseball and have fun. There are over 950 programs in 10 countries, equating to 30,000 participants (Little League of America, 2016).

Rules.   Because the Challenger Division is not a competitive program, flexibility and adaptability are important. Typical games last about one hour and are one to two innings long; everyone bats and fields in each inning. Several other modifications from traditional Little League programs exist. First, no score is kept, emphasizing the focus on fun. Second, as mentioned, buddies may assist participants but only as needed. These buddies should be at least nine years old. Third, participants do not pitch; rather, a player is designated to field the position. Fourth, each participant receives six pitches and the option to hit off a tee (Little League of America, 2016).

Classification.   No classifications are designated beyond the entry criteria that participants must have physical or intellectual disabilities and be between the ages of 4 and 18 (up to 22 if still enrolled in school). A Senior League Challenger Division exists for participants ages 15 and above (Little League of America, 2016).

Modifications.   Although Challenger baseball is designed to be highly accommodating, further modifications may be appropriate for children with more severe disabilities.

- For a chair user with limited upper-body strength, use a plastic bat and have the child hit a plastic ball off a tee. A buddy can then help propel the chair down the baseline.

- For a student who can drive a power chair but cannot grip a bat, attach the bat (or a hockey stick) to the chair, and then have the child rotate the chair to swing the bat at a ball resting on a tee.

- To simulate fielding, a student in a chair who cannot retrieve the ball from the floor or ground can toss a hula hoop around the ball to represent the fielding of the ball. A rule can be added that if the batter does not reach first base by the time the ball is hula-hooped, the batter is out.

Boccia

Boccia is a precision ball game named for the Italian word meaning "to bowl." Its roots go back to a game in ancient Greece in which participants threw large stones at a stone target. Egyptian tomb murals dating as far back as 5200 BCE depict a similar game. Millennia later, boccia included a version for people with cerebral palsy, which was introduced at the New York Paralympic Games in 1984. Now this disability sport is played in more than 50 countries (International

Paralympic Committee, 2016). Interestingly, boccia is one of the two Paralympic sports that does not have an Olympic counterpart; goalball is the other (Boccia International Sports Federation [BISFED], 2016).

Rules.   The goal of boccia is to throw leather balls so that they land as closely as possible to the white target ball called the jack. The match takes place on a court 41 by 21 feet (12.5 by 2 m) of empty space surrounding it. On one short end of the court are six rectangular throwing boxes from which the players must throw. Each team has its own set of six colored (red or blue) leather balls to throw at the jack per "end," which culminates when the jack and all 12 leather balls have been thrown. Individual (one-on-one) and partner (two-on-two) matches conclude after four ends, with the partners splitting their six throws during each end. In team competition, the match continues for six ends.

To start game play, the jack is thrown by one of the team members. After the toss, each team has a turn at throwing their leather balls; the first one by the team who threw the jack and then a throw from a team member from the other team. From here, the order of which side throws is determined by which team's leather balls are farther from the jack. The side whose ball is farther from the jack continues throwing until one of the balls is closer than the opponent's or until they throw all six, at which point the other side may throw their remaining balls to try to score more points. Scoring is tallied once all balls have been played (at the completion of the end). For each ball that one side has closer to the jack than the opponent's closest ball, 1 point is awarded. All the balls are then collected, and the side that did not throw the jack to start the first end throws it to start the second end. The ends continue in this manner until the completion of the designated number of ends, at which point the side with the higher number of points wins (BISFED, 2016). The websites in the appendix include a link to the full official rules for boccia.

Classification.   At the competitive level, boccia athletes are classified at four levels: BC1 (players throw or kick the ball with a hand or foot and may have assistance to adjust their chairs); BC2 (players throw the ball with a hand and may not have assistance); BC3 (players with very severe locomotor dysfunction in all limbs and who cannot propel a boccia ball onto the court are permitted to use a ramp and an assistant); and

BC4 (players with severe locomotor dysfunction in all limbs, in addition to poor trunk control, but who possess adequate dexterity to throw the ball, are not permitted assistance) (BISFED, 2016).

Modifications

- For students with very limited strength and range of motion of the upper limbs, attach a rubber mouthpiece to a stick (an "antenna") so they can push the boccia ball down a ramp more independently.
- For students with visual impairments, use beeping sound balls, which are available for boccia use (see appendix). For more information on functional assessments, see chapter 10.

Role of the Teacher and Coach in Disability Sport

Most physical education, adapted physical education (APE), and special education teachers, as well as coaches, understand the contribution of extracurricular activities such as sports to children's development. Children with disabilities, severe or otherwise, must not experience disability sports as disconnected from their overall educational programs. Physical education and APE teachers are charged with the task of providing appropriate skill development opportunities while instilling a sense of joy from participating in physical activities and sports in every student. How can you ensure that a child with severe spastic cerebral palsy, like Muhammad, has the prerequisite functional skills to participate in physical activity and sport, such as power soccer, beyond his APE services?

Although adhering to the official rules and regulations of a disability sport help children prepare for full participation in more competitive disability sport programs, a child with a severe disability may have different goals. For example, the most appropriate long-term goal for Muhammad may be to participate in power soccer at a scaled-down, more functional level with classmates or perhaps in a less competitive community setting. Ultimately, you should follow the popular pedagogical adage *Games are not sacred, kids are* (Morris & Stiehl, 1999). If a child needs the rules or equipment of a disability sport changed, even drastically, to succeed, then you should make those modifications.

> *Students with and without disabilities need to feel successful in sport programming. Adapt rules, equipment, and tasks so that successful, meaningful participation for everyone is the norm.*

How does a child gain self-determination while still receiving the best opportunity to participate in disability sport both within and outside of physical education? To answer this question, begin with the child's individual education plan (IEP) team (see chapter 1). Early in the child's educational career, parents, teachers, related service providers, and the child should consider what activities and sports best fit the child's interests and abilities, as well as the offerings of the local community (Block, 2016; Lieberman, & Houston-Wilson, 2018; Wilson & Colombo-Dougovito, 2015). Given Muhammad's interest in soccer and the availability of a small community power soccer program, the long-term plan that guides his entire educational program (and IEP goals) should include skill development in power soccer (Kelly & Melograno, 2004). Once the long-term plans are established, the IEP team, led by the physical education and APE teachers, can take steps in that direction.

Summary

Much like their typically developing peers in traditional sport programs, children with severe disabilities, such as Muhammad, can benefit from being included in disability sport programs. Muhammad could not participate in a traditional soccer league as some of his peers did. Instead, he found a power soccer program that supported his meaningful participation in sport. Other disability sports provide participants with opportunities to learn and be successful in activities such as para table tennis, table cricket, and power hockey. Regardless of the disability sport chosen, strive to make the activity accessible and meaningful for each child with a disability.

▷ ▷

Because Muhammed had played boccia with his siblings and neighbors in his backyard, this was a natural sport for his physical education teacher to add to the physical education curriculum and for Muhammed to play after school. The teacher also created an after school intramural program for students with and without disabilities. His athletic director is now looking for avenues for competition at the regional level as Muhammed has improved his skills and wants to pursue this activity further.

Review Questions

1. Why is disability sport such an important part of development for a child with a disability?
2. Choose one of your students. How might you modify one of the disability sports described in this chapter for that student?
3. How should the adage *Games are not sacred, kids are* drive your approach to teaching disability sport to a child with a severe disability?
4. What information should members of an IEP team consider when creating a long-term plan for a child's APE and recreational programing?

Modified Programming in Physical Education

Michelle Grenier
University of New Hampshire

Catherine Clermont
Cooperative Middle School, Stratham, New Hampshire

Eilleen Cuell
Cooperative Middle School, Stratham, New Hampshire

Chapter Objectives

By reading this chapter, you will:

▶ Gain an understanding of how to implement disability sports in the physical education curriculum.
▶ Identify essential elements for successful programming.
▶ Be able to provide functional skills assessment that addresses a variety of needs and abilities.

Sasha is an eighth grade student enrolled in the modified physical education class at Cooperative Middle School. Sasha was diagnosed with autism as well as speech and language impairment, which impact both his daily needs and learning. Sasha is a sensitive, loving, fourteen-year-old who enjoys spending time with friends and familiar teachers throughout his school day. Although he uses an iPad for communication, he has a great ability to imitate others, a valuable attribute when learning new concepts. He enjoys his modified physical education class, as well as his speech/language and occupational therapy group, lunch group, and his music therapy program. He loves to be active and involved with his peers but needs his learning tasks to be made as meaningful as possible in order to make connections and generalize his skills to the larger community.

One wish Sasha's parents have for him in his program is that his teacher, Ms. Cleary, teach him how to ride his beautiful, two wheeled Trek bike. To accomplish this, Ms. Cleary needed to assess his skills on his bike. After asking his parents to bring in his bike, Ms. Cleary's first step was to get Sasha on the bike. Although initially hesitant, he reluctantly complied as Ms. Cleary sat on the back tire to stabilize the bike. After many unsuccessful attempts, Ms. Cleary concluded she needed an alternative plan, as Sasha neither had the concept of pedaling, nor the balance to be successful.

Ms. Cleary decided to take the pedals off his bike so that he could scoot using his feet for balance and propelling the bike. She also rented a Trailmate Banana Peel Trike from a local recreational therapy and adapted sports program. Alternating between the Trike and the bike, Sasha soon found success.

As illustrated in the above example, sports can create a community through shared experiences. The growing appeal of disability sports, particularly in light of the emphasis on the Paralympic movement, make the sports an attractive addition to any physical education program (Davis, 2011). Disability sports, also known as adaptive sports, are sports played by individuals with disabilities. Generally the sports are adapted from existing traditional sports modified to the meet the individual's ability; however, not all sports are adapted. Several sports, such as goalball, have been specifically designed for people with disabilities. While many sports, such as goalball and sledge hockey, are unique to the specific disability, others sports, such as wheelchair basketball and sitting volleyball, are modifications of their traditional counterparts. When included in a general physical education program, these sports offer students with severe disabilities skills that enable them to participate in lifelong physical activity. For students who are often marginalized, there is the opportunity to know what it means to be an athlete with a disability. Additionally, when used in the general education setting, disability sports provide an avenue for teaching all students skills that impact the affective, psychomotor, and cognitive domains (Grenier & Kearns, 2012).

It is particularly important to devise activities for students with severe disabilities because they are less likely to exercise or participate in organized sporting activities (Ryan, Katsiyannis, Cadoret, Hodge & Markham, 2014). Students have limited opportunities to engage in recreational and athletic activities and oftentimes lack the same physical activity experiences as their peers without disabilities (Taub & Greer, 2000). All of these factors make it essential that sport and physical activity be designed to include all children, particularly those with severe disabilities.

Establishing Disability Sports Within the Physical Education Curriculum

Modified physical education programs are specifically designed to meet the needs of students with disabilities. The programs generally include students with and without disabilities and use disability and adapted sports as vehicles to reduce physical and social barriers.

Modified physical education falls within the categories of the least restrictive environment under the Individual With Disabilities Education Improvement Act (IDEIA) of 2004, which states that students with disabilities have access to the general education curriculum including health and physical education. The program provides the least restrictive environment for students and is fully inclusive. **Functional skills assessments** (examples to follow) are used as a form of data collection to determine individual student needs for instruction and equipment modifications.

Cooperative Middle School (CMS) in Stratham, New Hampshire, serves as a real-world example. In the spring of 2012, the Health & Physical Education Department brainstormed ways to meet the physical education needs of students who were not accessing the current curriculum to their fullest ability. Through multiple discussions, modified physical education was born. In modified physical education, the physical education teachers created a peer group learning environment with the common purpose of achieving health and physical fitness through sport. Funding for the program was secured through a grant program from IDEA.

As with many of the other programs highlighted in this text, the program is built on the principals of Universal Design for Learning (UDL). As mentioned in chapter 1, UDL is a strategy for eliminating barriers to students' learning that includes Universally Designed Instruction (UDI), Universally Designed Curriculum (UDC), and Universally Designed Assessment (Rapp, 2014). The program also uses the **Response To Intervention** (RTI) model to improve outcomes for all learners. The multi-level approach to instruction is aimed at providing immediate support to those who may be at risk for poor outcomes in a less proactive learning environment. The program assesses students through standard-based grading that coincides with each functional outcome and skill assessment for each activity. This is also a determining factor for which activities the program will provide.

Sports should be selected that encourage a lifetime of physical activity so that students will develop a love of fitness to be enjoyed with family and friends. Through selected activities, students come to appreciate their own athleticism. Some of the activities include biking, table tennis, snowshoeing, and Paralympic sports, including boccia, sitting volleyball, goalball, and court sports.

Incorporating goalball into the curriculum.

Prior to starting the program at CMS, student interest surveys were disseminated to students and parents to determine sporting interests. In addition to student interest, other factors including safety, paraeducation support, adaptability of the sport, and sufficient equipment rentals and resources were considerations. For the staff at CMS, it was important to partner with other staff members in creating a team approach for programming purposes. Setting a tone of teamwork, trust, respect, and collaboration from the start helped the students see all staff as valuable parts of their education.

Another vital asset to the program was community involvement. Modified physical education implemented volunteer outreach organizations, such as Tae Kwon Do, yoga, and skateboarding, to teach a variety of activities. The program also established a strong relationship with a nonprofit organization whose mission is to create an environment where individuals with disabilities can enjoy recreation with the same freedom of choice, quality of life, and independence as their nondisabled peers (Northeast Passage, 2016). Northeast Passage has provided the students with adaptive equipment for many of the disability sports offered in the program.

Modified physical education provides an enriching social connection for students through physical movement and play. Students in the seventh and eighth grade who have shown an interest and capacity for working with peers are selected for the program to work in a one-on-one situation. Students are taught how to deliver instruction, reinforce social cues, and provide feedback (Lieberman & Houston-Wilson, 2018). Peer tutors also gain leadership experience while encouraging positive socialization. For more information on peer tutors, see chapter 5.

Strive to create modified physical education programs that meet the needs of ALL students. Reach out to local sport and community recreation programs for support. They will be more than happy to help out!

The following list outlines the steps for developing the peer partner program:

1. Provide a detailed overview of the program to all faculty, parents, and the community.

2. Advocate and encourage students to apply through means of morning and afternoon announcements, school newsletters, assemblies, visual posters and flyers, and faculty support through classroom teachers and guidance counselors.

3. Create and provide an application for students to apply to the program. Within the application, include the expectations of peer partners, followed by questions addressing their availability, goals and qualities they possess, and their experience working or living with students with disabilities.

4. During the selection process, identify the gender, age, and personal characteristics of each peer partner. Documenting this information will provide for an ideal and successful pairing with their peer tutee.

5. Determine which type of peer tutoring will be implemented within the program. Different types of peer tutoring can include unidirectional (peer tutor teaches the entire time), bidirectional (a student with a disability and a student without a disability form a dyad with a student taking turns at being the tutor and tutee), and class wide (breaking the entire class into small pairs) (Lieberman & Houston-Wilson, 2018).

6. Provide a training session for the peer partner tutors. Include the paraeducator that is working with the peer partner tutee. The paraeducator can provide positive cues, techniques or relative information pertaining to the student with a disability, in order for the peer partner tutor to be successful with their partner. A training session should include proper techniques for visual and verbal cues.

7. Maintain peer partner progress throughout the program. Provide weekly, friendly reminders to peer partner tutors to exhibit cues and model appropriately. If desired, create a peer tutor process checklist for the peer tutee, as well as a peer tutor evaluation checklist. See chapter 5 for more information on peer tutoring.

Assessment in Disability Sport

The modified physical education program provides functional skills assessment for all students in the program. Functional skills assessments take into consideration the student's current skill level and functioning within the particular activity and the necessary supports for success. Figure 10.1 shows a functional assessment for table tennis.

The assessment process is constantly being revised in order to align with district standards based on grading policies. The original intent of the assessments were to provided communication to parents, case managers, and occupational and physical therapists on the progress of the student's ability in each activity or sport. In developing the assessments, the program used a multitude of resources and adaptations from various Special Olympics and Paralympic coaching guides, as well as language used by physical therapists. Table 10.1 presents additional examples of skills assessments for several different sports.

Summary

CMS is a wonderful example of how the physical education teachers designed a program to meet the specific needs of their students with disabilities in an environment supported by peers. The program falls within the category of the least restrictive environment as an option to the general education program. As described in the chapter, the teachers use disability and adapted sports as avenues of instruction to enrich the lives of their students with disabilities while accessing lifetime and recreational activities. The sports described in this chapter offer age-appropriate skills that highlight student's ability rather than their disability. With disability sports, the overall commitment is toward removing barriers while providing opportunities for physical activity and social interaction for students of all abilities.

FIGURE 10.1

Functional Skills Assessment for Table Tennis

Each skill incorporates the level of assistance needed to complete the activity. At the end of the assessment, include any additional comments and any equipment or accommodations provide to the student.

- F = Functional: The student can perform the task with or without adaptive equipment within the educational environment.
- S = Supervision/prompts: The student requires adult attention for safety or thoroughness and verbal, visual tactile, or gestural cues to perform the task.
- P = Physical assistance: The student requires hands-on assistance to perform all or part of the task.
- E = Emerging: The student is beginning to perform part of the task. Moderate to maximum assistance may be needed to complete the task.
- N/A = Not applicable: The assessment of the skill is not needed. The student is unable to perform the task due to developmental age, physical limitations, or cognitive ability. The student's needs are addressed through classroom curriculum or other existing services, which may include total assistance by school staff.

Student's ability to	F	S	P	E	N/A
HAND-EYE COORDINATION					
Recognize the spatial relationship between the racket and the ball					
Understand the relationship between the distance of the racket and the oncoming ball; proficient at making contact					
GRIPPING THE RACKET					
Time his or her swing to the approaching ball					
Rarely mishits a ball that he or she is in the proper position to strike					
Stroke with smooth hand control					
FOREHAND OR BACKHAND STROKES					
Recognize the spatial relationship between the racket and the ball					
Proficiently make contact with the ball without misses					
SERVE					
Demonstrate a proper forehand serve					
Demonstrate a proper backhand serve					
SERVE RETURN					
Stand in a ready position					
Watch the server and oncoming serve					
Hit with movement					

TABLE 10.1 Skills to Assess for Selected Sports

Sport skill	Assessment criteria
SNOWSHOEING	
Stretching	• Know stretches for calves, hamstrings, groin, quadriceps, triceps, and shoulders • Perform stretches
Putting on snowshoes	• Identify left and right snowshoes • Loosen binding straps • Place foot in proper position on snowshoe • Tighten bindings properly
Remove snowshoes	• Loosen binding straps • Move heel strap down off of heel • Slide foot out of binding and snowshoe
Moving forward	• Stand without assistance • Move forward without assistance • Increase stride length • Increase stride rate
Avoiding snowshoe overlap	• Walk without stepping on the other snowshoe • Accelerate to a jog without stepping on the other snowshoe
Stopping	• Gradually decrease stride length and rate over distance • Stop without losing balance • Stop without assistance
Falling	• Fall safely • Be aware of arm and hand placement when falling
Getting up	• Get up correctly • Get up in a reasonable amount of time
Turning	• Take successive steps to the side • Keep snowshoe flat and balance • Turn without causing overlap on tips or tails
Climbing	• Take shorter steps • Avoid snowshoe overlap • Keep weight forward and on balls of feet • Climb up hills without slipping or falling • Climb up moderate hills without using hands • Pump arms to power up hill • Identify the fall line, if necessary • Use the fall line, if necessary
Descending hills	• Keep weight forward and on balls of feet • Maintain traction • Maintain balance • Keep knees slightly bent • Avoid overlap • Run down the hill • Identify the fall line, if necessary • Use the fall line, if necessary
PARALYMPICS-BOCCIA	
Equipment selection	• Recognize a bocce ball • Recognize the color differences of the bocce balls • Recognize the pallina

Sport skill	Assessment criteria
Scoring	• Understand the point scoring system used in the game of bocce
Rules of the game	• Know not to cross the foul line • Show an understanding of the game • Know to play only when indicated by the official
Sportsmanship and etiquette	• Take turns with other team members • Select and uses the same color balls throughout the game • Exhibit sportsmanship and etiquette at all times
Retrieving the ball	• Identify own ball by the color • Collect bocce ball from court • Hold bocce ball back at starting position
Grip	• Place fingers and thumb evenly around the ball (left or right) • Use thumb to hold ball in place • Hold the ball in front portion of hand
Stance	• Stand with feet shoulder width apart • Demonstrate proper foot placement (left or right foot forward opposite of throwing hand)
Delivery and release	• Bring arm straight back and forward to release ball • Deliver ball over the foul line toward the pallina or target • Execute proper follow-through with arm swing
PARALYMPICS-SITTING VOLLEYBALL	
Serve	• Make contact with the ball • Get an underhand serve over the net • Get an underhand serve over the net and inbounds
Forearm passing (Bump)	• Create a consistent platform • Demonstrate proper athletic stance • Pass the ball tossed directly to him or her • Pass the ball served directly to him or her • Accurately pass the ball to a designated spot on the court
Overhead passing (Set)	• Create a consistent overhead hand position • Demonstrate proper athletic stance • Pass the ball tossed directly to him or her • Pass the ball served directly to him or her • Accurately pass the ball to a designated spot on the court
Communication	• Communicate with team members during play
Scoring	• Understand concept of rally scoring • Can keep record of score
PARALYMPICS-WHEELCHAIR COURT: HANDBALL	
Catching and passing	• Pass the ball to teammate while sitting in chair • Catch the ball while sitting in chair • Perform a pass while wheelchair is moving • Make long passes • Make short passes
Shooting	• Make a shot in place • Use his or her arm, trunk, or wrist while making the shot • Fake to an opponent

(continued)

Table 10.1   *(continued)*

Sport skill	Assessment criteria
Offensive and defensive movements	• Properly perform defense movements • Steal the ball • Screen the opponent without a ball • Screen with a ball
Maneuvering	• Self-propel wheelchair • Maneuver safely in wheelchair • Follow direction of play
Communication	• Communicate with team members during play
Scoring	• Understand concept of rally scoring • Can keep record of score
PARALYMPICS-GOALBALL	
Throwing	• Grasp goalball with one or both hands • Bring arm straight back and forward to release ball • Execute proper follow-through with arm swing • Roll or bowl goalball on ground
Anticipation	• Maneuver position changes • Hands ready out to the side
Blocking	• Follow auditory perception to the left or right • Lean left or right to block ball with hands, arms or trunk • Grasp, hold, and maintain goalball
Rules of the game	• Show an understanding of the game • Know to play only when indicated by the official • Maintain quiet during game place

▷ ▷

After several weeks of practice, Ms. Cleary finally felt Sasha's modified physical education plan was coming together; Sasha was becoming a capable bike rider. An indication of his success came one day after participating in his modified physical education class. After being escorted to the lunchroom, Sasha immediately went to the table where his friends were eating. He put down his iPad and verbally reported, "I bike." All of his friends erupted in celebration of his success.

Review Questions

1. Identify three benefits for implementing disability sports into your program for students with disabilities.
2. Describe four essential elements for building the program.
3. What role do peers play in a disability sport unit?
4. What are functional assessments, and how are they used in analyzing students' performance?

Transitioning to Recreational Opportunities Beyond School

Amaury Samalot-Rivera
The College at Brockport, State University of New York

Rocco Aiello
St. Mary's County Public Schools, Maryland

Chapter Objectives

By reading this chapter, you will:

- ▶ Learn how to implement an appropriate transition process from the physical education class to the community for students with severe disabilities.
- ▶ Provide information on recreational activities that students with disabilities can participate in within their communities.
- ▶ Understand how to train key personnel in the community integration process to work with students with disabilities.

Donte is a ninth-grade student with a severe cognitive disability, along with other health impairments. He receives adapted physical education three times a week in an inclusive physical education setting and one time per week for 30 minutes in a separate adapted physical education class. The adapted physical education teacher, Mr. Copsey, has been teaching Donte basic manipulative skills as indicated on his individual education plan (IEP). At the beginning of the school year, Mr. Copsey sent home a physical activity survey form for Donte's parents to fill out. This form provided valuable information to help Mr. Copsey establish appropriate long-term goals and transition plans for Donte. On the survey, the parents indicated that they were very interested in seeing Donte strike a ball off a tee stand.

Mr. Copsey worked with Donte the entire school year and was able to teach him how to strike a ball off a tee stand in three out of five trials. Mr. Copsey recorded the sequence of Donte striking the ball and shared the video with Donte's parents. A few weeks later, Donte's parents contacted Mr. Copsey to inform him that

Donte had participated in a tee ball game with friends and family at a neighbor's picnic. The parents were elated that, for the first time, family members were able to interact with Donte in physical activity.

The family, including Donte, spent some time educating the staff at the local YMCA about Donte's physical and emotional needs so that he could be included in a tee ball game. The staff training included two 1-hour sessions and one weekend day for all involved staff. This process, required by law, is called transition services.

Transition Services and Individuals' Rights

Public Law 108-466, the Individuals With Disabilities Education Improvement Act, requires that all individuals diagnosed with a disability (ages 3 to 21) be provided with a free and appropriate public education in the least restrictive environment. Furthermore, this law requires that transition services be provided to these individuals at age 16. **Transition services** are intended to provide young people with disabilities with the skills they need to transition from school to the community, where they can be independent, active, and healthy. These services must be provided in school settings as part of an IEP through **an individual transition plan (ITP)**. This official document is used as a guide to help youth with disabilities achieve their short- and long-term goals in relation to their life after high school at age 21. Based on Public Law 108-466, transition services are defined as follows:

> The term "transition services" means a coordinated set of activities for a student with a disability, that: (A) is designed within an outcome-oriented process, that promotes movement from school to post-school activities, including postsecondary education, vocational training, integrated employment (including supported employment), continuing and adult education, adult services, independent living, or community participation; (B) is based on the student's needs, taking into account the student's preferences and interests; and (C) includes instruction, community experiences, the development of employment and other post-school objectives, and, when appropriate, acquisition of daily living skills and functional vocational evaluation. (Education for All Handicapped Children Act Amendments of 1990, P.L. 101-476, 20 U.S.C. § 1401)

> *Knowing about individual's rights related to recreation and leisure is important to promote successful community integration.*

The transition definition provided by this law describes recreational activities as an essential part of the ITP in the area of community experiences. An appropriate transition plan helps ensure that students with disabilities become active members of society once they complete their school years at age 21.

Another important piece of legislation that supports participation in sports for individuals with disabilities is the U.S. Department of Education, Office for Civil Rights' "Dear Colleague Letter" (2013). Arnhold, Young, and Lakowski (2013) clarified the obligations of school districts to provide equal participation opportunities to students with disabilities in extracurricular activities including athletics, clubs, and intramurals. The letter also pointed out the responsibility of school districts

1. to review the general legal requirements of the Rehab Act of 1973, Section 504,
2. to ensure equal opportunities in after-school athletics and sports, and
3. to offer separate or different athletic opportunities if reasonable accommodations and supplementary aids and services cannot ensure effective participation (Davis, 2013).

Initiating the Transition Plan

One way to collect pertinent data is to ask the family of a student with a disability to fill out a physical activity survey (see figure 11.1).

By completing this survey, parents can help adapted or general physical educators understand the needs and expectations for their children with disabilities. In the case of Donte, the information from his parents helped shape the physical edu-

---

FIGURE 11.1

Physical Activity Survey

Name _____ Age _____ School _____

Date _____

Dear Parent(s) or Guardian(s):

Please take a few moments to fill out this survey. You can send it directly back to Mr. Asher, the adapted physical education teacher.

Check all that apply:

Activity	Involved in	Interested in	Activity	Involved in	Interested in
Aerobics			Roller skating		
Archery			Running or jogging		
Badminton			Skateboarding		
Baseball			Skiing or snowboarding		
Basketball			Soccer		
Bicycling			Softball		
Bowling			Special Olympics		
Canoeing			Swimming		
Cycling			Tee ball		
Dance			Tennis		
Fishing			Ultimate		
Football			Volleyball		
Disc golf			Walking		
Kayaking			Other:		

---

cation program while increasing his community involvement.

Another way general and adapted physical educators can assist students with disabilities in their transition process is by including after-school sport objectives in their transition planning. Every IEP has a section for transition planning to be completed once the student reaches age 16, or earlier, if determined by the IEP team. This transition planning must include appropriate, measurable postsecondary goals based on age-appropriate transition assessments related to education and training, employment, and independent living. In addition, it must state the transition services needed to help the student reach goals related to instruction; related services; such as occupational therapy, physical or speech therapy; community experiences (leisure and recreation); employment and other postschool adult living situations; daily living skills; and functional vocational assessments. After-school sports and recreation should be an integral part of the community experience

> *Collecting data on a student with a disability in the area of motor development and sports is one of the most important steps in helping that student transition from school to community recreation, leisure, and sport activities.*

in leisure and recreation to be developed for an effective transition and therefore included on the IEP and any transition plans.

Transition Processes in Physical Education

Finding appropriate sport, recreation, and leisure programs for students with disabilities can be a daunting process, particularly given the limited number of choices (Samalot & Lieberman, 2016). The process can be even more difficult for students with severe disabilities, particularly those who want to be involved in community programs. One of the biggest concerns that parents of students with disabilities report is not knowing what to do once their children reach age 21, when they are no longer eligible for school-provided services. Many parents worry that their children will not be able to integrate into and be active members of their communities, and they do not know where to get information about appropriate programs in their local communities.

The following five steps can help parents and others select a sport or recreational program that will promote a student's transition into the community Samalot-Rivera & Lieberman (2016):

1. Determine the needs and skills of the student.
2. Take into consideration the student's and family members' interests.
3. Identify available community-based programs.

Learn what types of activities are available in the community for people with disabilities. Collaborations between parents and school, district, and community recreation programs and clubs are key to successful community integration.

4. Identify support personnel willing to collaborate.
5. Assess the student's level of satisfaction and progress over time.

Table 11.1 provides detailed information on these steps.

Training Personnel for Community-Based Programs

Training personnel, from parents to administrators, staff, and volunteers, both in school and in the community, is key for proper community integration of students with disabilities. Here are six steps for training key personnel:

1. Analyze the facility to determine whether there are any physical barriers.
2. Discuss the goals of the program.
3. Assess the student's abilities and needs.
4. Review modification and instructional variables.
5. Implement the program.
6. Adjust and review as needed.

Making sure facilities are accessible and staff are well-trained is necessary for transition experiences.

TABLE 11.1 Steps for Selecting a Sport or Recreational Program for Students With Disabilities

Steps to consider	Actions to take to meet the student's needs
1. Determine the needs and skills of the student.	Identify mobility, communication, and self-help needs.
2. Take into consideration the student's and family members' interests.	Taking the student's interests into consideration increases the likelihood that they will reach their goals. It is also important to know parents' and other family members' interests. If the student's disability is very severe, participation may be limited to accompanying family members to activities that they enjoy. Either way, it is important to make sure the activity is something the student enjoys.
3. Identify available community-based programs.	Once you know what the student can and cannot do, contact a local recreation community department or YMCA to see what programs are available. A university or college program that provides free services to children and youth with disabilities may be available. The physical education or recreation departments of local institutions may be aware of programs.
4. Identify support personal willing to collaborate.	Know the people willing to collaborate and help with the student's integration into the community. Collaborate with a nurse or volunteer, if needed. Coordinate transportation needs with others to ensure it is confirmed.
5. Assess the student's level of satisfaction and progress over time.	Periodic assessments can provide information on areas in need of improvement and adaptations needed to ensure that transition goals are achieved. Collaboration is the key to success. Consult adapted physical educators, therapeutic recreationists, or other personnel to make sure this important process takes place.

Other resources for training personnel include consultant services, one-day workshops with follow-up communication, and Web-based video consultations (Samalot-Rivera & Lieberman 2016). Make sure to include parents and the student in the process when appropriate.

In many cases, the adapted or physical education teacher or the parents, or both, need to work closely with the staff at the community facility to train them to include the student with a disability. They may need to provide guidance in positioning the student, modifying or acquiring equipment, motivating the student, helping the student socialize, and establishing goals. This training should begin with a meeting with the facility staff and administrators before the program starts.

Summary

Educators must advocate for their students, particularly those with disabilities, to help them gain access to sport and recreational activities beyond their formal schooling. This chapter addressed the legal requirement for transition and explained how to help students appropriately transition from the physical education class to the community. This chapter also provided information on recreational activities for students with disabilities within their communities and strategies for training support personnel. The successful transition of students with disabilities from school to community can contribute to their well-being and help families become more engaged in the community.

▷ ▷

Through skill development and access to community programs, Donte's teacher laid the groundwork for a successful transition program. Much to his family's excitement, Donte now regularly participates in modified tee ball games at their local YMCA. Donte's adapted physical education teacher's collaboration with the family and the community was essential to ensure that his participation in after-school recreation and sport programs will lead to a lifetime of quality involvement. The ultimate goal for all of us is to ensure that everyone with a disability, including those with severe disabilities, can be active members of society in a satisfactory and safe manner.

Review Questions

1. Why is important to know about transition services when working with students with disabilities?
2. What are the recommended steps to promote an effective transition and community integration?
3. What are some of the strategies and key personnel that can facilitate the process of community integration for students with disabilities?

Aquatics for Students With Disabilities

Pamela Arnhold
Slippery Rock University of Pennsylvania

David G. Lorenzi
Indiana University of Pennsylvania

Chapter Objectives

By reading this chapter, you will:

▶ Learn the benefits of an aquatic program for students with disabilities.
▶ Identify ways to assess students with disabilities in the pool.
▶ Learn to develop goals for students in an aquatic environment.
▶ Identify equipment that may help students with disabilities communicate and achieve success in the water.
▶ Learn strategies for modifying swim stroke development programs.

Mr. and Mrs. Flores recently moved to the Green Valley School District when Mr. Flores took a position at the Pine Tree Nuclear Company. Mrs. Flores is a special education teacher but is currently taking care of their youngest son, Esteban. This will be the first time Esteban is attending a public school now that he is five years old. Esteban has spastic quadriplegia cerebral palsy with a mild visual impairment.

The school district has invited the Floreses to the school to create an individual education plan (IEP) based on information provided by the early intervention program at Esteban's previous school and with recommendations from his physical, occupational, and speech therapists and his physician. Based on the assessments administered at Green Valley School and Mrs. Flores' knowledge of the law pertaining to special education, the team hopes to create an IEP that will guide Esteban's teachers and help him succeed in school.

The team discusses the type of physical education Esteban will receive. The physical education teacher, Mrs. Kelly, is excited to share with the Flores family that the school district has an extensive aquatic program. She believes that Esteban can benefit from this opportunity. However, the Floreses are not certain of the benefits for Esteban given the severity of his disability. They are concerned for his safety and cannot imagine him being able to participate in an aquatic program.

Mrs. Kelly explains the program and the connection the students have with high school students who are trained volunteers, as well as the support they can offer Esteban in the pool. The Floreses are encouraged to visit one of the aquatic classes to see why staff members are so excited about the program. A date is set for a visit, and the entire Flores family is looking forward to it.

Aquatics can help all students improve their cardiorespiratory endurance, agility, strength, coordination, flexibility, and socialization. It can also improve all swimming skills including diving. This chapter presents strategies teachers and paraeducators can use when teaching students with disabilities in an aquatic environment.

> Involvement in aquatic programs can improve quality of life by increasing endurance, developing motor skills, fostering psychological health, and increasing self-help and independence.

Benefits of Aquatics

Individuals with disabilities are limited frequently in their movement and range of motion. This is especially true for those with orthopedic impairments, but it can also be true of people with other types of disabilities including cerebral palsy, spina bifida, spinal cord injury, and traumatic brain injury. Movement limitations can be profound on land; however, an aquatic environment affords a greater opportunity for movement and physical activity (Arnhold & Lepore, 2017; Lepore, Columna, & Friedlander Litzner, 2015). Because the buoyancy of water lessens the effect of gravity, those with movement limitations can sometimes move in the water in ways they cannot on land (Kelly & Darrah, 2005; Watson, Cummings, Quan, Bratton, & Weiss, 2001).

In addition to the freedom of movement an aquatic environment affords, participation in aquatic activities has shown to improve muscle strength, coordination, flexibility and range of motion, cardiorespiratory endurance, postural stability and trunk control, breath control, and overall health-related physical fitness (Archer, 2002; Arnhold, & Lepore, 2017; Binkley & Schoyer, 2002; Darby & Yaekle, 2000). Improving cardiorespiratory endurance helps people with disabilities more easily perform activities of daily living (Schlough, Nawoczenski, Case, Nolan, & Wiggleworth 2005; Shinohara, Suzuki, Oba, Kawasumi, Kimizuka, & Mita, 2002). Movement in water not only improves flexibility and range of motion but also may provide pain relief while enhancing locomotor skill development and overall motor coordination. Aquatic activities can also enhance sensory perception and integration for those with sensory issues.

The aquatic environment provides a variety of psychological benefits, including improved mood, enhanced self-esteem and body image, and decreased anxiety and depression. The freedom of movement that water provides not only enhances morale but also provides a level of independence that a student with a disability often cannot achieve on land (Arnhold & Lepore, 2017). A child who cannot walk, jump, throw, or bat on land may be able to perform these gross motor skills with the support of the water. This enhanced level of independence can foster a wide range of positive effects including an increased sense of self-efficacy and self-esteem (Block & Conatser, 2007; Johnson, 2005).

Lastly, aquatics affords opportunities for learning to care for one's own personal hygiene. Dressing and undressing in the locker room, showering after a program, and using personal hygiene products after swimming can promote a sense of independence that is so important to feelings of autonomy. Students with disabilities can benefit from opportunities to brush their hair and put on socks, shoes, and clothing during and after aquatic classes.

Medical Issues, Precautions, and Safety Issues

Medical information about students with disabilities should be obtained before any program in the water begins. Parents, guardians, and

Photo courtesy of Maleda Funk.

Swimming programs allow students to connect with others while engaging in physical activity.

classroom teachers can provide information to ensure that they are as safe as possible in the water. The following are possible concerns in an aquatic environment:

- *Oral motor control.* Some students have difficulty closing their mouths as a result of a disability or muscle control. A speech therapist can help set goals both in and out of the water to increase one's ability to close the mouth. Drinking a lot of pool water can cause abdominal discomfort or even aspiration of water into the lungs, so it is imperative to come up with a solution for this issue.

- *Seizures.* For a student diagnosed with seizures, all pool personnel should have information about the type of seizures the student may have, as well as the protocol for taking the medication. The first aid objectives for helping a person having a seizure in the pool are to keep the face above water, maintain an open airway, and prevent injury by providing support with a minimal amount of restraint (Lepore, Gayle, & Stevens, 2007). If a seizure happens, immediately announce it to the lifeguard and have someone time the seizure. If the seizure lasts longer than five minutes (or the child's typical time span for a seizure), call for emergency assistance, following the standard operating procedures for the facility.

- *Spasticity and retention of infantile reflex patterns.* Some students exhibit spasticity as a result of a congenital disability, disease, or trauma. You may need to adapt or modify swim strokes for students with this issue. Confer with the staff and the student to come up with a position that is as streamlined as possible to improve movement in the water. For example, Esteban has spastic flexion in both arms. When performing the breaststroke, he should start by pulling the water in with his hands facing his chest, rather than face his hands out and pull, as in a traditional stroke. With this simple functional change, Esteban can perform the breaststroke with a flotation device and some support at the waist. To ensure the student's safety, be aware that splashing or loud noises may elicit reflex patterns.

Assessment in Aquatics

A proper assessment of a student in an aquatic environment yields a great deal of information that can be used to plan an instructional program (Lepore et al., 2015). An assessment provides a clear picture of the student's strengths, weaknesses, and present level of performance. It also provides information about the types of equipment, modifications, and support services that might be necessary.

Before conducting an aquatic assessment, determine the skills you will assess and match the assessment to those skills. The following are some questions to ask prior to conducting an assessment (Arnhold & Lepore, 2017):

- What is the student interested in learning?
- What skills do the parents or caregivers believe are important for the student to acquire (e.g., balance, grip strength, cardiorespiratory endurance, leg strength)?
- Where will the student use the learned skills (e.g., standing in a prone stander, pushing a wheelchair, performing daily activities, walking up stairs)?
- What are typically developing peers doing in aquatic classes?
- What equipment is available to the family?
- What are the student's medical, therapeutic, educational, and recreational needs?

An ecological assessment is common for people with disabilities in an aquatic environment. It addresses skills people need in both the current and the future environment. In an aquatic environment, an ecological assessment would include skills such as changing in the locker room, entering and exiting the water, using appropriate language in a swim group, performing stretching exercises before swimming, swimming in a lane, using a flotation device, clearing the mouth of water, understanding the rules of the pool, and other functional skills appropriate to swimming and overall independence (Arnhold & Lepore, 2017). See chapter 4 for more information on conducting ecological assessments. You may want to determine the student's overall comfort level in the water by assessing skills such as splashing water on the body and face and putting the mouth, nose, eyes, face, and body in the water. This can be a good starting point for planning aquatic instruction. You should also assess social skills such as interactions with teachers and peers.

An appropriate assessment will help you determine the equipment, teaching aids, and **support personnel** needed to create a safe and successful aquatic experience for a student with a disability. Assessment should be both formal and informal, and the results should help you plan instruction and write goals for the student. Select an assessment that will yield the information you need to plan your aquatic program (see table 12.1).

Before conducting an aquatic assessment, determine the skills you will assess and match the assessment to those skills (see figure 12.1). Select an assessment that will yield the information you need to plan your aquatic program.

TABLE 12.1 Examples of Aquatic Assessments

Assessment	Population and age	Where to find it
Special Olympics Aquatics Coaching Guide (Special Olympics, Inc.)	Students with intellectual disabilities	A PDF file of this test can be found by searching the title online.
Conatser Adapted Aquatics Swimming Screening Test, Second Edition (Conatser, 2009)	Children with autism, cerebral palsy, or intellectual disabilities	www.adaptedaquatics.org/assesment.htm
Aquatics Readiness Assessment	Beginning swimmers	Langendorfer & Bruya, 1994
Modified TWU Aquatics Assessment	All ages and abilities	Lepore, Columna, & Friedlander Litzner, 2015

FIGURE 12.1

Aquatic Skills Checklist

Student: _____ Age: _____ Date: _____

Instructor: _____

	Independent	Needs assistance	Total assistance
POOL PREPARATION			
Demonstrates proper behavior en route to pool			
Takes clothes off			
Hangs clothes in locker			
Puts bathing suit on			
Takes shower			
Awaits directions before entering pool			
POOL ENTRY			
Sits at edge of pool with feet in water			
Puts water on body			
Lowers self into pool			
Climbs down stairs and enters pool			
ADJUSTMENT TO WATER			
Splashes water around with no fear			
Holds gutter and kicks legs			
Kicks while lying on front and being towed			
Kicks while lying on back and being towed			
Moves arms and legs in swimming motion while being towed			
Blows bubbles			
Treads water for 30 seconds			
Puts whole face in water for 5 seconds			
Holds breath while submerged for 10 seconds			
Bobs up and down five times			
Engages in continuous rhythmic breathing while holding side of pool and turning head to side 10 times			
Engages in continuous rhythmic breathing from prone position while kicking with kickboard for 20 feet (6.1 meters)			
FLOATING SKILLS			
Floats while lying on front and holding kickboard with arms fully extended and face submerged			
Does front float			
Does back float			

(continued)

Figure 12.1 *(continued)*

BASIC PROPULSION			
Flutter-kicks with kickboard while on front for 15 feet (4.6 meters)			
Glides on front with push-off, holds kickboard with arms extended, and flutter-kicks for 15 feet			
Glides on front with push-off and flutter kicks with no kickboard for 15 feet			
Glides on front with push-off and flutter-kicks with face submerged and no kickboard for 15 feet			
Glides on back with push-off, holds kickboard with arms extended, and flutter-kicks for 15 feet			
Glides on back with push-off and flutter-kicks with no kickboard for 15 feet			
Rolls over, front to back, while gliding			
Rolls over, back to front, while gliding			
SWIMMING STROKES			
Does freestyle stroke using arms only with face out of water for 10 strokes			
Does freestyle stroke using arms only with face submerged for 10 strokes			
Does freestyle stroke using arms and legs with face submerged for 10 strokes			
Does freestyle stroke using arms and legs with rhythmic breathing for 10 strokes			
Swims underwater for 10 feet (3 meters)			
Does sidestroke on either side for 10 feet			
Does breaststroke for 10 feet			
Does back crawl stroke using arms only for 10 strokes			
Does back crawl stroke using arms and legs for 10 strokes			
DIVING SKILLS			
Dives from a sitting position			
Dives from squatting or crouched position			
Dives from standing position with knees slightly bent			
Dives from standing position with spring and arm action			
Performs standing dive from end of low board			
WATER SAFETY AND DEEP WATER SKILLS			
Bobs 15 times			
Treads water for 30 seconds			
Performs survival floats			
Jumps feetfirst into water, surfaces, and swims back to side of pool			
Changes directions while swimming			
Changes position while floating and swimming (rolls from front to back)			
Changes from horizontal to vertical position while treading water			
Dives off side and swims underwater for 15 feet			

Reprinted, by permission, from L.J. Lieberman and C. Houston-Wilson, 2009, *Strategies for inclusions,* 2nd ed. (Champaign, IL: Human Kinetics), 133, 134.

Planning Goals

Assessment, as previously described, is used to determine instructional goals. The results will help you determine what to teach and highlight the student's strengths and weaknesses to facilitate your instructional planning. Aquatic goals for students with disabilities might range from being comfortable in the water to performing more complex swim strokes. Affective goals can be included such as interaction with peers and increased awareness and attention.

To plan for instruction in an aquatic environment, you need to prioritize the skills you will teach based on the assessment results, and develop both long- and short-term goals. The long-term goals are based on the short-term goals, as outlined in the individual plans for each lesson. For Esteban, the student in the opening scenario, this may look like the following:

1. *Floating for time:* Esteban will float while on his front holding on to the instructor for 15 seconds.
2. *Kicking for distance:* Esteban will kick while on his front holding on to the instructor for 15 seconds.
3. *Gliding for distance:* Esteban will push off the wall with his legs and glide for 10 feet (3 m) with a flotation device and with physical assistance at the waist.
4. *Blowing bubbles for time while kicking on front:* Esteban will kick on his front with a flotation device and with physical assistance at the hips while blowing bubbles for five seconds.
5. *Standing independently for time with support:* Esteban will stand while holding the gutter with physical assistance at the hands for one minute.

The organization of the lesson plan will have a direct result on the learning and success of the student. The lesson plan should include goals that are compatible with the individual aquatic program plan. A description of specific activities that will be used to meet the stated goals should be included along with a timetable for completing each activity. Additionally, the lesson plan should include any relevant medical and safety information so that all teachers and support personnel are aware of these issues.

> *The lesson plan should include goals that are compatible with the student's aquatic program plan.*

The following are some questions to ask when developing aquatic lesson plans (Lepore et al., 2007):

- Are the long-and short-term objectives compatible with the student's aquatic program plan?
- Do performance objectives contain conditions, observable behaviors, and criteria?
- Do performance objectives reflect functional behaviors?
- Does the plan include specific interventions for learning in the affective and cognitive domains in addition to the psychomotor domain?
- Does the plan include an assessment that will help the teacher know when the student achieves short-term and long-term goals?

Teaching and Safety Strategies

The number one priority in teaching aquatics to students with disabilities is having the proper ratio of students to instructors. Whereas those without disabilities may be successful in a 1:10 or 1:12 ratio, students with disabilities, particularly those with severe disabilities, typically need a 1:1 or even 1:2 ratio (Lepore et al., 2015). Ideally, having one instructor position or support the student and one teach the student with demonstrations and physical assistance yields the best results. Anything less may not provide the support or instructional guidance the student needs to succeed. Make an effort to ensure appropriate ratios before developing lessons.

Your assessment of the child both in and out of the pool should be based on information from the family, classroom teachers, paraeducators, therapists who work with the child, and the child's physician. You will be looking for the best way to help the child change clothes, transfer to an aquatic-ready wheelchair, and enter the pool. In addition, you need to know what movements the child can perform independently or with support once in the water.

The following are strategies to help students with disabilities in an aquatic program:

- Help the student explore the freedom of movement an aquatic environment provides, particularly the feeling of less gravity on the body, with support if necessary. You might provide a life jacket or place flotation devices, such as pool noodles, under body parts that may need support.

- Once you have determined that the student is safe, provide as little support as possible so that the student can begin to move independently. You might begin by offering physical support, and then step back to let the student use just flotation devices.

- Continue to reassess the student throughout the program, and eliminate supports if possible. Removing one or more of the flotation devices when the student is ready can engender more confidence. The goal is to have the student be as independently active as possible.

Communication in the Pool

Communication between you and the student is an important aspect of instruction. Identifying the student's preferred form of communication before entering the pool will help the student understand your directions.

Students who are nonverbal may use facial expressions, hand signals, or sign language. Using a dry erase board or laminated pictures attached to a foam board may facilitate communication with these students. See chapter 4 for a more in-depth discussion on communication.

Some students use technology-based communication. Computer-generated speaking, such as through a Tobii Dynavox, can be used in the locker room or before entering the water. A tablet in a water-resistant sleeve can help you and the student exchange thoughts and ideas in and around the pool.

Physical Supports and Equipment

The sense of weightlessness in the water is enriching for children who are physically weak or paralyzed by neuromuscular disease (Pearn & Franklin, 2013). Those with severe disabilities may need support from either people or equipment. The goal should be to discover the minimal amount of assistance a student needs to encourage as much independence as possible. According to Patterson and Grosse (2013), the appropriate use of equipment during aquatic activities not only facilitates engagement but also fosters independence in motor skills and ultimately improved physical fitness.

Students with disabilities may need flotation devices to participate in a swimming program. Choose devices that fit the swimmer's ability, range of motion, strength, buoyancy, swimming style, and experience in the water (Lepore et al., 2015). Support can be in the form of **personal flotation devices (PFDs)**, flotation devices designed for people with disabilities, or equipment already available in the pool (e.g., aqua joggers for keeping the hips near the surface for better horizontal movement). You might need to be creative and design a system using what you have available. A life jacket that clipped in the front enabled Esteban to use his arms as much as possible. This was helpful because he needed to work on flexibility and arm control.

Entering and Exiting the Pool

Children with disabilities may enter a pool themselves by walking down a ramp, transferring from a personal wheelchair to an aquatic-ready chair and then wheeling themselves down a ramp, or moving with a Hoyer lift. All staff should be trained in these methods so the appropriate one is chosen.

General Tips

- The first concern is safety (of the student and of the person lifting the student).
- Tell the person you are lifting what you plan to do before you do it.
- Lock the wheelchair brakes.
- Move the foot rests out of the way as needed.
- Clear away any obstacles from your path.
- The distance the person is lifted should be as small as possible.
- Bend your knees and lift with your legs.
- Avoid bending and twisting at the same time; stand and then pivot.
- Use both hands to help lift.
- If more than one person is lifting, make sure that you work together, with the leader giving commands.
- Wear suitable clothing and footwear when lifting; flat shoes are best.

Student Transferring Independently

- Be close by to assist if necessary.
- Encourage the student to transfer independently.
- Lock the wheelchair brakes.
- Move the foot rests out of the way.
- Clear a path.
- Give the student verbal cues for transfer (e.g., push up on the arm rest, stand up, pivot, reach for the support base).

One Person Transferring the Student With Pivot Support

- Lock the wheelchair brakes.
- Place a gait belt around the student's waist to use as a firm surface to hold onto.
- The new surface should be at the same level or height as the wheelchair the student is transferring from.
- Move the foot rests out of the way.
- Place the wheelchair as close to the new surface as possible. The wheelchair should be at a 90-degree angle to the new surface.
- Help the student scoot to the edge of the wheelchair.
- Place the student's feet flat on the floor.
- Place the student's arms around your upper back or elbows—*not your neck*.
- Place your hands on the gait belt.
- Count to three, rocking forward on each number. Come to a standing position on the number three as you straighten your legs and lift the student from the wheelchair.
- When the student is upright and under control, pivot your feet toward the new surface, rotating the student as you pivot.
- Slowly lower the student's body onto the new surface. Have the student reach back to the surface to help lower himself or herself down.
- Hold the student until he or she is stable and secure.

Two People Transferring the Student Using an Arms and Legs Lift

- Lock the wheelchair brakes.
- Move the foot rests out of the way.
- *First lifter:* Stand behind the student. Help the student cross his or her arms over the chest. Place your arms under the student's upper arms.
- *Second lifter:* Place both hands under the student's lower thighs. Initiate and lead the lift with a prearranged count (1, 2, 3, lift).
- *Both lifters:* Using your leg and arm muscles, and bending your back as little as possible, gently lift the student's torso and legs at the same time.
- Move the student to the new surface. Position the student on the new surface, maintaining contact until the student is stable and secure.

Two People Transferring the Student Using a Side Lift

- Lock the wheelchair brakes.
- Move the foot rests out of the way.
- *Both lifters:* Stand beside the student. Help the student cross his or her arms over the chest. Place the arm nearest the student's head around his or her back and the other arm under the thigh. Initiate and lead the lift with a prearranged count (1, 2, 3, lift). Using your leg and arm muscles, and bending your back as little as possible, gently lift the student's torso and legs at the same time.
- Move the student to the new surface. Position the student on the new surface, maintaining contact until the student is stable and secure.

Adjusting to the Water

Many people, and perhaps especially people with disabilities, need some time to adjust to the water before beginning an aquatic activity. This process may begin with sitting on the side of the pool independently or being physically supported by a staff member. You might gently place water on the student's legs and arms with a sponge or by cupping water in your hands. Once acclimated to the water, the student may be escorted into the water via a ramp or from the side of the pool into another staff member's grasp. In the water, you might assist with bouncing or swaying while making sure the student does not inhale water or become fearful.

Water Temperature

Students with varying disabilities respond differently to the air and water temperatures in a pool environment. People with spasticity relax and experience more freedom of movement in warmer water. Those with multiple sclerosis perform better in cooler water because they are sensitive to high temperature while exercising.

Wearing a rash guard, a T-shirt, or even a Wet Vest can keep a person warm during an aquatic program. Have a large beach towel at the ready when a student with sensitivity to cold air comes out of the water.

Water varying from 83 to 86 °F (28 to 30 °C) is the most comfortable for typical water fitness classes and general aquatic programming. This allows the body to react and respond normally to the onset of exercise and the accompanying increase in body temperature. Cooling benefits are still felt, and there is little risk of overheating. Program modifications will be required for water temperatures outside the recommended range. Aquatic fitness professionals should know the water temperature and modify the program based on the population and the program format (USA Swimming, n.d.). In the case of Esteban, the teacher requested an increase in the pool temperature to 85 °F (30 °C) on his swim days because of his cerebral palsy.

Transitioning to Aquatics in the Community

The ultimate goal of an aquatic program is to help students be as independent and successful as possible inside and outside of the school environment. This is now possible as more facilities become accessible as a result of the reauthorization of the Americans with Disabilities Act (ADA). ADA Standards (2010) for Accessible Design contained accessibility requirements for certain types of recreation facilities, including the requirement to provide accessible means of entry and exit to swimming pools, wading pools, and spas (ADA, n.d.). As a result, accessibility to aquatic facilities has improved; many hotels and recreation facilities now provide swimming pool lifts. Ramps and zero entry or beach entry pools also provide accessibility to those with disabilities. When students are exposed in school to the opportunities water can provide, their parents may be more willing to participate in aquatics outside of the school day for recreational purposes or even on family vacations.

Summary

Students with disabilities should be welcomed in aquatic facilities and aquatic physical education programs. Because of their buoyancy, students may feel successful and experience more freedom of movement in the water than they do on land. Your job is to consider adaptations and modifications, ensure appropriate student-to-instructor ratios, check water temperatures, assess student progress, provide flotation devices, and use appropriate instructional strategies to ensure student success. With some time, energy, and planning, all children can benefit from the aquatic environment.

The Flores family discovered that Esteban's physical education program was enhanced by his aquatic experiences. His team determined that the safest and quickest transfer into the pool was via a Hoyer lift, assisted by his instructor and paraeducator. As a result of his aquatic program, Esteban became more independent, had more stamina, and began to socialize more with his peers and teachers. Everyone on the team learned the benefits of offering aquatics to all children. With their knowledge of proper transfers and of their son's goals and abilities, Esteban's parents now feel comfortable taking him to community pools.

Review Questions

1. What is one physical benefit, one social benefit, one activity of daily living benefit, and one cognitive benefit of participating in an aquatic program?

2. How would you assess a student with a disability in an aquatic environment?

3. Why is it important to create goals for a student with a disability who is enrolled in an aquatic program?

4. What would be an inexpensive way to communicate directions at a station in the aquatic environment?

5. What is the best instructional ratio in the pool for a student with a disability?

6. What is the best plan for assisting a person who is having a seizure in the water?

PART III

Sample Lessons Using Universal Design for Learning

Part III offers a blueprint for delivering lessons using a Universal Design for Learning (UDL) format. The lessons included in part III are divided into two categories: (1) team sports and target games and (2) lifetime and health-related activities. We encourage you to use UDL concepts to plan lessons that create flexible learning environments to accommodate students' unique learning styles and needs. When designing lessons using UDL, consider the following guidelines:

1. *Use multiple modalities.* Because students take in information in diverse ways, consider presenting lessons visually (e.g., by modeling and demonstrating, using a video model, or using task cards), auditorily, tactilely, multilingually, and representationally (e.g., with pictures, words, symbols).

2. *Provide multiple means of action and expression.* Provide multiple ways for each student to express what they know for assessment purposes. Students could show that they can serve for volleyball from the service line, half court, or throw the ball over the net. Students could show that they know how to rotate positions in volleyball by drawing a picture or typing the directions into a device.

3. *Provide multiple means of engagement.* Learners differ significantly in what attracts their attention and engages their interest.

When determining what to teach students with disabilities, begin with the general physical education curriculum. Analyze the skills to determine appropriate fit. Chapters 2, 4 and 7 offer strategies to determine how to align the student's strength with the curricula. For example, if general physical education students are working on jump rope skills, consider using a task analysis to include skills such as jumping and bouncing. You might use fitness balls, fitness ramps, split ropes, or jump rope kits. Be sure to include progressions and regressions related to the skills you are focused on.

When delivering instruction, consider motivational strategies to encourage cooperation and competition between peers. In many cases, students with disabilities want to engage meaningful ways with their peers.

Be aware of the environmental conditions to ensure safe conditions for learning. You may need to decrease extraneous sounds and change lighting fixtures to reduce stimulation. Promote social responsibility through peer and teacher modeling, and above all, have high expectations for student learning. Make sure assistive devices are routinely available, and offer choices and variety of equipment (in weight, color, texture, sound) to all learners.

When assessing your students, consider multiple means of gathering information such as a physical demonstration, a verbal explanation of a concept, or an electronic assessment. See chapter 3 for assessment ideas.

Special thanks to Anne Griffin for her input on suggestions for Universally Designing Lessons section.

Team Sports and Target Games

SHAPE America's National Standards & Grade-Level Outcomes provide the blueprint for student learning in developing the lessons for team sports and target games presented in this chapter. The lessons are presented as outlines to be adapted or modified to accommodate students with a wide range of skills and abilities. Suggestions for peer and paraeducator support are provided so that the lessons can be used in a variety of settings.

Team Sports

This section presents lessons in soccer, floor hockey, basketball, and hurdles. These team sports enable students with disabilities to engage in activities with peers with simple modifications to the equipment and game structure. Because these sports are typically taught in physical education programs, aligning standards and modifying outcomes is easy. The lesson on hurdles provides a unique modification of the skills of hurdling that encourages students to use tracking and arm movements to conquer the hurdle.

SOCCER: PASSING

Contributed by Toni Bader, Morgan Wescliff, and Joy Rose

APPLICABLE UNITS

Soccer

Eye–foot coordination

AGE GROUP

Elementary school students. This lesson can easily be adapted for middle and high school students.

OBJECTIVE

Students will be able to kick to a target, working individually or with a partner.

NATIONAL STANDARDS MET

Standard 1: The physically literate individual demonstrates competency in a variety of motor skills and movement patterns.

Standard 3: The physically literate individual demonstrates the knowledge and skills to achieve and maintain a health-enhancing level of physical activity and fitness.

Standard 4: The physically literate individual exhibits responsible personal and social behavior that respects self and others.

Standard 5: The physically literate individual recognizes the value of physical activity for health, enjoyment, challenge, self-expression and/or social interaction.

GRADE-LEVEL OUTCOMES

S1.E19: Manipulative—Passing and receiving with feet

S3.E2: Engages in physical activity

S4.E4: Working with others

S5.E3: Self-enjoyment

ACCEPTABLE OUTCOME VARIATIONS

Students with disabilities hit the target, kick in the direction of the target, or pass a ball to a partner.

EQUIPMENT

Wedge mat, soccer ball, tape roll to put ball on, bells, beepers, hoops made into targets or bowling pins

DESCRIPTION

Set students up across from each other. Place the tape roll flat on the wedge mat and the soccer ball on top of it. Students in wheelchairs kick the ball off the wedge mat at a target or a partner (see figure 13.1).

Instructor can have multiple stations of partner passing and target practice. Ramps may be used to send balls to a target, a partner, or a small group. Place bells or beepers on the targets to add a sensory response.

Students should have ample time to strike the ball depending on their skills and abilities. Sensory equipment, such as bells, may be attached to a student's foot or the target.

SPATIAL CONSIDERATIONS

Students' ability to strike the ball determines the length of the court. Students can be in lanes or in small groups with targets in the middle.

INSTRUCTIONS FOR PEERS

Support the student with a disability to the best of your ability. Recognize communication patterns

Figure 13.1 Setup for passing soccer.

when the student is communicating a desire to play the game with you (looking at you, using sounds or gestures). Be aware of the slower pace of the activity, and provide feedback on foot direction and the amount of force needed to propel the ball. Also, assist with target setup.

INSTRUCTIONS FOR PARAEDUCATORS

Support students with verbal cues and physical support. Facilitate interactions between students with disabilities and their peers. Give positive specific and general feedback throughout the activity to students with disabilities to support skill development and facilitate interactions.

BASKETBALL: SPOT REMOVER

Contributed by Nancy Miller and Toni Bader

APPLICABLE UNIT

Basketball

AGE GROUP

Elementary school students. This can easily be adapted for middle school and high school students.

OBJECTIVES

Students work as a team and use correct basketball shooting form to score baskets and remove as many spots from the floor as possible.

NATIONAL STANDARDS MET

Standard 1: The physically literate individual demonstrates competency in a variety of motor skills and movement patterns.

Standard 5: The physically literate individual recognizes the value of physical activity for health, enjoyment, challenge, self-expression and/or social interaction.

GRADE-LEVEL OUTCOMES

S1.E16: Manipulative—Catching

S1.E17: Manipulative—Dribbling/ball control with hands

S1.E20: Manipulative—Dribbling in combination

S5.E4: Social interaction

ACCEPTABLE OUTCOME VARIATIONS

Students with disabilities choose between two sensory-engaging balls and practice reaching, holding, and releasing from a three-ring binder ramp. They may also strike or push a ball off a tray table or ball holder to score a basket. Other options are shooting through a hanging hoop or into a bucket.

EQUIPMENT

Balls of different sizes (basketballs, light balls), baskets at various heights, six poly spots

Modified equipment: Variety of sensory-engaging balls; variety of lap trays; three-ring binder ramp; low, medium, and high targets (e.g., buckets); hoops to shoot into

DESCRIPTION

Students are part of a team at a designated basket, with each student having a ball. Students work on proper shooting technique to score baskets; spots are removed each time a teammate scores a basket.

Poly spots are scattered in an arch on the floor in front of each team's basket (see figure 13.2). Each student has a ball and stands on one of the spots in a shooting position. On the "Go" signal, each student shoots at the basket; there may be multiple basket variations for each group, if desired, such as a bucket, hula hoop, or mini basket, being careful to shoot only when no one is in front of them. Encourage students to use correct shooting technique with pads of fingers on ball and helping hand on ball. Cues for the activity include *Push with the legs, Make an L with your hands, Wave goodbye*.

Students who make baskets remove the spot they were standing on for a team point. Teams try to remove all the spots using correct shooting form.

A student with a disability, with or without the assistance of a paraeducator or peer, holds a ball and, with the support of a tray or three-ring binder ramp, releases it to score into the team basket. When a ball that is released hits a target, a spot is removed.

SPATIAL CONSIDERATIONS

Buckets and targets on the floor that serve as modified baskets should be should be strategically placed to ensure safety.

INSTRUCTIONS FOR PEERS

Support the student with a disability to the best of your ability. Recognize when the student is communicating a desire to play the game with you (looking at you, using sounds or gestures). Cue the student to hold the ball as you place it in front of his or her

Figure 13.2   Setup for spot remover basketball.

hand. Other cues include *Hold the ball* and *Score a basket*. Give positive specific and general feedback.

INSTRUCTIONS FOR PARAEDUCATORS

Recognize when the student with a disability is communicating a desire to play the game with you or a peer (looking at you or a peer, using sounds or gestures). Give the student visual, manual, and verbal cues such as *Hold the ball* and *Let go*. Give positive specific and general feedback. Facilitate interactions with peers. Give positive specific and general feedback throughout to the student with a disability and to their peers to support skill development and facilitate interactions.

HOCKEY: RIP OFF

Contributed by Nancy Miller

APPLICABLE UNITS

Floor hockey

Striking with a long-handled implement

AGE GROUP

Elementary school students. This can easily be adapted for middle school and high school students.

OBJECTIVES

Students work on dribbling, dodging, faking, and ball handling to gain and keep possession of a ball or puck.

NATIONAL STANDARDS MET

Standard 1: The physically literate individual demonstrates competency in a variety of motor skills and movement patterns.

Standard 2: The physically literate individual applies knowledge of concepts, principles, strategies and tactics related to movement and performance.

Standard 4: The physically literate individual exhibits responsible personal and social behavior that respects self and others.

GRADE-LEVEL OUTCOMES

S1.E6: Locomotor—Combinations

S1.E25: Manipulative—Striking, long implement

S2.E5: Movement concepts—Strategies and tactics

S4.E6: Safety

ACCEPTABLE OUTCOME VARIATIONS

Students with disabilities can use gestures or their vision to communication directions to paraeducators or peers. They can make choices to travel on open pathways and to pursue players, pucks, or balls to gain and keep possession. A paraeducator gives verbal, visual, and manual cues to help students hold modified hockey sticks and to draw attention to the ball or puck.

EQUIPMENT

Floor hockey sticks, balls or pucks

Modified equipment: Double hockey stick connected with pool noodles along the blades and at the top, larger pucks and balls

DESCRIPTION

This activity can be done individually, in pairs, or on a team.

Everyone starts in a home space with a hockey stick. Two thirds of the students start with a puck or ball. On the "Go" signal, players with pucks or balls use their stick-handling, dribbling, faking, and dodging skills to maintain possession. The players without pucks or balls use their stick-handling skills to mark and try to gain possession. On each "Stop" signal, players in possession earn a point, after which you restart the game. Games can be played with two partners or two teams.

Students with disabilities hold on to modified hockey sticks (see figure 13.3) while pursuing peers, balls, or pucks that they are visually choosing with

assistance. A paraeducator can give visual, verbal, and manual cues when needed to help a student hold a hockey stick and to draw attention to the ball or puck. The paraeducator can also help the student pursue peers and the ball or puck of the student's choosing.

SPATIAL CONSIDERATIONS

Everyone starts in a home space and moves in open pathways while attempting to gain and keep possession of a ball or puck as long as possible.

INSTRUCTIONS FOR PEERS

Support the student with a disability to the best of your ability. Give visual and verbal cues, such as *My turn* when you steal the student's ball or *Your turn*, when the student steals your ball. Give positive specific and general feedback.

INSTRUCTIONS FOR PARAEDUCATORS

Support the student with a disability by facilitating skill performance and interactions with peers. Give visual, auditory, and verbal cues to hold the hockey stick, and manual assistance when needed to perform skills. Allow the student to choose what to pursue (ball, puck, or peers). To facilitate interactions with peers, give positive specific and general feedback throughout regarding holding the stick and looking to peers.

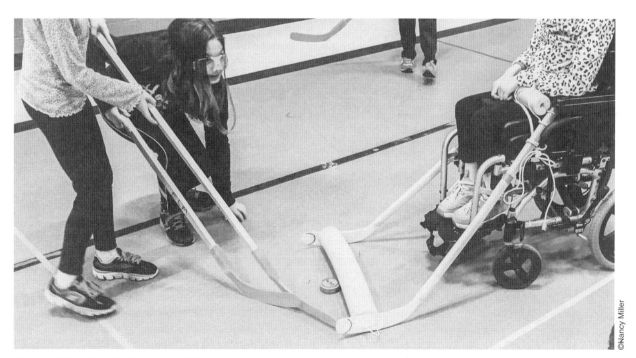

Figure 13.3 Modified hockey stick.

©Nancy Miller

TRACK AND FIELD: HURDLING

Contributed by Nancy Miller

APPLICABLE UNITS

Running

Jumping

Landing

AGE GROUP

Elementary school students. This can easily be adapted for middle school and high school students.

OBJECTIVES

Students use correct form to run, jump, hurdle, and land.

NATIONAL STANDARDS MET

Standard 1: The physically literate individual demonstrates competency in a variety of motor skills and movement patterns.

Standard 2: The physically literate individual applies knowledge of concepts, principles, strategies and tactics related to movement and performance.

Standard 4: The physically literate individual exhibits responsible personal and social behavior that respects self and others.

GRADE-LEVEL OUTCOMES

S1.E2: Locomotor—Jogging, running

S1.E3: Locomotor—Jumping and landing, horizontal plane

S1.E10: Nonlocomotor (stability)—Curling and stretching, twisting and bending

S2.E2: Movement concepts—Pathways, shapes, levels

S2.E3: Movement concepts—Speed, direction, force

S4.E3: Accepting feedback

ACCEPTABLE OUTCOME VARIATION

Students with disabilities make visual contact and reach with their hands to push hurdles out of the way.

EQUIPMENT

Age-appropriate high hurdles (cones and plastic L hurdles)

Modified equipment: Cones (wheelchair height), adapted hurdles, and pool noodles to create turnstile hurdles; cones, pool noodles, streamers, and poles can be used to create an overhead sensory hurdle

DESCRIPTION

Each student lines up on the starting line in a lane. Students with disabilities are in a lane with modified sensory-engaging hurdles.

On the "Go" signal, students without disabilities use correct form to leap over a hurdle and land on one foot. Proper hurdling technique is as follows: Lift the lead knee higher than the hurdle, kick the leg forward, stretch and reach with the opposite hand forward, bend the trail leg at the knee to the side to clear the hurdle, land on the lead foot, snap the trail-leg foot down, and continue with proper running form. Arms are always in opposition to the legs.

Students with disabilities may be supported by paraeducators or peers as they travel down their lane using their eyes to track the hurdles. They should stretch, reach, and push to move the hurdles out of the way to represent passing over them (see figure 13.4).

SPATIAL CONSIDERATIONS

Students start on the starting line before a lane of hurdles.

INSTRUCTIONS FOR PEERS

Support the student with a disability to the best of your ability. Recognize when the student is communicating a desire to play the game with you (by using sounds or gestures). Give the student verbal cues to look at the hurdles during the approach; give cues to reach out or up and to push the hurdle out of the way. Give positive specific and general feedback.

INSTRUCTIONS FOR PARAEDUCATORS

Recognize when the student is communicating a desire to play the game with you or a peer using sounds or gestures. Give the student verbal cues to look, to reach up or out, and to push the hurdles out of the way during the approach. Facilitate interactions between students with disabilities and their peers. Give positive specific and general feedback throughout to students with disabilities and to their peers to support skill development and facilitate interactions.

©Nancy Miller

Figure 13.4   Modified hurdling with assistance from a paraeducator.

Target Games

Target games are wonderful activities that can be enjoyed by all. In particular, golf, bowling, and archery are suitable recreational sports for students with disabilities and their families. Regardless of the variations presented in these lessons, hitting a target provides motivational and visual feedback that engages the students.

Golf

Golf is a satisfying long-handled activity that can be enjoyed by people of all ages and abilities. These games can be played inside or outside with easy modifications and with game play that includes a variety of shots. This section presents four golf lessons.

GOLF: PUTTING

Contributed by Brad M. Weiner

APPLICABLE UNIT

Golf

AGE GROUP

High school students

OBJECTIVE

Students analyze and refine their putting technique (grip, stance, swing, follow-through, and accuracy) to engage in a six-hole competitive miniature golf activity with peers.

NATIONAL STANDARDS MET

Standard 1: The physically literate individual demonstrates competency in a variety of motor skills and movement patterns.

Standard 5: The physically literate individual recognizes the value of physical activity for health, enjoyment, challenge, self-expression and/or social interaction.

GRADE-LEVEL OUTCOMES

S1.H1: Lifetime activities

S5.H2.L2: Challenge

ACCEPTABLE OUTCOME VARIATIONS

Students with disabilities demonstrate the following:

- Extension and accuracy of the arm and hand when pressing a button switch to activate a device to propel the golf ball toward the hole
- Maintaining a grip on a golf ball, as well as accuracy, coordination, and flexibility when extending the arm to drop the ball down a ramp toward the hole
- Maintaining a grip on the golf club while striking a switch that activates a device to propel the golf ball toward the hole
- Maintaining a grip on the golf club with one hand and swinging it in a pendulum motion to strike the golf ball toward the target

EQUIPMENT

Golf putters, golf holes or small circular targets of various sizes, course obstacles, practice golf balls (soft foam), traditional golf balls, powerlink device, button switch activator, air blower, ball ramp, modified ball return, exercise step, table tennis paddle, lollipop paddle, 4- to 6-inch (10 to 15 cm) foam ball

DESCRIPTION

In groups of four, students take turns striking the golf ball toward each of the six holes, following the rules of miniature golf. A scorecard is used to record the number of strikes it takes each student to complete each hole. Encourage students to provide verbal corrective and positive feedback and to model putting technique and angles for students with disabilities. Students with limited range of motion and grasping ability press a button switch with their fingers or head to activate a blower. Students with limited range of motion who can grip a small object grasp and release the golf ball down a ramp toward the target.

Students with some arm range of motion grasp the golf club and swing it into a button switch that activates a blower to propel the ball toward the target.

Students with bilateral coordination difficulty can use one hand to grasp the golf club, or a short-handled implement (a table tennis or lollipop paddle). Elevate the golf ball to within arm's reach.

Students may choose to strike a 4- to 6-inch (10 to 15 cm) foam ball toward various targets (e.g., between two cones, hit the ring of a hula hoop).

Set up obstacles for students to move in a linear pathway to the hole if the original hole or course is too difficult.

Use peer modeling, video modeling, communication systems with pictures, repeated verbal directions, cues, prompts, including verbal cues, demonstration, physical assistance, and feedback.

Students work in pairs or small groups.

Students with short-term focus and high energy can stand on a heightened surface (e.g., exercise step, low balance beam) with the ball elevated as needed to help them focus on the task.

SPATIAL CONSIDERATIONS

The area around each hole needs to accommodate students using wheelchairs or other assistive walking devices. As much as possible, spread out the holes on the course to decrease confusion.

INSTRUCTIONS FOR PEERS

Support everyone in the group using corrective and positive feedback. When beneficial and appropriate, help students with disabilities grasp short-handled implements or help them bring their arms up so they can drop the ball down the ramp. It may help to hold the button switch in place.

INSTRUCTIONS FOR PARAEDUCATORS

Using appropriate wait times and communication devices, provide corrective and positive feedback. Help students attend to the task, and promote positive on-task behaviors. Use a variety of prompts including visual, verbal, and physical to provide the best opportunities for independence.

GOLF: STATIONS

Contributed by Toni Bader, Morgan Wescliff, and Joy Rose

APPLICABLE UNITS
Golf

Striking with a long implement

AGE GROUP
Elementary school students. This can easily be adapted for middle school and high school students.

OBJECTIVE
Students hit objects to targets using either short or long-handled objects

NATIONAL STANDARDS MET
Standard 1: The physically literate individual demonstrates competency in a variety of motor skills and movement patterns.

Standard 3: The physically literate individual demonstrates the knowledge and skills to achieve and maintain a health-enhancing level of physical activity and fitness.

Standard 4: The physically literate individual exhibits responsible personal and social behavior that respects self and others.

Standard 5: The physically literate individual recognizes the value of physical activity for health, enjoyment, challenge, self-expression and/or social interaction.

GRADE-LEVEL OUTCOMES
S1.E25: Manipulative—Striking, long implement

S4.E4: Working with others

S4.E5: Rules and etiquette

S4.E6: Safety

ACCEPTABLE OUTCOME VARIATIONS
Students with disabilities put or chip objects to targets of various sizes from different distances. Options include either hitting the targets, or grasping or holding the golf club.

EQUIPMENT
Pendulum station: two chairs, three TheraBands, a golf putter, a cone to put the ball on, and a target

Auditory sensory stations: tambourine, bells, variety of balls and target sizes

DESCRIPTION
Set students up at a variety of putting stations with targets in front of them. One station should provide a pendulum activity. At the pendulum station, a student with a disability (in a wheelchair, walker, or standing) is holding a club. A peer pulls a string attached to the head of a club and gives the string to the student. Have the student practice at each station for two to three minutes, and then rotate. Each station can have a different target or put length.

Students can have multiple stations for putting or chipping. They can also have choices of putters and balls at each station (e.g., extended putters with poles taped on them, pendulum putters, regular putters, ramps for rolling balls on, larger balls, bell balls). Bells can be placed on targets to add a sensory response. Music can also direct students to targets. Construction paper or hula hoops can be used as targets.

SPATIAL CONSIDERATIONS
Students' ability to hit the ball and their strength should determine the length of the putt. Students perform individually or in small groups with targets in the middle.

INSTRUCTIONS FOR PEERS
Recognize the slow pace of the activity, and provide feedback on ball direction. Give positive reinforcement throughout the activity. Assist with station setup and write scores on a whiteboard to show students how they performed.

INSTRUCTIONS FOR PARAEDUCATORS
Facilitate students' skill performances and interactions with peers. Support students with disabilities who can stand to gain balance and stamina, and provide positive reinforcement. Help all students, or rotate with a student with a disability.

GOLF: ALIEN INVASION

Contributed by Nancy Miller

APPLICABLE UNITS

Golf

Striking with a long implement

AGE GROUP

Elementary school students. This can easily be adapted for middle school and high school students.

OBJECTIVES

Students work in teams using proper putting form to strike a ball, hit disc targets, and collect balls for the team. Students focus on speed, direction, force, and personal responsibility while working alone or with partners.

NATIONAL STANDARDS MET

Standard 1: The physically literate individual demonstrates competency in a variety of motor skills and movement patterns.

Standard 2: The physically literate individual applies knowledge of concepts, principles, strategies and tactics related to movement and performance.

Standard 4: The physically literate individual exhibits responsible personal and social behavior that respects self and others.

GRADE-LEVEL OUTCOMES

S1.E25: Manipulative—Striking, long implement

S2.E3: Movement concepts—Speed, direction, force

S4.E1: Personal responsibility

ACCEPTABLE OUTCOME VARIATIONS

Students with disabilities use their vision to track, reach, and grasp a bell to release a string and golf club. Paraeducators give verbal, visual, and manual assistance when needed to help students engage in putting.

EQUIPMENT

Putter golf clubs with red and yellow markings on the handles to help with proper grip; bull's-eyes on the heads of the clubs, golf balls, and discs

Modified putter: Club with a hole drilled through in which to place a wooden dowel, two cones, bells, string, sensory-engaging balls (see figure 13.5)

Figure 13.5 Modified putter.

DESCRIPTION

In teams of four, students are paired up and take turns putting with partners. Discs that represent spaceships are scattered on the floor. The objective is to use correct putting form to strike golf balls to hit the spaceships and collect them for the team.

Each student has a putter and a ball in a home space on the striking line. Partners work together using proper putting form to strike their balls with the correct amount of force and directionality to hit disc targets on the floor. Students retrieve the balls and discs and return to switch places with their partners on a waiting line.

- Grip cues: *Left on red, Right on yellow,* and *Glue together*
- Stance cues: *A* (athletic), *Y* (arms and club), *Dot the eye* (hit the ball with the bull's-eye on the head of the club)
- Putting cue: *Brush tick tock*

A student with a disability works with a paraeducator or peer. A putter is suspended between two cones with a string attached to the head of the club and a bell attached to the end of the string. The student grasps and swings the club to propel the club forward to strike a ball. Bells are also attached to the head of the club, and a variety of sensory-engaging balls are used. The student uses vision and hearing to track the club, and then uses reaching, grasping, and releasing skills to hold and release the bell string to strike a sensory-engaging ball to hit a spaceship (disc). Peers then proceed to take their turns putting. A paraeducator can retrieve balls from discs and reset balls. Cues are *Reach, Hold,* and *Release.*

SPATIAL CONSIDERATIONS

Students are paired up and share a putting area on the striking line.

The striking equipment for students with disabilities is set up alongside peers' equipment on the striking line.

INSTRUCTIONS FOR PEERS

Support the student with a disability to the best of your ability. Give the student visual and auditory cues. Verbal cues might be *Reach, Hold bell,* and *Let go.* Give positive specific and general feedback.

INSTRUCTIONS FOR PARAEDUCATORS

Facilitate students' skill performances and interactions with peers. Give visual, auditory, and verbal cues, such as *Reach, Hold bell, and Let go,* as well as physical assistance when needed to perform skills. Give positive specific and general feedback throughout to support skill development and facilitate peer interactions.

THROLF (THROWING GOLF)

Contributed by Ken Black

APPLICABLE UNITS

Golf

Manipulative

AGE GROUP

Elementary and middle school students

OBJECTIVE

Students throw underhand at a target. This activity adapts the fundamental concept and rules of golf to create the platform for an inclusive game that can be differentiated to support students with a wide range of abilities (see acceptable outcome variations).

NATIONAL STANDARDS MET

Standard 1: The physically literate individual demonstrates competency in a variety of motor skills and movement patterns.

Standard 2: The physically literate individual applies knowledge of concepts, principles, strategies and tactics related to movement and performance.

Standard 4: The physically literate individual exhibits responsible personal and social behavior that respects self and others.

GRADE-LEVEL OUTCOMES

S1.E13.K: Throws underhand with opposite foot forward

S2.M9.6: Shot selection

S4.M6: Rules and etiquette

ACCEPTABLE OUTCOME VARIATIONS

Substitute any propelling method appropriate for the student. For example, a student with limited hand or arm control can push or kick a large ball toward the target, or release a ball toward a target using a ramp or gutter device.

EQUIPMENT

Throwing implements: beanbags, boccia balls, paper or yarn balls, large soccer or Swiss balls

Targets: plastic hoops or circles marked on the floor or ground, or common items such as cardboard boxes, large buckets, or other containers (must be clean)

DESCRIPTION

Students can participate individually, in pairs, in small groups, or teams. Partners might use one ball or beanbag, alternating throws to try to land as close to the target as possible. The number of throws students make to each target (hole) are recorded by the paraeducator, peer tutor, or teacher.

This activity follows the basic rules of golf. Students try to throw a ball or beanbag around an improvised golf course consisting of a variety of targets (holes). The object is to complete the course in the fewest number of throws (strokes) possible. Students throw from the tee (throwing line) toward the target; each subsequent throw is made from where the ball or beanbag lands until the target is reached.

Variations

- You can vary the distance to the targets based on players' functional ability.
- Students can choose to throw or send objects in different ways according to their ability or as a challenge. For example, some students might use their nondominant hand. The targets can also vary (e.g., be set at different heights, require different throwing actions).
- The number of targets, and the distance to be covered, can also vary. Additionally, the throlf course can be located either indoors or outdoors.

SPATIAL CONSIDERATIONS

Partners and peers can support students with vision or spatial or perceptual impairments by calling or clapping from just behind each target.

You can also use fluttering flags or colored material to identify the targets (holes) more clearly.

INSTRUCTIONS FOR PEERS

In pairs or small groups, work together to create target holes using available materials. All the targets combined make up the throlf course. Challenge each other as you play.

INSTRUCTIONS FOR PARAEDUCATORS

Use this activity to introduce the basic rules and etiquette of golf, such as the following:

- Turn taking
- Silence and respect when another student is playing
- Honesty when recording scores

Bowling

Most students enjoy bowling. This section includes three bowling lessons that uses a variety of equipment to both propel the ball. Depending on the outcomes or goals of the activity, each lesson presents a variety of movement experiences that motivate students to engage with peers.

BOWLING FOR JUNK

Contributed by Ann Griffin

APPLICABLE UNITS

Bowling

Manipulatives

Ball skills

AGE GROUP

Elementary school students. This can easily be adapted for middle school and high school students.

OBJECTIVE

Students use a variety of throws to propel objects toward a target or peer.

NATIONAL STANDARDS MET

Standard 1: The physically literate individual demonstrates competency in a variety of motor skills and movement patterns.

Standard 3: The physically literate individual demonstrates the knowledge and skills to achieve and maintain a health-enhancing level of physical activity and fitness.

Standard 4: The physically literate individual exhibits responsible personal and social behavior that respects self and others.

GRADE-LEVEL OUTCOMES

S1.E13: Manipulative—Underhand throw (roll)

S3.E2: Engages in physical activity

S4.E1 and E2: Personal responsibility

S4.E4: Working with others

ACCEPTABLE OUTCOME VARIATIONS

Students with disabilities move independently or with other supportive equipment and increase accuracy by knocking down the pins.

EQUIPMENT

- A variety of targets including bowling pins, recycled plastic 2-liter bottles, empty water bottles, coffee containers, plastic juice bottles, plastic milk jugs, soda cans, empty tennis ball or Pringles cans, small pill bottles, film canisters, yogurt containers
- One tennis ball per group
- One hula hoop per group
- One cone per group
- One score sheet for each group (laminate for longer use)
- Lively music
- A variety of balls, bocce ramps, bowling ramps, and switch-activated ramps
- Paper and pencil, calculator, or iPad for keeping score

DESCRIPTION

This activity can be done individually, in pairs, or as part of a team. Place a variety of objects a suitable distance from the bowlers depending on their age and ability. Each group lines up behind a cone with a hoop in front. Determine a foul line that the bowlers may not cross.

On your signal, the first bowler from each group rolls a tennis ball at an object trying to knock it down. If the object is knocked down, the bowler runs and picks up the knocked-down object, along with the tennis ball, and returns to the group to place the object in the hoop.

The next bowler repeats the activity. If an object is not knocked down, the bowler runs and picks up only the ball and returns to the group. Bowlers may move anywhere behind the foul line when rolling. Have students play for a designated amount of time or until all of the objects have been knocked down. Teams add up their scores as indicated on the score sheet.

SPATIAL CONSIDERATIONS

Set the restraining line diagonally to give all students a choice of distance from which to roll the ball.

INSTRUCTIONS FOR PEERS

Give the student with a disability visual and verbal cues such as *Reach, Hold,* and *Let go.* Give positive specific and general feedback.

INSTRUCTIONS FOR PARAEDUCATORS

Help students, if necessary, with physical supports and verbal prompts. You may also support all class members with strategy development to knock down as many targets as possible.

Bowling for Junk Score Sheet

White bowling pin: 1 point

Red bowling pin: 2 points

Pringles can: 3 points

Tennis ball container: 3 points

Large water or milk jug: 4 points

Soda or Gatorade bottle: 5 points

Small water bottle: 6 points

Energy drink bottle: 7 points

Cone: 8 points

Soda can: 9 points

Yogurt container: 9 points

Film canister or small pill bottle: 10 points

BOWLING: BATTLESHIPS

Contributed by Matthew Mescall

APPLICABLE UNITS

Bowling

Games and sports

Target games

AGE GROUP

All age groups

OBJECTIVE

Students roll balls down a ramp or bowl the balls toward a target in an attempt to "sink" the opposing team's battleships.

NATIONAL STANDARDS MET

Standard 1: The physically literate individual demonstrates competency in a variety of motor skills and movement patterns.

Standard 2: The physically literate individual applies knowledge of concepts, principles, strategies and tactics related to movement and performance.

Standard 4: The physically literate individual exhibits responsible personal and social behavior that respects self and others.

Standard 5: The physically literate individual recognizes the value of physical activity for health, enjoyment, challenge, self-expression and/or social interaction.

GRADE-LEVEL OUTCOMES

S1.E13: Manipulative—Underhand throw

S1.M12: Games & sports—Net/wall games

S2.E5: Movement concepts—Strategies and tactics

S4.E2: Personal responsibility

S5.E2: Challenge

ACCEPTABLE OUTCOME VARIATIONS

Students can use a variety of throwing or propelling techniques to hit the targets. Bowling ramps or other assistive devices can be used to assist anyone with rolling.

EQUIPMENT

Pieces of battleships (see figure 13.6), 32 poly spots, 32 pins, 1 ball per 2 students, bowling ramps (if needed), a mat if possible (to keep teams from seeing each other's setup)

DESCRIPTION

Set up poly spots in a four-by-four grid that can safely be set up in the gymnasium space on both sides of the gym, and place a pin on each poly spot. Divide the class into two teams. Each team strategically places two pieces of each battleship under the poly spots. Team members should not see where the other team's battleship pieces are hidden. Each ship piece must be next to the other piece of the same ship to complete the ship. Once all ships are hidden and both teams are ready, the game can begin.

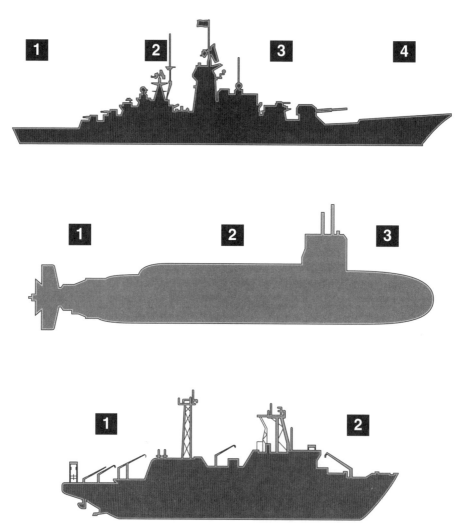

Figure 13.6 Battleship pieces.

Students from one team take turns rolling a ball in an attempt to hit pins. When a pin falls, the other team reveals what is under that spot. If there is nothing, it is a miss. If there is one (or more) pieces of a ship, it is a hit. The ship is sunk when all its pieces are revealed. Once all members of one team roll, it is the other team's turn. The team to sink all the battleships first is the winner.

SPATIAL CONSIDERATIONS

The playing space should be roughly the size of a volleyball court.

INSTRUCTIONS FOR PEERS

Help each other create strategies for concealing ship pieces and for aiming at specific targets when rolling. Support the student with a disability with skill performance and interactions with peers.

INSTRUCTIONS FOR PARAEDUCATORS

Help students, if necessary, with physical supports and verbal prompts. You may also support all class members with strategy development.

BOWLING FOR BUCKS

Contributed by Nancy Miller and Toni Bader

APPLICABLE UNITS

Bowling

Throwing

AGE GROUP

All age groups

OBJECTIVE

In teams, students take turns using proper underhand bowling technique to knock down pins and score bucks for their teams.

NATIONAL STANDARDS MET

Standard 1: The physically literate individual demonstrates competency in a variety of motor skills and movement patterns.

Standard 2: The physically literate individual applies knowledge of concepts, principles, strategies and tactics related to movement and performance.

Standard 4: The physically literate individual exhibits responsible personal and social behavior that respects self and others.

GRADE-LEVEL OUTCOMES

S1.E13: Manipulative—Underhand throw

S2.E3: Movement concepts—Speed, direction, force

S5.E4: Social interaction

ACCEPTABLE OUTCOME VARIATIONS

Students with disabilities use their vision to reach, grasp, and release a ball down a ramp. A paraeducator gives verbal, visual, and manual cues when needed.

EQUIPMENT

Bowling pins, backstop, bowling balls or softballs, cash box, and bucks (money)

Modified equipment: Ramp made from a cardboard box filled with a variety of sensory-engaging balls (sound, texture, color)

DESCRIPTION

This activity can be done individually, in pairs, or as part of a team of two to four players. On the "Go" signal, students take turns bowling two balls using a three-step approach (tick, tock, and follow-through) to try to score points for their team. After bowling, each player runs to the banker (teacher or paraeducator) to collect one buck for each pin knocked down; then places the money in the team cash box and resets the pins for a teammate. Teams of four have a bowler, pin setter, ball retriever, and an additional person who all rotate turns. On the "Stop" signal, teams reset the pins and count their bucks.

The student with a disability uses a ramp and grasps, holds, and releases sensory-engaging balls to knock down pins and score bucks for the team. A paraeducator or peer provides verbal and visual cues (see figure 13.7). The paraeducator also gives manual assists as needed.

SPATIAL CONSIDERATIONS

Each team of two to four players has its own bowling lane, cash box, and two balls. Students with disabilities bowl at the same lane as teammates; they are stationed at the foul line with a ramp and a box of sensory-engaging balls to choose from.

INSTRUCTIONS FOR PEERS

Support the student with a disability to the best of your ability using visual and verbal cues such as

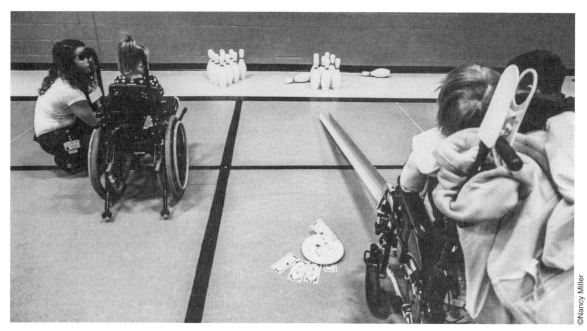

©Nancy Miller

Figure 13.7   Modified bowling with ramps and paraeducators to assist.

Reach, Hold, and *Let go.* Give positive specific and general feedback.

INSTRUCTIONS FOR PARAEDUCATORS

Facilitate the student's skill performance and interactions with peer. Provide visual, auditory, and verbal cues, as well as manual assistance when needed. Give positive specific and general feedback throughout to support skill development and facilitate peer interactions.

Archery

Archery is one of the world's oldest sports and is fairly easy to adapt. Most anyone can participate competitively or for fun. We present two lessons on archery; one addresses following safety commands, and the other offers unique modifications of both equipment and game play.

ARCHERY: SAFETY FIRST

Contributed by Eilleen Cuell

APPLICABLE UNIT

Archery

AGE GROUP

Middle and high school students

OBJECTIVE

Students demonstrate safety protocols for archery.

NATIONAL STANDARDS MET

Standard 1: The physically literate individual demonstrates competency in a variety of motor skills and movement patterns.

Standard 2: The physically literate individual applies knowledge of concepts, principles, strategies and tactics related to movement and performance.

Standard 4: The physically literate individual exhibits responsible personal and social behavior that respects self and others.

Standard 5: The physically literate individual recognizes the value of physical activity for health, enjoyment, challenge, self-expression and/or social interaction.

GRADE-LEVEL OUTCOMES

S1.M22: Outdoor pursuits

S1.H: Lifetime activities

S2.M13: Outdoor pursuits—Movement concepts

S4.H5: Safety

S4.M1: Personal responsibility

S4.M7: Safety

S5.M6: Social interaction

ACCEPTABLE OUTCOME VARIATION

Students with disabilities mirror peers performing the safety protocols presented by the archery instructor.

EQUIPMENT

Cones, ropes, arrows, left- and right-handed compound or recurve bow, targets, balloons, a heavy mesh curtain and a standard to hold it up (to prevent arrows from going too far past the targets)

Modified equipment: Bow secured to stationary dolly, wrist clip to release trigger, chair

DESCRIPTION

Students are arranged in groups of five or six that are designated as a firing group, an on-deck group, and side activity groups (to limit wait time). Students with disabilities are placed in each of these groups with a peer partner (see figure 13.8). (Depending on the availability of modified equipment, this decreases wait time for students with disabilities.)

The instructor explains how to set up the bows, what the ropes on the floor represent (firing line and waiting line), and how to notch a bow, emphasizing that all bows need to be facing downrange toward the targets.

The instructor commands are as follows:

1. "Bowmen, you may approach the firing line (from the waiting line)."
2. "Bowmen, you may pick up your bow and arrows."
3. When the student has notched the bow: "You may fire when ready."

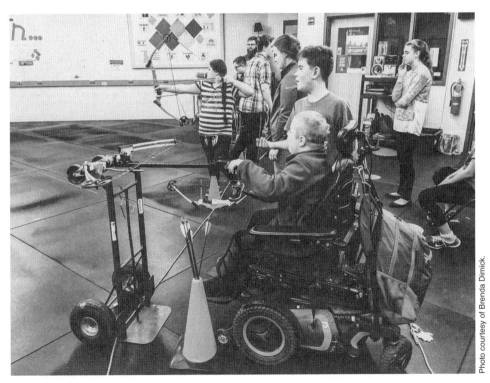

Figure 13.8 Setup for safety first archery.

Photo courtesy of Brenda Dimick.

For students with disabilities, decrease the amount of tension on the bow. This provides increased velocity and distance which will create more draw on the bow.

After all arrows have been released from the designated cones in front of each bowman, the instructor tells them to lower their bows. After they do so, the instructor says, "You may retrieve your arrows." All bowmen may now step over the firing line.

Bowmen place six arrows in the cone where they were shooting. The next group is waiting behind the waiting line. Those who have just fired their arrows now play a side activity (e.g., boccia), and the side activity group moves up to wait behind the waiting line.

The second group now waits for the instructor to give the command, "Bowmen, you may approach the firing line."

SAFETY PROCEDURES

Listen to the instructor's commands before approaching the firing area.

Do not go beyond the firing line when students are firing their bows.

When nocking arrows (i.e., placing on bowstring), make sure the color fletching (feather) faces the ceiling or faces out.

Always face downrange when nocking arrows.

If an arrow falls out or past the firing line, *do not* go and retrieve it, even if it is only 1 foot (30 cm) over the firing line.

Before firing, stand sideways: one foot forward and one foot back. Hold the bow in your nondominant hand, and pull the string back with your dominant hand. Straighten the dominant hand while pointing the arrow downrange. Grab the string with your nondominant hand; it should rest between your index and middle fingers. Pull the string toward your cheek. Your thumb should be resting on your lower cheek bone. Then breathe and release.

After all students have fired their bows, place your bow on the ground and wait for the instructor to say "Bowmen, you may retrieve your arrows."

When retrieving arrows, collect six arrows and place them back in the cone.

When pulling arrows from the target, grab them as close to the target as possible and pull straight back and out.

INSTRUCTIONS FOR PEERS

Provide positive role modeling for your peers with and without disabilities. Provide positive reinforcement and positive general feedback to your peer with a disability. Prompt the student with verbal cues such as *Bows down, Approach the firing line, You may retrieve your arrows,* and *Colored fletching out.*

INSTRUCTIONS FOR PARAEDUCATORS

Facilitate interactions between students with disabilities and their peers. Give positive specific and general feedback to all students to support skill development and facilitate interactions. Give the student with a disability visual, manual, and verbal cues such as *Bows down, Approach the firing line,* and *You may retrieve your arrows.* Reinforce positive role modeling for all students, such as not talking when the instructor is giving directions.

ARCHERY: ADD IT UP

Contributed by Nancy Miller

APPLICABLE UNITS

Archery

Hitting a target with manipulatives

AGE GROUP

Elementary school students. This can easily be adapted for middle and high school students.

OBJECTIVE

Students work in teams to safely use a bow and arrows and execute proper shooting form to hit the target and score points.

NATIONAL STANDARDS MET

Standard 2: The physically literate individual applies knowledge of concepts, principles, strategies and tactics related to movement and performance.

Standard 4: The physically literate individual exhibits responsible personal and social behavior that respects self and others.

Standard 5: The physically literate individual recognizes the value of physical activity for health, enjoyment, challenge, self-expression and/or social interaction.

GRADE-LEVEL OUTCOMES

S2.E4: Movement concepts—Alignment and muscular tension

S4.E4: Working with others

S4.E5: Rules and etiquette

S4.E6: Safety

S5.E2: Challenge

ACCEPTABLE OUTCOMES VARIATIONS

Students with disabilities use vision, reaching, grasping, pulling, and releasing to shoot from a modified mounted bow. A paraeducator gives verbal, visual, and manual cues when needed.

EQUIPMENT

Archery bows, arrows, arm guards, ground quivers, backstop targets, 10-ring paper targets, netting, shooting line, waiting line, scorecards, pencils

Modified equipment: Small bow mounted horizontally with a clamp onto a scooter board (see figure 13.9), bowstring with bell attached, large sensory-engaging felt tips on arrows, large sensory-engaging Velcro target on chair close to student

DESCRIPTION

This activity can be done individually, in pairs, or as part of a team of four. While one partner is shooting, the other is waiting behind the waiting line. Students without disabilities use recurve bows, arrows, arm guards, and targets to demonstrate safe and proper shooting technique to score points for their teams.

Each student with a disability works with a paraeducator and a peer assistant. Students with disabilities use a smaller bow mounted horizontally on a scooter positioned on the lap (see figure 13.10). The bowstring has a bell, and arrows have large visually engaging felt tips. Large visually engaging targets are placed closer than their peers' targets. The paraeducator provides manual assists as needed.

Teams consist of two pairs of players who take turns shooting three arrows each. Each team has its own target. The objective is to use safe and correct shooting form to hit as close as possible to the bull's-eye to score points for the team.

Following whistle commands, one partner at a time steps forward to take a turn safely shooting, scoring, and retrieving arrows. Setup cues are *Stance*, *Grip*, and *Nock arrow*. Shooting cues are *Draw hand*, *Predraw*, *Draw*, *Anchor*, *Aim*, *Release*, and *Follow through*. The other partner then takes a turn.

The student with a disability works with a paraeducator and a peer from the team. The student uses visual and auditory senses to reach, grasp, and release the bell on the bowstring to shoot arrows. The peer or paraeducator uses the verbal cues *Reach*, *Hold bell*, *Pull*, and *Let go* to help the student shoot from the bow mounted on the scooter on the lap. The paraeducator gives manual assistance as needed. Peer partners then take turns shooting.

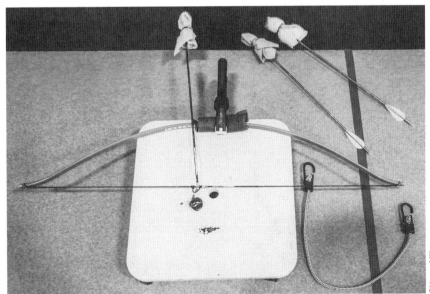

Figure 13.9 Modified archery equipment.

Figure 13.10   Bow mounted on a flat surface positioned on the student's lap.

SPATIAL CONSIDERATIONS

Partners share a bow. While one partner is shooting, the other is waiting safely behind the waiting line. Students with disabilities have archery equipment set up on their laps or on tray tables. When it is their turn to shoot, they move up to the shooting line.

INSTRUCTIONS FOR PEERS

Support the student with a disability to the best of your ability. Point out the visual and auditory cue of the bell on the string. Give verbal cues, *Reach, Hold bell, Pull,* and *Let go,* and give positive specific and general feedback.

INSTRUCTIONS FOR PARAEDUCATORS

Give visual, auditory, and verbal cues, *Reach, Hold bell, Pull,* and *Let go,* as well as physical assists when needed. Give positive specific and general feedback throughout to support the student's skill development and facilitate peer interactions.

Lifetime
and Health-Related
Activities

This chapter includes lesson plans for lifetime and health-related activities designed for school-age students. The lessons are presented as outlines to be adapted or modified to accommodate students with a wide range of skills and abilities. All of the lessons are aligned with SHAPE America's National Standards & Grade-Level Outcomes and have additional accepted outcomes for students with disabilities. Suggestions for peer and paraeducator support are provided so that you can use the lessons in a variety of settings.

RED LIGHT, GREEN LIGHT

Contributed by Debbie Phillips

APPLICABLE UNIT
Tracking

AGE GROUP
All levels

OBJECTIVES
Students work on head control and visual spanning.

NATIONAL STANDARD MET
Standard 2: The physically literate individual applies knowledge of concepts, principles, strategies and tactics related to movement and performance.

GRADE-LEVEL OUTCOMES
S2.E1: Movement concepts—Space

S2.E2: Movement concepts—Pathways, shapes, levels

ACCEPTABLE OUTCOME VARIATIONS
This activity can be used as a one-on-one activity or in small groups. Students with limited head control play a game that practices controlling head movement.

EQUIPMENT
Helmet (or hat) with a laser light on top; wall with a track design; words, letters, numbers, or shapes

DESCRIPTION
The object of this game is for the student with limited movement to use a laser light on his or her head to point to objects. A word search game is created by tapping different words (or pictures, numbers, letters, shapes) on the wall (see figure 14.1). The student looks for a particular word and, when found, shines the light on it for three seconds. Students go on the green light and stop on the red light. (Students will have already been taught that a green light means go and a red light means stop.)

For students with limited hand control, the game should be adjusted by placing a laser pointer in the student's hand.

SPATIAL CONSIDERATIONS
Students may need to be at different distances from the wall, depending on their flexibility and range of movement of the head and neck.

INSTRUCTIONS FOR PEERS
Remind the students of the expectation of good sportsmanship and how to give positive feedback.

INSTRUCTIONS FOR PARAEDUCATORS
Paraeducators will help facilitate the activity and the interaction between the student with the disability and the rest of the class. Paraprofessionals should also provide positive and constructive feedback to students about their game play and interaction with each other.

©Debbie Phillips.

Figure 14.1   Setup for red light, green light.

HAND FUNCTION CHALLENGES

Contributed by Ken Black

APPLICABLE UNITS

Locomotor

Nonlocomotor

Manipulative

AGE GROUP

Elementary school students. Activities can be enhanced to create more challenge for older students.

OBJECTIVES

These activities (and the following activity, Hand Functions for Sports) give students with disabilities opportunities to explore and develop basic manipulative skills. These skills can be applied in a range of other movement-based and sport-specific activities.

NATIONAL STANDARDS MET

Standard 1: The physically literate individual demonstrates competency in a variety of motor skills and movement patterns.

Standard 3: The physically literate individual demonstrates the knowledge and skills to achieve and maintain a health-enhancing level of physical activity and fitness.

GRADE-LEVEL OUTCOMES

S1.E1: Locomotor

S1.E7: Nonlocomotor (stability)—Balance

S3.E2: Engages in physical activity

ACCEPTABLE OUTCOME VARIATIONS

Students with disabilities have the time and space to work on their manipulative skills while participating in fun, engaging tasks and mini-games. The skill development focus is on, among other things, wiping, sweeping, feeling, searching, pulling, pushing, grasping and releasing, pinching, and coordination. These activities often precede integration into mixed-ability environments, enabling students to enter at a higher level of competence.

EQUIPMENT

Absorbent cotton or cotton balls; small, smooth-edged mirror(s); small cloth; paper or plastic bags; a variety of small objects, such as erasers, pencils, paper clips, beanbags, sponge paper, or tennis balls; old newspapers or comic books; strong rope or cord; string of varying thicknesses

DESCRIPTION

These activities can be done individually, with a partner, or as part of a small group.

The skills can be performed as stand-alone challenges or as an introduction to other manipulative and sport-specific activities (see the examples in Hand Function 2).

Students with disabilities can work with typically developing partners or paraeducators to increase motivation. The activities can be modified to stimulate and challenge all learners.

DIRECTIONS

Wiping and Sweeping

To clear a lap tray of cotton balls or absorbent cotton pieces, students use a wiping or sweeping movement of the hand(s) or arm(s). As a challenge, a partner puts the cotton balls back on the tray; clearing the tray completely signifies a win! A fun variation is to use a flat, smooth-edged mirror and cover it with shaving foam or a similar substance. The student clears the foam using sweeping or wiping movements.

Feeling and Searching

Students feel in a bag to grasp and retrieve a range of small objects. They try to identify these by touch before placing them on a lap tray, on a table, or in a receptacle.

Grasping and Releasing

The student grasps a small, soft object, such as a beanbag, lifts it from the table surface, and then drops it (releasing).

Pulling and Coordination

Depending on muscular strength and coordination, students pull objects, attached to a cord, toward themselves. They can use one or both hands and should try to establish a rhythmic movement. As an extension activity, students with some upper-body strength can pull themselves along a strong rope tethered horizontally to a wall bar or similar apparatus. Other options are pulling themselves forward while in a lightweight chair on a FreeWheel, or sliding across a mat or a smooth floor.

Pushing and Coordination

Students push small objects away from themselves across a flat surface (lap tray, table, or lap). Increase resistance by using heavier, denser objects, or by asking students to increase the force they exert to push the objects a greater distance.

Pinching

Students pick up objects using thumb and forefinger or any two fingers on one hand, or by grasping them between the fingers of both hands.

Squeezing

Students develop hand strength by squeezing (e.g., a sponge ball, water from a bath sponge into a plastic bowl).

Scraping and Scratching

Students perform tasks such as gathering small objects together with the fingers.

Separating

Students separate and spread small objects on a table or a lap tray using the fingers or the side of the hand.

Screwing and Unscrewing

Students practice screwing and unscrewing the lid of a jar. Lids can be loosely attached initially and then gradually screwed down more as students' strength and coordination improve.

Tying and Untying

Students tie and untie simple or loosely tied knots.

SPATIAL CONSIDERATIONS

Students can work in their own personal spaces (e.g., using their own lap trays) or in a small group setting around a table. The feeling and searching activity can be done in a group by placing small objects under a cloth, towel, or small sheet loosely spread over all students, who race to pull them out from under the sheet and place them in front of themselves.

INSTRUCTIONS FOR PEERS

Ask students to perform the activities with students with disabilities (e.g., both pull on a cord to bring a small object toward them). In wiping and sweeping activities, a student with a disability can try to clear a lap tray or table before the other student clears objects from a space on the floor (by running to pick up an object and returning it to a hoop or bucket).

Encourage students to both support and challenge each other.

INSTRUCTIONS FOR PARAEDUCATORS

Use gestures, facial expressions, and sound cues to encourage students with disabilities in their tasks or games. Encourage them to increase their range of movement or intensity within each task or game.

Find ways of moving students from individual activities to partner or group-based games that involve all students.

HAND FUNCTIONS FOR SPORTS

Contributed by Ken Black

APPLICABLE UNITS

Locomotor

Nonlocomotor

Manipulative

AGE GROUP

Elementary school students. This lesson can also be adapted to accommodate middle and high school students.

OBJECTIVES

These activities build on the manipulative skills in hand function challenges, enabling students to apply these to a range of sport-specific skills.

NATIONAL STANDARDS MET

Standard 1: The physically literate individual demonstrates competency in a variety of motor skills and movement patterns.

Standard 3: The physically literate individual demonstrates the knowledge and skills to achieve and maintain a health-enhancing level of physical activity and fitness.

Standard 4: The physically literate individual exhibits responsible personal and social behavior that respects self and others.

GRADE-LEVEL OUTCOMES

S1.E7: Nonlocomotor (stability)—Balance

S1.E13: Manipulative

S1.E24: Striking

S3.E2: Engages in physical activity

S4.E4: Working with others

ACCEPTABLE OUTCOME VARIATIONS

Students with disabilities work independently and with peers to apply manipulative and hand function skills to sport-specific activities, progressing at their own level of participation with minimal or no instruction, individually and with others.

EQUIPMENT

Old newspapers or comic books; beach ball(s); balloon(s) with tether(s); paddles; short-handled rackets and bats that can be attached to the hand or arm; bowling pins ; empty plastic water bottles (targets); boccia balls; paper balls

DESCRIPTION

These activities can be done individually, with a partner, or as part of a small group. They can be used as stand-alone developmental activities or as part of a sport-specific lesson (e.g., striking activities using the hand can progress to grasping and using a paddle or racket).

DIRECTIONS

Gripping and Parrying

Students clasp or grab a rolled-up newspaper to strike a sponge ball or balloon suspended overhead. A fun variation using a partner is newspaper fencing; a peer moves slowly initially, encouraging the student with a disability to parry.

Striking

Students strike a tethered beach ball or balloon. Put seeds or rice inside to create sound cues. They can also strike an object from an improvised tee (e.g., a marker cone). Students with disabilities try to increase the distance they can strike the object. A large floor or wall target can provide motivation. The action can be progressive, from striking with the hand to striking with a paddle and then with a small racket. If grip is impaired (or absent), but arm function is good, a bat can be attached to the arm by wrapping material around both and securing it with tape (tape should not directly contact the skin).

Aiming and Eye–Hand Coordination

Students toss or throw soft balls or beanbags at homemade targets (such as empty plastic water bottles). A partner can help a student with a disability release the ball at the optimal moment by using verbal or sound cues (e.g., tapping a tambourine).

Ball-Sending Games

Students can propel balls using a chute or ramp. The activity can be made into a group game by gathering all students into a circle with targets (plastic jugs or bottles) in the center. Individually or in teams, students throw or roll balls to knock down the targets.

Introducing Control

Students attempt to knock down targets placed in a big circle. As the students get better and increase accuracy, reduce the number of targets and the size of the circle, thereby increasing the level of control needed. Use an assortment of balls appropriate to students' functional ability.

Rolling and Flattening

Students practice rolling and flattening play putty or dough; they can progress to a soft boccia (bocce) ball.

SPATIAL CONSIDERATIONS

Students with disabilities require working space for movement. Those using wheelchairs can have the arms and supporting straps of the chairs removed or loosened so they can move more freely.

In target activities, students can be positioned at different distances and angles from the target, based on ability and mobility.

INSTRUCTIONS FOR PEERS

Perform parallel or similar activities alongside students with disabilities to provide support. For example, some students might use their hands to strike tethered balloons, some might use small-handled rackets to hit a balloon upward, and others might balance or strike a tennis ball with a regular racket.

Try to both support and challenge your partner.

INSTRUCTIONS FOR PARAEDUCATORS

Use gestures, facial expressions, and sound cues to encourage students with disabilities in tasks and games.

Provide early success by using implements, objects, and targets that can be easily controlled by students with disabilities (e.g., have them send a large ball down a ramp toward closely packed targets). However, always increase the challenge once they are achieving regular success. In this example, move the targets farther away or spread them out.

Find ways to make individual activities into partner or group-based games that involve all students.

SCOOTER TRAIN

Contributed by Lauren J. Lieberman

APPLICABLE UNITS

Scooter activities

Mobility

Core strength

Gross motor coordination

AGE GROUP

Elementary school students

OBJECTIVE

In teams, students move from one place to another, possibly around cones and through an obstacle course.

NATIONAL STANDARD MET

Standard 2: The physically literate individual applies knowledge of concepts, principles, strategies and tactics related to movement and performance.

GRADE-LEVEL OUTCOMES

S2.E1: Movement concepts—Space

S2.E2: Movement concepts—Pathways, shapes, levels

S2.E3: Movement concepts—Speed, direction, force

EQUIPMENT

A variety of scooters, cones, hula hoops, and poly spots

DESCRIPTION

This activity can be done individually, in pairs, or as a group. Scooters can be large, with backs, or small, with handles. Students with disabilities can have a paraeducator or peer assistant or perform independently with a wall or without. They can travel while seated or lying prone (see figure 14.2) or be pulled on a scooter with a rope or a hula hoop.

DIRECTIONS

Students get on their scooters in the position they prefer. They are given the direction to either push themselves (seated or lying prone) or be pulled across the gym. This activity can be performed in a group, in pairs, or individually, for time or just for fun. Students then go through a scooter obstacle course (under hula hoop tunnels, around cones, over poly spots, etc.). You can even add throwing (into hoops) or kicking with small or large balls.

SPATIAL CONSIDERATIONS

Determine whether the children need boundary markers such as cones or mats. Give them enough room to move and to challenge themselves.

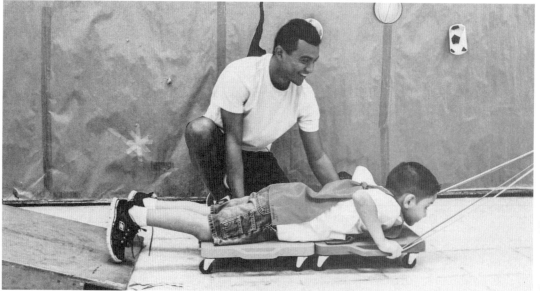

Figure 14.2 Traveling on a scooter with help from paraeducators.

Photo courtesy of Christian Martinez.

INSTRUCTIONS FOR PEERS

Support the student with a disability to the best of your ability. Instruct them to push and move (or be pulled) across the gym. Provide positive specific and general feedback.

INSTRUCTIONS FOR PARAEDUCATORS

Instruct students to push and move across the gym and then through the obstacle course. Give positive specific and general feedback throughout the activity (including to peer tutors when appropriate).

CLIMBING WALL: PERIWINKLE RESCUE

Contributed by Nancy Miller

APPLICABLE UNITS

Fitness

Gymnastics

AGE GROUP

Elementary school students. This can easily be adapted for middle and high school students.

OBJECTIVES

Students use balance, weight transferring, movement concepts, upper-body and lower-body strength, and endurance to traverse the climbing wall while stretching, bending, and twisting to remove objects from the wall and drop or throw them into buckets. Peers can also drop objects into the hula hoops or buckets.

NATIONAL STANDARDS MET

Standard 1: The physically literate individual demonstrates competency in a variety of motor skills and movement patterns.

Standard 2: The physically literate individual applies knowledge of concepts, principles, strategies and tactics related to movement and performance.

Standard 3: The physically literate individual demonstrates the knowledge and skills to achieve and maintain a health-enhancing level of physical activity and fitness.

GRADE-LEVEL OUTCOMES

S1.E7: Nonlocomotor (stability)—Balance

S1.E8: Nonlocomotor (stability)—Weight transfer

S1.E10: Nonlocomotor (stability)—Curling & stretching; twisting & bending

S2.E1: Movement concepts—Space

S2.E2: Movement concepts—Pathways, shapes, levels

S3.E2: Engages in physical activity

ACCEPTABLE OUTCOME VARIATIONS

Students with disabilities reach, grasp, pull, and manipulate the sensory-engaging equipment that protrudes from the wall. They may use their vision to track, reach, or grasp, when choosing equipment on the wall. The paraeducator uses visual, verbal, and manual cues to engage these students.

EQUIPMENT

A variety of sensory-engaging objects that stick out from the wall, yarn balls, deck rings, hula hoops (see figure 14.3)

DESCRIPTION

This activity can be done individually, in pairs, or as a group. Typically developing students start in a home space at the wall and traverse the wall, climbing on various pathways and levels to stretch, bend, reach, and grasp periwinkles (objects) on the wall to throw or drop into tidal pools (hoops or buckets). Students with disabilities, working independently or with a paraeducator or peer tutor, travel alongside the wall to stretch, bend, reach, and grasp sensory-engaging objects (periwinkles) on the wall and hold them, place them on lap trays, or drop them into tidal pools (hula hoops or buckets).

DIRECTIONS

The description used for the activity is that at high tide all the periwinkles (objects on the wall) adhere to the rocks. The task for students is to traverse the wall and rescue (remove) the periwinkles and drop or throw them back into a tidal pool (hoop). Each student removes one periwinkle on each panel of the wall. At the end of the wall, each student travels back to the first panel and starts again. Once all the periwinkles are rescued, count the number of periwinkles in the hoops to determine a score. The game can be scored individually, in pairs, or as a team. Reset to play again. Student with disabilities collect larger sensory-engaging objects that they

©Nancy Miller

Figure 14.3   Climbing wall set up with a variety of sensory-engaging objects.

can either hold or drop into the hoops depending on their abilities.

SPATIAL CONSIDERATIONS

Each student starts at a wall panel and traverses from right to left staying on the panel until the peer in front has moved to the next panel.

INSTRUCTIONS FOR PEERS

Support the student with a disability to the best of your ability. Recognize when the student is communicating a desire to play the game by looking at you or using sounds or gestures. Give the stu-

dent visual and verbal cues to reach, grasp, and pull objects. Give positive specific and general feedback.

INSTRUCTIONS FOR PARAEDUCATORS

Recognize when the student is communicating a desire to play the game by looking at you or a peer or using sounds or gestures. Give the student verbal cues to reach, grasp, and pull objects. Facilitate interactions between student with disabilities and peers. Give positive specific and general feedback throughout the activity to students with disabilities and their peers.

HORSESHOES

Contributed by Ken Black

APPLICABLE UNIT

Manipulative

AGE GROUP

Elementary and middle school students

OBJECTIVE

Students throw with a reasonable amount of accuracy at a target.

NATIONAL STANDARDS MET

Standard 1: The physically literate individual demonstrates competency in a variety of motor skills and movement patterns.

Standard 4: The physically literate individual exhibits responsible personal and social behavior that respects self and others.

Standard 5: The physically literate individual recognizes the value of physical activity for health, enjoyment, challenge, self-expression and/or social interaction.

GRADE-LEVEL OUTCOMES

S1.E13: Manipulative—Underhand throw

S2.E3: Movement concepts—Speed, direction, force

S4.E4: Working with others

ACCEPTABLE OUTCOME VARIATIONS

Students can send in any acceptable manner appropriate to their functional or cognitive ability (e.g., using a ball-sending ramp or gutter if throwing by hand is not an option).

EQUIPMENT

Throwing implements: plastic horseshoes, beanbags, boccia balls, paper or yarn balls

Targets: plastic hoops, throw-down marker strips or improvised targets such as chalk circles, cardboard boxes, or other containers. Plastic bowling pins or empty water bottles that make a noise when knocked over may motivate some students and help them estimate distance.

DESCRIPTION

Students can take part in these activities as individuals, in pairs or small groups or as a team. Pairing a student who has a disability with a peer tutor can establish a positive platform for cooperation and understanding.

DIRECTIONS

The game of horseshoes can be played with modified rules.

Two targets are separated by an agreed-on distance (suggested maximum of 5 meters). Players are positioned beside one target and throw twice toward the opposite target. On completion of their throws, players move to the target to count their points; they then throw back toward the other target.

Alternatively, students throw toward one target from a throwing line. They then collect their beanbags or balls before returning to the throwing line to start again.

Partners can throw from different distances from the target based on functional ability; for example, a student without a disability can throw from 5 feet (152 cm) away, and a student with a disability can throw from 1 foot (30 cm) away.

Students can send the ball in different ways; for example, students without disabilities can be challenged to use the nondominant hand.

Students for whom a hand throw is not appropriate can push a large ball with a foot toward the target (e.g., a large box placed on its side, or a series of lines on the floor designating different scores).

A student with a severe impairment can sit close to or above the target and drop a beanbag or cloth onto the target using a pinch grip or by opening the hand.

SPATIAL CONSIDERATIONS

Adequate spatial area for a variety of target distances.

INSTRUCTIONS FOR PEERS

Some students may need help locating the target. A peer can call, clap, use a beeper from just behind the target to help students who have vision or spatial/perceptual impairments.

INSTRUCTIONS FOR PARAEDUCATORS

You may need to work with the student with a disability to identify the optimal throwing angle of the chair or wheelchair. Parts of a wheelchair (e.g., arm rests) can be removed, if safe to do so, to enable free movement of the arm.

Use gestures, facial expressions, and sound cues to encourage students with disabilities. Also, encourage them to increase their range of movement or intensity level within the parameters of the game.

BICYCLING: RULES OF THE ROAD

Contributed by Eileen Cuell and Nancy Miller

APPLICABLE UNIT

Cycling

AGE GROUP

Elementary, middle, and high school students

OBJECTIVE

Students learn the biking rules of the road by following and leading each other through a closed marked course.

NATIONAL STANDARDS MET

Standard 1: The physically literate individual demonstrates competency in a variety of motor skills and movement patterns.

Standard 2: The physically literate individual applies knowledge of concepts, principles, strategies and tactics related to movement and performance.

Standard 4: The physically literate individual exhibits responsible personal and social behavior that respects self and others.

Standard 5: The physically literate individual recognizes the value of physical activity for health, enjoyment, challenge, self-expression and/or social interaction.

GRADE-LEVEL OUTCOMES

S1.E6: Locomotor—Combinations

S2.E2: Movement concepts—Pathways, shapes, levels

S1.M22: Outdoor pursuits

S4.M1: Personal responsibility

S5.M6: Social interaction

S1.H1: Lifetime activities

ACCEPTABLE OUTCOME VARIATIONS

Students with disabilities learn to ride on the right side of the road, stop at stop signs, and signal left or right while following a peer tutor or paraeducator.

EQUIPMENT

Helmets, two-wheel cycles, cones, map of closed marked route, stop signs

Modified equipment: Recumbent bike, tandem bike, trike, two-wheel cycle, hand crank cycle. Rentals can be provided by a local disability sport resource outreach center.

DESCRIPTION

Students work in pairs, taking turns playing follow-the-leader through a closed marked bike route. Students with disabilities perform the task with a peer tutor or paraeducator (or both). They use bikes appropriate to their needs (e.g., carrier, recumbent bike, tandem bike, trike, two-wheel cycle, hand crank cycle). After completing a few repetitions of the route, the partners switch roles if desired. All students should demonstrate appropriate safety checks as administered by the teacher or paraeducator.

DIRECTIONS

Students study the map of the closed loop route and play follow-the-leader through all traffic and safety stops (see figure 14.4). A student who violates a traffic or safety stop must remain there and act as a police guards until that student's partner has made a full loop back to the same stop. Students with disabilities who violate a traffic or safety stop must stop with the peer tutor or paraeducator and mirror the verbal and hand signals for the next three pairs to pass through the stop. Review the marked closed route with the class. Remind all students to follow the rules of the road. Have all students demonstrate

Figure 14.4   Biking with paraeducator and peers.

left, right, and stop hand signals. All students must check in at the pit stop to be assessed for their knowledge of the traffic safety signals. Students with disabilities mirror the signals that the peer tutor or paraeducator has provided.

SPATIAL CONSIDERATIONS

Create a smaller closed route within view of the teacher for students with disabilities.

INSTRUCTIONS FOR PEERS

Be a positive role model and provide positive reinforcement and positive general feedback. Prompt the student with a disability with verbal cues such as *Stop, Signal left (or right), Stay on the right side of the road,* and *Follow the leader.*

INSTRUCTIONS FOR PARAEDUCATORS

Facilitate interactions between students with disabilities and their peers. Give positive specific and general feedback throughout to students with disabilities and their peers. Give students with disabilities visual, manual, and verbal cues such as *Stop, Hand signal left (or right),* and *Follow your partner.* Reinforce positive role modeling for all students (e.g., wearing a helmet, following traffic rules, maintaining an appropriate distance between bikes).

TENNIS: FOREHAND STROKE

Contributed by Brad M. Weiner

APPLICABLE UNIT

Tennis

AGE GROUP

High school students

OBJECTIVE

Students analyze and refine their forehand stroke technique to engage in noncompetitive rallies with peers.

NATIONAL STANDARD MET

Standard 1: The physically literate individual demonstrates competency in a variety of motor skills and movement patterns.

GRADE-LEVEL OUTCOMES

S1.E13: Manipulative

S1.E24: Striking

S3.E2: Engages in physical activity

S4.E4: Working with others

S1.H1: Lifetime activities

ACCEPTABLE OUTCOME VARIATIONS

Students demonstrate the following:

- Swinging the arm and hand to strike a suspended ball or large lightweight ball and accepting corrective feedback to refine performance.
- Swinging the arm and hand in a forehand movement to knock a tennis ball off a cone and accepting corrective feedback to refine performance.
- Swinging a short-handled implement in a forehand movement to knock a ball off a cone and accepting corrective feedback to refine performance.

DESCRIPTION

Students work in pairs; one is on the side tossing a ball to the other, who performs a forehand stroke. Students with physical disabilities work on grasping, releasing, range of motion, force production, and accuracy to propel the ball to a partner. Students using a chair tray can push the ball off the tray to a partner.

DIRECTIONS

Students using a tennis racket practice the forehand stroke to strike a suspended large lightweight ball to a partner, who uses a hand to strike it back.

In pairs, one student performs a forehand strike to knock five balls off a cone before a partner strikes five balls over the net. They should count how many consecutive forehand strokes they perform during a rally. Students using wheelchairs with enough force production and range of motion should participate in the rally with a peer, either with a net or using a line on the floor.

Students with more significant physical limitations use a hand or short-handled implement to strike balls off a cone and over a line on the floor. They should count the number of times they send a ball over the line.

Students with difficulty with reaction time, grasping a short-handled implement, or open activities with variables (such as tennis or volleyball) should strike a suspended ball with a peer standing on the other side of a line. They should count the consecutive strokes of the rally.

Students with severe disabilities work on extending a hand and coordinating the body to press a switch that sends the ball to a peer. Plugging a tennis-ball-launching machine into the powerlink device (AbleNet product) enables students to "strike" using a button switch activator.

EQUIPMENT

Tennis rackets, lollipop paddles, table tennis paddles, tennis balls, beach balls, balloons, 4-inch (10 cm) squeezable soft balls, tall cones or tees, powerlink device with button switch activator (see figure 14.5), tennis ball launcher, rope and string (for suspending balls), plastic balls (for suspending inside)

SPATIAL CONSIDERATIONS

When engaged in a rally, students with advanced skills should cover larger spaces than lesser-skilled students. They should also be required to strike the ball into smaller areas. Use the wired fencing of the tennis court to tie rope and string to suspend lightweight balls. When striking the balls off the cones, students should be challenged to produce enough force that the ball goes over a line on the floor (an imaginary net).

©Brad Weiner

Figure 14.5   Powerlink device with button switch activator.

INSTRUCTIONS FOR PEERS

Support students with disabilities with corrective and positive feedback. When beneficial and appropriate, help them grasp a short-handled implement, or guide their hand through the motion to strike the ball.

INSTRUCTIONS FOR PARAEDUCATORS

Using appropriate wait time and communication devices, support students with disabilities using corrective and positive feedback. Help them attend to the task, and promote positive on-task behaviors. Use the least restrictive prompt hierarchy (verbal instruction/cue, demonstration, physical assistance, feedback) to promote maximal independence.

TABLETOP SHUFFLEBOARD

Contributed by Lauren J. Lieberman

APPLICABLE UNIT

Lifetime activities

AGE GROUP

Middle school and high school

OBJECTIVE

Students push, hit, or bat a puck to the other end of a shuffleboard table and score points in the scoring area of the game surface.

NATIONAL STANDARDS MET

Standard 1: The physically literate individual demonstrates competency in a variety of motor skills and movement patterns.

Standard 4: The physically literate individual exhibits responsible personal and social behavior that respects self and others.

GRADE-LEVEL OUTCOMES

S4.E4: Working with others

S4.E5: Rules & etiquette

S1.M24: Individual-performance activities

EQUIPMENT

Tabletop shuffleboard, eight pucks per player, small stick or bat if necessary

DESCRIPTION

Create a shuffleboard playing area using a large piece of cardboard or plywood that can fit on top of a table that is waist height (e.g., table tennis or meeting table). Use juice lids or small hockey pucks as the playing pieces, which students push or bat with the hand or a stick depending on their abilities.

DIRECTIONS

Players play in pairs, and choose their puck colors before starting. Player A begins the game by shooting a puck; player B then shoots a puck of a different color. The two players then rotate shots until they have each shot all eight pucks. If a puck doesn't cross the foul line closest to the player shooting, it must be removed, and the shot is forfeited.

After all pucks have been shot, the players determine who scored by counting only the pucks closest to the end of the table that are the same color. If a player has more than one puck closer to the end of the table than the opponent's puck, those pucks also count.

Remember, only one color can score per frame. A puck must be completely inside the score zone to receive the points in that zone.

Participants can push or hit the puck with a hand or hit it with a stick. They can have physical assistance and help with scoring if necessary. Do not start counting until all players have finished their turns.

SPATIAL CONSIDERATIONS

The game surface must fit safely and securely on top of a table at a height that is within the reach of all players.

INSTRUCTIONS FOR PEERS

Use verbal encouragement, demonstrations, physical assistance, and guidance when needed. If the student with a disability needs help adding up points, use a whiteboard or an index card.

INSTRUCTIONS FOR PARAEDUCATORS

Use verbal encouragement, demonstrations, physical assistance, and guidance when needed. Encourage peer-to-peer support rather than adult support. If the student with a disability needs help adding up points, encourage the peer tutor to help with a whiteboard or an index card.

PERSONAL PHYSICAL FITNESS PLAN

Contributed by Brad M. Weiner

APPLICABLE UNIT

Personal fitness

AGE GROUP

High school

OBJECTIVE

Students analyze, reflect on, and modify (as needed) the goals and activities in their personal physical fitness plans.

NATIONAL STANDARD MET

Standard 3: The physically literate individual demonstrates the knowledge and skills to achieve and maintain a health-enhancing level of physical activity and fitness.

GRADE-LEVEL OUTCOMES

S3.H5: Physical activity knowledge

S3.H6: Engages in physical activity

ACCEPTABLE OUTCOME VARIATIONS

Plans can be simplified by using pictures, easier vocabulary, larger text, and less text and imagery per page. Students use bingo markers to choose exercises, physical activity tasks, the number of sets and reps, and how long to perform the tasks. A variety of exercise tasks per fitness component are offered. Peer tutors may help students with disabilities develop and analyze their plans. When appropriate, they may help them create plans by writing down what they communicate. Some students with disabilities may use personal communication systems

(e.g., voice output devices or picture communication symbols) to communicate with tutors.

DESCRIPTION

Students work on their own within the community of the class. While analyzing and reflecting on their personal physical fitness plans, students with disabilities may ask peers to help them review their plans or understand the correlations between tasks and goals. Students identify exercises that address personal fitness goals related to muscular strength, muscular endurance, cardiorespiratory endurance, and flexibility.

DIRECTIONS

Students with severe disabilities focus on the skills they need to perform daily physical and leisure activities, such as grasping, releasing, flexing and extending joints, increasing range of motion, visual tracking, finger dexterity, body posture, grip strength, and balance. Students with ritualistic behavior patterns should have schedule boards showing the desired exercises.

Based on their fitness data results, personal interests, and personal goals, students develop three SMART (specific, measurable, attainable, realistic, and time sensitive) goals, each of which includes exercises that address muscular strength, muscular endurance, flexibility, and cardiorespiratory endurance.

Students analyze their plans while engaging in the exercises, reflect on their plans with classmates, and adjust their plans accordingly. They identify how often and where they will engage in their fitness activities outside of physical education, as well as the amount of time they will spend in each exercise session.

EQUIPMENT

Paper or electronic-based personal physical fitness plans with the necessary writing utensils or technology; fitness equipment required for performing personal physical fitness plan exercises (regulated by the teacher); if appropriate, fitness room equipment; stopwatches; measuring tape

SPATIAL CONSIDERATIONS

Divide the room into quadrants for each fitness component (muscular strength, muscular endurance, flexibility, and cardiorespiratory endurance).

INSTRUCTIONS FOR PEERS

Collaborate with each other, ask for feedback, and practice providing positive and corrective feedback. Have three peers review your fitness plans and provide feedback. If needed, help students with disabilities develop their fitness plans.

INSTRUCTIONS FOR PARAEDUCATORS

Using appropriate wait time and communication devices, help students with disabilities create their personal physical fitness plans based on their choices. Help them maneuver throughout the room and engage in exercises with the least prompt hierarchy (verbal instruction/cue, modeling, physical assistance, feedback) needed for maximal independence.

CUP RACING

Contributed by Debbie Phillips

APPLICABLE UNIT

Locomotor patterns

AGE GROUP

Elementary school students

OBJECTIVE

The students will take turns guiding a cup to the other end of the string. A variety of locomotive movements can be used.

NATIONAL STANDARDS MET

Standard 1: The physically literate individual demonstrates competency in a variety of motor skills and movement patterns.

Standard 2: The physically literate individual applies knowledge of concepts, principles, strategies and tactics related to movement and performance.

Standard 5: The physically literate individual recognizes the value of physical activity for health, enjoyment, challenge, self-expression and/or social interaction.

GRADE-LEVEL OUTCOMES

S1.E6: Locomotor—Combinations

S2.E2: Movement concepts—Pathways, shapes, level

S2.E3: Movement concepts—Speed, direction, force

ACCEPTABLE OUTCOME VARIATIONS

Students will engage in a cup racing activity by moving a string-guided cup, demonstrating a variety of gripping and locomotive movements.

EQUIPMENT

Wax coated string, about 24 plastic cups covered in colored duct tape, two volleyball standards to tie the string to

DESCRIPTION

Students perform this activity individually or competitively in groups. The string provides a straight line for the student to follow, and the cup on the string provides both vibration and noise to motivate students (see figure 14.6).

DIRECTIONS

The students run, walk, or moved in a preferred manner along the string, one at a time, moving the cup from one end to the other. The game promotes taking turns, communicating, and following directions. To make it more enjoyable, the activity can be set up with two strings, lined up next to each other, so two teams can race against each other. The teacher calls out a different locomotor skill for each time the students take turns. The locomotor skills must be within the students' ability levels.

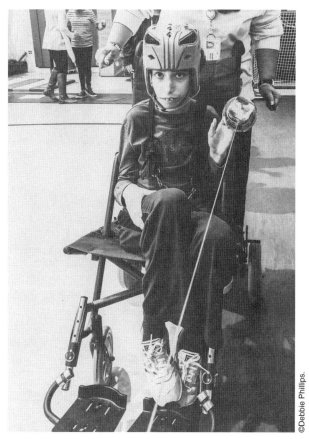

Figure 14.6   Setup for cup racing.

SPATIAL CONSIDERATIONS

Make sure that the students are keeping a safe distance from each other when switching off. Students should be shown a visual marker to indicate where they should start to slow down so they don't run into the next person.

INSTRUCTIONS FOR PEERS

Support the student with a disability to the best of your ability. Recognize communication patterns when the student is communicating a desire to play the game with you (looking at you, using sounds or gestures).

INSTRUCTIONS FOR PARAEDUCATORS

Support students with verbal cues and physical support. Facilitate interactions between students with disabilities and their peers. Give positive specific and general feedback throughout the activity to students with disabilities to support skill development and facilitate interactions.

SWIMMING THROUGH THE OCEAN

Contributed by Sheyla G. Martinez-Rivera

APPLICABLE UNIT

Movement concepts

AGE GROUP

Elementary school students

OBJECTIVES

Students will work individually, using a scooter while applying the movement concepts of levels, pathways, directions, and relationships.

NATIONAL STANDARDS MET

Standard 2: The physically literate individual applies knowledge of concepts, principles, strategies and tactics related to movement and performance.

Standard 4: The physically literate individual exhibits responsible personal and social behavior that respects self and others.

Standard 5: The physically literate individual recognizes the value of physical activity for health, enjoyment, challenge, self-expression and/or social interaction.

GRADE-LEVEL OUTCOMES

S2.E1: Movement concepts—Space

S2.E2: Movement concepts—Pathways, shapes, level

S2.E3: Movement concepts—Speed, direction, force

S4.E4: Working with others

S4.E6: Safety

S5.E3: Self-expression & enjoyment

ACCEPTABLE OUTCOME VARIATIONS

Students use visual cards to perform the skills at the stations. Using this strategy, the teacher would ensure the processing of information related to the task.

EQUIPMENT

Cones, scooters, multicolored domes, bean bags, ramps, cue cards

Modified equipment: Provide a variety of scooters to accommodate differences in student height, weight, and postural angle. Bright color during the activity will motivate and guide the student through the path of the circuit. At the last station, it is important that the physical educator use one particular color to represent the reef to ensure that students understand it is the end of the course. Grasping gloves can be provided to those individuals who need extra assistance with grasping.

DESCRIPTION

The PE teacher will include a variety of instructional strategies to ensure an inclusive environment. For example, the PE teacher can have the peer tutors and paraeducators use different words related to movement concepts. Each station will have a cue card that teaches the movement concept.

DIRECTIONS

The teacher splits the group into two teams of three students. Each student will have a peer tutor or paraeducator assigned. The students should be told to wait until the PE teacher uses the starting signal (a whistle or a visual cue) to start the activity.

At the starting signal, each student with a scooter will start to follow the path of the circuit, following the arrows on the floor and going to each station in numeric order (see figure 14.7). On each station of the circuit, the student will learn a specific movement concept:

- Station 1: direction (up/down)
- Station 2: pathways (straight and zigzag)
- Station 3: relationship with object (over/under)
- Station 4: location (self-space and general space)
- Station 5: grasping marine animals

The station will include the station number and brief instructions for what activity to perform. At the fifth and final station, the student should try to grasp the picture of a particular marine animal that the paraeducator calls out, such as a shark, globe fish, octopus, or clownfish. (For those individuals who have difficulty grasping, the teacher will provide a special glove to facilitate grasping the marine animal images.) After all team members have done the circuit, each team will count the collected animals and read the name of each animal.

SPATIAL CONSIDERATIONS

The main consideration should be scooter use. Each scooter should be assigned according to the student's height, weight, and posture. This activ-

Photo courtesy of Christian Martinez.

Figure 14.7   Setup for swimming through the ocean.

ity should be performed in an open space such as a gymnasium or a playground with a firm floor. The instructor should place the stations at least 7 feet apart to prevent collisions. Once a teammate completes the third station, the next student would start the path.

INSTRUCTIONS FOR PEERS

Master positive behavior strategies. Understand how to provide clear and concise instructions, such as saying, "Holvin, it's your turn to start the adventure", or "Sheyla, look at that globefish at your right". Learn specific cues related to performing a task correctly—for example, "Luis, keep your trunk in the middle of the scooter."

INSTRUCTIONS FOR PARAEDUCATORS

Provide a short training about the activity, emphasizing visual and verbal. Use verbal and visual cues related to movement concepts: up, down, zigzag, straight, over, under, self-space, and general space. Use cues for the name of a marine animal image: octopus, clown fish, shark, or globe fish. Provide visual, verbal, and physical assistance only if necessary (using a system of least prompts) to ensure independent performance. Ensure the student uses an appropriate posture on the scooter. Provide physical prompting (e.g., tapping the shoulder that the student should use in order to reach the object) and verbal prompting ("Christian, remember to keep your chest on the middle of the scooter," "Thalia, nice stroke, but remember to extend your arms in order to reach the image that you want to collect"). Provide positive praise (e.g., "good job," "great," "awesome") and feedback ("reach your left hand to reach the tennis ball at your side") and correct mistakes ("you pushed the scooter well, but you did not follow the images of the animals").

Appendix

Resources

Wesley J. Wilson

Sports

Books

DePauw, K.P., & Gavron, S.J. (2005). *Disability sport* (2nd ed.). Champaign, IL: Human Kinetics.

Winnick, J.P., & Porretta, D.L. (Eds.). (2017). *Adapted physical education and sport* (6th ed.). Champaign, IL: Human Kinetics.

Websites

Special Olympic Resources (essential resources about sports and unified sports): http://resources.specialolympics.org/ResourcesDefault.aspx

Motor Activity Training Program: Special Olympics Coaching Guide: http://digitalguides.specialolympics.org/matp/?#/0

Disabled Sports USA: Adaptive Sports: www.disabledsportsusa.org/sports/adaptive-sports

Para table tennis
- http://ittfnorthamerica.com
- www.paralympic.org/table-tennis

Power soccer
- www.powersoccerusa.org
- http://powersoccershop.com
- www.powersoccerteamusa.net

Power hockey
- http://powerchairhockey.org
- http://powerhockey.com

Table cricket
- www.lordstaverners.org
- www.daviessports.co.uk

Sitting volleyball
- www.worldparavolley.org

Challenger baseball
- www.littleleague.org

Boccia
- www.bisfed.com
- https://usaboccia.org
- www.handilifesport.com/en/Boccia
- www.bisfed.com

Shuffleboard
- www.shuffleboard.net/

Videos

Blaze Sports America: Sport & Coaching, program development videos: www.blazesports.org/what-we-do/training-and-education/training-tools

Disabled Sports USA: Disabled sports in the media: www.disabledsportsusa.org/about/news

Programs

Special Olympics: www.specialolympics.org

World ParaVolley: www.worldparavolley.org

United States Power Soccer Association: www.powersoccerteamusa.net

Power Hockey: http://powerhockey.com

ITTF Para Table Tennis: www.ipttc.org

Wheelchair Tennis: www.usta.com/Adult-Tennis/Wheelchair-Tennis/grassroots_camps

Little League Challenger Division Baseball: www.littleleague.org/media/challenger.htm

The Miracle League Baseball: www.themiracleleague.net

Disabled Sports USA: School-Based Athletics: www.disabledsportsusa.org/sports/youth-programs/school-based-athletics

Boccia International Sports Federation: www.bisfed.com

American Youth Soccer Organization: www.ayso.org/VIP

Equipment

Super Switch Hitter: www.switchintime.com

Adaptive Equipment: www.disabledsportsusa.org/sports/adaptive-equipment

Boccia equipment: www.handilifesport.com/en/Boccia

Recreation, Physical Activity, and Adapted Physical Education

Books

Canales, L., & Lytle, R.K. (2011). *Physical activities for young people with severe disabilities*. Champaign, IL: Human Kinetics.

Davis, E.A. (2012). *Physical activities in the wheelchair and out: An illustrated guide to personalizing participation*. Champaign, IL: Human Kinetics.

Delaney, T. (2009). *101 games and activities for children with autism, Asperger's, and sensory processing disorders*. New York, NY: McGraw-Hill.

Orelove, F.P., Sobsey, R., & Gilles, D.L. (Eds.). (2017). *Educating students with severe and multiple disabilities: A collaborative approach*. Baltimore, MD: Paul H. Brookes.

SHAPE America. (2014). *National Standards & Grade-Level Outcomes for K-12 Physical Education*. Champaign, IL: Human Kinetics.

Sullivan, T., Slagle, C., Hapshie, T.J., Brevard, D., & Brevard, V. (2012). *Build it so they can play: Affordable equipment for adapted physical education*. Champaign, IL: Human Kinetics.

Websites

Commit to Inclusion: http://committoinclusion.org

Teaching Adapted Physical Education & Activity: www.teachingadaptedpe.com

Support Real Teachers: Resources for Adapted Physical Education: www.supportrealteachers.org/adapted-physical-education.html

Universal Design for Learning: www.cast.org/our-work/about-udl.html#.WHUXBlNVhHy

National Center on Universal Design for Learning: www.udlcenter.org

Videos

National Center on Health, Physical Activity and Disability, video catalog: www.nchpad.org/Videos

PE Central: Adapted PE Videos: www.pecentral.org/mediacenter/adaptedPEvideos.html

Teaching Adapted Physical Education & Activity: Video Examples: www.teachingadaptedpe.com/video-examples.html

Programs

Adaptive Adventures: https://adaptiveadventures.org

President's Council on Fitness, Sports & Nutrition: I Can Do It, You Can Do It!: www.fitness.gov/participate-in-programs/i-can-do-it-you-can-do-it

Equipment

Leap T.V. Educational Active Video Game System (with games such as Dance and Learn, and Sports): www.google.com/#q=Leaptv+Educational+Active+Video+Game+System&tbm=shop

Active video games such as Wii Sports (bowling, tennis, boxing) and Dance Dance Revolution

Adapted recreation equipment: www.achievableconcepts.com.au

Climbing wall equipment: http://everlastclimbing.com

Physical Education and Recreation Equipment

- US Games: www.usgames.com
- Sportime: www.sportime.com
- Gopher: www.gophersport.com
- FlagHouse: www.flaghouse.com

Aquatics

Books

Lepore, M., Gayle, G.W., & Stevens, S.F. (2007). *Adapted aquatics programming: A professional guide* (2nd ed.). Champaign, IL: Human Kinetics.

Lepore, M., Columna, L., & Friedlander Litzner, L. (2015). *Assessment and activities for teaching swimming.* Champaign, IL: Human Kinetics.

Websites

Adapted Aquatics Organization: www.adaptedaquatics.org

Special Olympics: Swimming: www.specialolympics.org/Sections/Sports-and-Games/Coaching_Guides/Aquatics.aspx

USA Disability Swimming Resources: www.usaswimming.org

Videos

Introduction to Adapted Aquatics DVD: www.humankinetics.com/products/all-products/Introduction-to-Adapted-Aquatics-DVD

National Center on Health, Physical Activity and Disability: Teaching Adapted Aquatics: www.nchpad.org/273/1732/Teaching~Adapted~Aquatics

Programs

Special Olympics: www.specialolympics.org

USA Disabled Water Ski: www.usawaterski.org/pages/divisions/WSDA/main.asp

USA Swimming: www.usaswimming.org

Equipment

My Pool Pal (special needs swimwear): www.mypoolpal.com/store/search-results.cfm?specialneeds

Theraquatics: Pool Access Equipment: www.theraquatics.com/pool-access-equipment.html

Aqua Mentor: ADA Equipment: www.aquamentor.com/products/ada-equipment

Life Jacket-Adapted, Inc.: www.pfd-a.com/index.html

AccessRec: www.accessrec.com

United Spinal Association: www.usatechguide.org

Danmar Products: www.danmarproducts.com

Para Mobility: www.paramobility.com.au

Recreonics: www.recreonics.com

SprintAquatics: www.sprintaquatics.com

Glossary

adapted equipment—Equipment that is modified to meet the unique needs and abilities of students with disabilities.

adaptive behaviors—The collection of conceptual, social, and practical skills that all people learn to function in their daily lives.

alternative assessments—Modified assessments conducted in lieu of the assessments used by the general class participants for students with more severe disabilities.

American Sign Language (ASL)—A communication technique commonly used by people who are deaf; it is a separate and distinct language consisting of manual signs, spelled-out language, gestures, facial expressions, and body movements.

auditory system—The system through which we receive and process sound; a stimulation is received through the peripheral receptors and then transmitted to the central auditory nervous system.

authentic assessment—An ongoing feedback system that monitors and records student learning and outcomes under what are termed *authentic conditions;* that is, those things that the student typically does in a sports and recreation environment.

basic skills assessment (BSA)—An assessment used to assess a heterogeneous population of students— from those with severe disabilities to typically developing students—in a variety of curricular units.

boccia—A precision ball game in which each team tries to throw leather balls closer to the target ball than the other team. Ramps are used for players who do not have enough upper-body strength or range of motion to throw the ball.

Challenger baseball—A noncompetitive variation of baseball in which participants are paired up with buddies who help them hit, field, and run the bases.

chromosomal abnormalities—Rare chromosome disorders that include extra, missing, or rearranged chromosome material. The larger the defect is, the more severe the disorder tends to be.

collaboration—The practice of working on an interdisciplinary team to learn about the unique skills and abilities of students with disabilities in order to provide them the best education possible.

communicative dictionary—A dictionary that identifies the visual skills, physical gestures, and movement language a student uses to communicate.

contraindications—Symptoms or conditions that would make activities harmful or not recommended for the student.

curriculum-based assessments—Assessments that relate to the content areas taught in physical education.

differentiated instruction—Instruction that addresses students' specific learning styles and needs (Ellis et al., 2009).

direct selection—A communication technique in which a learner points to a desired symbol on a communication board.

disability sports—Typical sports modified to accommodate the individuals and their disability. Paralympic sports, such as goalball and sledge hockey, are specifically designed for the disability population.

dynamic communication devices—Communication devices that include active displays that are typically accessed using touchscreen technology.

ecological task analysis (ETA)—An alternative form of task analysis that provides strategies for individualizing instruction to give students choices, enhance decision making, increase teacher observation, and foster discovery.

eye gaze—A communication system in which the learner stares at a symbol to select it.

floating—The skill of lying on the front or back and staying above water.

foundational skills—The skills that make up the more complex movements and higher-order concepts that allow people to participate in leisure pursuits, sports, and activities of daily living.

functional activities—Activities that occur in the everyday life of the student.

functional assessment of students with severe disabilities (FASSD)—An assessment for students with severe disabilities and extremely limited mobility. It assesses basic functional movement, positioning, mobility, physical fitness, and sensory abilities.

functional cardiorespiratory endurance—A measure of a person's cardiorespiratory function (e.g., how many steps a student can take in a gait trainer before needing to rest; how long a student can push a wheelchair before needing to rest; how long a student can participate in physical activities before getting tired).

functional flexibility—A measure of the general range of motion in arms and legs with reference to basic physical activities such as reaching to grasp an object or pushing a ball down a ramp.

functional physical fitness—A measure of basic strength, flexibility, and cardiorespiratory endurance with reference to daily activities.

functional skills assessments—Assessments that take into consideration the student's current skill level and functioning within the particular activity and the necessary supports for success.

gestural communication—A form of communication that involves physical gestures that are commonly understood by members of a particular group or culture.

gliding—The act of pushing off a wall and floating forward on the front or the back.

individual education plan (IEP)—A comprehensive education plan specifically designed for a child with a disability.

individual transition plan (ITP)—A plan designed to assist children with disabilities transition to adulthood with the necessary skills to be as successful as possible. This must begin no later than the age of 16.

interdisciplinary team—Educational professionals from general and special education who work in a coordinated fashion toward a common goal for the student.

kicking—The act of moving the feet up and down while floating on the front or the back for the purpose of propulsion.

limited response repertoire—Students with severe disabilities may have a limited ability to respond to prompts because of hearing, vision, processing, muscular, or expressive issues.

modified physical education—An alternative to general physical education programs specifically designed to meet the needs of students with disabilities. Modified physical education is a peer-supported program that uses sport as a vehicle to reduce physical and social barriers.

multidisciplinary team—The team that supports an individual student such as physical therapists, vision teachers, and speech therapists; often includes the child.

multiple disabilities—A combination of disabilities, such as intellectual, visual, and orthopedic impairments, that result in extensive educational needs.

paraeducator—A support person who assists the teacher in providing educational services to students with disabilities.

para table tennis—Table tennis modified for people with a wide range of physical and intellectual disabilities. Some players even use their mouths to hold the paddle.

peer tutoring programs—The process of pairing a student with a disability with a peer who is trained to work with the student one-on-one. The peer tutor works on instruction and feedback with the direction of the physical education teacher.

performance-based approach—An approach to testing in which students are evaluated on skills directly related to the curricular content.

personal flotation devices (PFDs)—Supportive devices that help students float, such as life jackets, water wings, buoyancy belts, and full body supports.

picture exchange communication system (PECS)—A form of augmented communication that uses icons rather than words to help learners communicate.

power hockey—A form of hockey in which players operate motorized chairs. Depending on a player's upper-body strength and range of motion, modifications may be made such as attaching the hockey stick to the chair.

power soccer—A form of soccer played by people who operate power chairs. Participants may have a variety of disabilities such as quadriplegia, multiple sclerosis, muscular dystrophy, and cerebral palsy.

proprioceptive system—The system that receives sensations from receptors in the muscles, joints, skin, tendons, and underlying tissue. It is through this system that a person can sense a static position within dynamic movement.

response to intervention—Educational practices that integrate assessment and intervention strategies to maximize student achievement and reduce behavior problems.

rubric—A form of assessment used to measure the attainment of skills, knowledge, or performance against a consistent set of criteria.

scanning—A process by which a learner is given a menu of choices; when the desired choice is presented, the learner produces a voluntary response to signal the listener.

SENSE—An acronym for determining the appropriateness of equipment or a learning activity: **S**afe, **E**ducational (related to SHAPE America's National Standards), affords a high **N**umber of practice trials, ensures **S**uccess, and **E**njoyable.

sensory integration—Cheatum and Hammond (2000) described sensory integration as "the ability to receive, organize, interpret, and use the vast amount of sensory information that enters the body and neurological system through both external and internal stimuli" (p. 132).

severe disabilities—Extensive difficulties that result in the requirement of significant levels of support for participation in educational settings.

shared goals—Ability, skill, and educational goals that can be taught and reinforced across a number of settings.

sitting volleyball—A version of para volleyball in which all participants sit on the floor or ground.

six Ss model of equipment adaptation—A model for adapting equipment that reminds educators to consider size, sound, support, surface, speed, and switches.

static communication devices—Communication devices that have fixed displays that represent needed or desired items.

support personnel—Personnel such as para-educators, peer tutors, college students, and even parents who can help with one-on-one instruction in the aquatic environment.

switch-activated equipment—Equipment that can be activated with less force than is normally needed or using an alternative movement by the child. Switches can be high or low tech.

table cricket—Derived from the popular English bat-and-ball game of cricket, table cricket shrinks the game so that it can be played on a table tennis table by players of all abilities.

tactile sign language—A gestural communication option based on a standard manual signing system in which the receiver's hand is placed lightly on the hand of the signer to receive signs.

tactile system—The system that receives information when something comes in contact with the skin. Seven types of skin receptors are stimulated by pressure, temperature, and pain.

task analysis assessment (TAA)—A measure that identifies the level of assistance required for each skill and assigns a score of independence.

traditional task analysis—A form of analysis in which a motor skill is broken down into its discrete and underlying parts.

transition services—The process of providing young people with disabilities with the skills they need to transition from school to the community, where they can be independent, active, and healthy.

tutee—A student with a disability who is being taught in a peer tutoring program.

Universal Design for Learning (UDL)—A strategy for eliminating barriers to students' learning that includes Universally Designed Instruction (UDI), Universally Designed Curriculum (UDC), and Universally Designed Assessment (UDA).

universally designed—Designed using forethought to accommodate all learners before being presented to learners, not after the fact.

vestibular system—The system that informs the nervous system where the body is in relationship to the pull of gravity so that the person can maintain equilibrium.

visual system—The system that, through a learned process, changes images gained through acuity into useful information.

References

Preface

Block, M., & Obrusnikova, I. (2007). Inclusion in physical education: A review of the literature from 1995-2005. *Adapted Physical Activity Quarterly, 24*(2), 103-124.

Haegele, J.A., & Sutherland S. (2015). Perspectives of students with disabilities toward physical education: A qualitative inquiry review. *Quest, 67*(3), 255-273.

Hodge, S.R., Ammah, J.O., Casebolt, K., LaMaster, K., & O'Sullivan, M. (2004). High school general physical education teachers' behaviors and beliefs associated with inclusion. *Sport, Education & Society, 9*, 395-419.

Ryndak, D., Jackson, L., & White, J. (2013). Involvement and progress in the general education curriculum for students with extensive support needs: K-12 inclusive education research and implications for the future. *Inclusion, 1*(1), 28-49.

Chapter 1

Batshaw, M. (2002). *Children with disabilities* (5th ed.). Baltimore, MD: Paul H. Brookes.

Block, M.E., & Obrusnikova, I. (2007). Inclusion in physical education: A review of the literature from 1995-2005. *Adapted Physical Activity Quarterly, 24*(2), 103-124.

Carpenter, B., Egerton, J., Cockbill, B., Bloom, T., Fotheringham, J., Rawson, H., & Thistlethwaite, J. (2015). *Engaging learners with complex learning difficulties and disabilities: A resource book for teachers and teaching assistants.* London, England: Routledge.

Couturier, L., Chepko, S., & Holt/Hale, S. (2014). National standards & grade-level outcomes for K-12 physical education (pp. 13, 17, 27, 30, 32, 36, 39, 43, 53, 58). Champaign, IL: Human Kinetics.

Gray, P. (2006). *National audit of service, support and provision for children with low-incidence SEN.* London, England: DfES.

Hodge, S., Lieberman, L.J., Murata, N. (2012). *Essentials of teaching physical education: Culture, diversity, and inclusion.* New York, NY: Routledge Taylor & Francis Group.

Individuals with Disabilities Education Improvement Act, H.R. 1350, Pub. L. No. P.L. 108-446. (2004).

Kwon, K., Elicker, J., & Kontos, S. (2011). Social IEP objectives, teacher-talk, and peer interaction in inclusive and segregated preschool settings. *Early Childhood Education Journal, 39*, 267-277. doi:10.1007/s10643-011-0469-6

Lieberman, L.J., Lytle, R., & Clarcq, J. (2008). Getting it right from the start: Employing the Universal Design for Learning into your curriculum. *Journal of Physical Education, Recreation & Dance, 79*, 32-39.

Lieberman, L.J., Cavanagh, L., Haegele, J.A., Aiello, R., & Wilson, W. (2017). The modified physical education class: An option for the least restrictive environment. *Journal of Physical Education, Recreation and Dance, 88*, 10-16.

McLeskey, J., Landers, E., Williamson, P., & Hoppey, D. (2012). Are we moving toward educating students with disabilities in less restrictive settings? *Journal of Special Education, 46*, 131-140.

Nakken, H., & Vlaskamp, C. (2007). A need for a taxonomy for profound intellectual and multiple disabilities. *Journal of Policy and Practice in Intellectual Disabilities, 4*, 83-87.

Odom, S.L., Brantlinger, E., Gersten, R., Horner, R.H., Thompson, B., & Harris, K.R. (2005). Research in special education: Scientific methods and evidence-based practices. *Exceptional Children, 71*(2), 137-148.

Perez, K. (2014). *The new inclusion: Differentiated strategies to engage ALL students.* New York, NY: Teachers College Press.

Rapp, W. (2014). *Universal Design for Learning in action.* Baltimore, MD: Paul H. Brookes.

Rapp, W., & Arndt, K. (2012). *Teaching everyone: An introduction to inclusive education.* Baltimore, MD: Paul H. Brookes.

Rose, D.H., & Meyer, A. (2006). *A practical reader in Universal Design for Learning.* Cambridge, MA: Harvard Education Press.

Seymour, H., Reid, G., & Bloom, G.A. (2009). Friendship in inclusive PE. *Adapted Physical Activity Quarterly, 26*, 201-219.

Spooner, F., Baker, J., Harris, A., Ahlgrim-Delzell, L., & Browder, D. (2007). Effects of training in Universal Design for Learning on lesson plan development. *Remedial and Special Education, 28*, 108-116.

U.S. Department of Education. (2009). 28th annual report to Congress on the implementation of the Individuals with Disabilities Education Act, 2006. Washington, DC: Author.

Westling, D., & Fox, L. (2009). *Teaching students with severe disabilities* (4th ed.). Upper Saddle River, NJ: Merrill Prentice Hall.

Chapter 2

Calculator, S. (2009). Augmentative and alternative communication (AAC) and inclusive education for students with the most severe disabilities. *International Journal of Inclusive Education, 13*(1), 93-113.

Cervantes, C., Lieberman, L., Magnesio, B., & Wood, J. (2013). Peer tutoring: Meeting the demands of inclusion in physical education today. *Journal of Physical Education, Recreation and Dance, 84*(3), 43-48.

Grenier, M., & Miller, N. (2015). Using peers as natural supports for students with severe disabilities in general physical education, *Palaestra, 29*(1), 22-26.

Kelly, L. (2011). Connecting the GPE and APE curricula for students with mild to moderate disabilities. *Journal of Physical Education, Recreation, and Dance, 82*(9), 34-40.

Seaman, J., DePauw, K., Morton, K., & Omoto, K. (2007). *Making connections: From theory to practice in adapted physical education.* Scottsdale, AZ: Holcomb Hathaway.

Sherrill, C., Heikinaro-Johansson, P., & Slininger, D. (1994). Equal-status in the gym. *Journal of Physical Education, Recreation, and Dance, 65*(1), 27-31, 56.

U.S. Department of Education. (2009). 28th annual report to Congress on the implementation of the Individuals with Disabilities Education Act, 2006. Washington, DC: Author.

Chapter 3

Block. M.E., Lauer, J., & Jones, K. (2004, April). *Functional assessment of students with severe disabilities.* Presentation at the Annual American Alliance of Health. Physical Education. Recreation and Dance Convention, New Orleans, LA.

Block, M.E., Lieberman, L.J., & Connor-Kuntz, F. (1998). Authentic assessment in adapted physical education, *Journal of Physical Education, Recreation, & Dance, 69*(3), 48-56.

Block, M., & Obrusnikova, I. (2007). Inclusion in physical education: A review 20 of the literature from 1995-2005. *Adapted Physical Activity Quarterly, 24*(2), 103-124.

Carson, L.M., Bulger, S.M., & Townsend, J.S. (2007). Enhancing responsible decision making in physical activity. In W.A. Davis & G.D. Broadhead (Eds.), *Ecological task analysis and movement* (pp. 141-147). Champaign, IL: Human Kinetics.

Horvat, M., Block, M.E., Kelly, L., & Croce, R. (2018). *Developmental and adapted physical activity assessment.* Champaign, IL: Human Kinetics.

Houston-Wilson, C. (1994). *Physical best for students with disabilities.* Reston, VA: AAHPERD.

Kowalski, E., Houston-Wilson, C., & Daggett, S. (in press). The basic skills assessment. Brockport, NY: The College at Brockport.

Mitchell, S., & Oslin, J. (2007). Ecological task analysis in games teaching: Tactical games model. In W.A. Davis & G.D. Broadhead (Eds.), *Ecological task analysis and movement* (pp. 161-177). Champaign, IL: Human Kinetics.

Ulrich, D.A. (2017). *Test of Gross Motor Development-3.* Austin, TX: PRO-ED.

Winnick, J.P., & Short, F.X. (2016). *The Brockport Physical Fitness Test.* Champaign, IL: Human Kinetics.

Chapter 4

Best, C., Lieberman, L., & Arndt, K. (2002). The use of interpreters in physical education. *Journal of Physical Education, Recreation, & Dance, 73*(8), 45-50.

Block, M.E. (1992). What is appropriate physical education for students with profound disabilities? *Adapted Physical Activity Quarterly, 9,* 197-213.

Downing, J.E., & Peckham-Hardin, K. (2007). Supporting inclusive education for students with severe disabilities in rural areas. *Rural Special Education Quarterly, 26*(2), 10-15.

Hodge, S.R., Lieberman, L.J., & Murata, N.M. (2012). *Essentials of teaching adapted physical education.* Scottsdale, AZ: Holcomb Hathaway.

Lieberman, L.J., Ponchillia, P., & Ponchillia, S. (2013). *Physical education and sports for people with visual impairments and deafblindness.* New York, NY: AFB Press

Reichle, J., York, J., & Sigafoos, J. (1991). *Implementing augmentative and alternative communication: Strategies for learners with severe disabilities.* Baltimore, MD: Paul H. Brookes.

Chapter 5

Byrd, D.E. (1990). Peer tutoring with the learning disabled: A critical review. *Journal of Education Research, 84*(2), 115-118.

Carter, E.W., Cushing, L.S., Clark, N.M., & Kennedy, C.H. (2005). Effects of peer support interventions on students' access to the general curriculum and social interactions. *Research and Practice for Persons with Severe Disabilities, 30,* 15-25.

Carter, E. W., & Kennedy, C. H. (2007). Promoting access to the general curriculum using peer support strategies. *Research and Practice for Persons with Severe Disabilities, 31,* 284-292.

Cervantes, C.M., Lieberman, L.J., Magnesio, B., & Wood, J. (2013). Peer tutoring: Meeting the demands of inclusion in today's general physical education settings**. *Journal of Physical Education, Recreation & Dance, 84,* 43-48.

Downing, J.E. (2008). *Including students with severe and multiple disabilities in typical classrooms.* Baltimore, MD: Paul H. Brookes.

Giangreco, M.F., Halvorsen, A., Doyle, M.B., & Broer, S.M. (2004). Alternatives to overreliance on paraprofessionals in inclusive schools. *Journal of Special Education Leadership,17*(2), 82-90.

Hodge, S., Lieberman, L.J., & Murata, N. (2012). *Essentials of teaching physical education: Culture, diversity, and inclusion.* Scottsdale, AZ: Holcomb Hathaway.

Houston-Wilson, C., Lieberman, L., Horton, M., & Kasser, S. (1997). Peer tutoring: A plan for instructing children of all abilities. *Journal of Physical Education, Recreation & Dance, 68,* 39-44.

Klavina, A., & Block, M. (2008). The effect of peer tutoring on interaction behaviors in inclusive physical education. *Adapted Physical Activity Quarterly, 25,* 132-158.

Klavina, A. (2011). Development and initial validation of the computerized evaluation protocol of interactions in physical education. Measurement in Physical Education and Exercise Science, 15, 26–46.

Klavina, A., Kristen, L., Hammar, L., Jerlinder, K., & Soulie, T. (2013). Cooperation oriented learning in inclusive physical education. *European Journal of Special Education, 29,* 119-134.

Klavina, A., & Rodionova, K. (2015). The effect of peer tutoring in physical education for middle school students with severe disabilities. *European Journal of Adapted Physical Activity, 8*(2), 3-17.

Lieberman, L.J., Dunn, J.M., Mars, H., & McCubbin, J. (2000). Peer tutors' on activity levels of deaf children in inclusive elementary physical education. *Adapted Physical Activity Quarterly, 17*, 20-39.

Lieberman, L.J., & Houston-Wilson, C. (2018). *Strategies for inclusion: A handbook for physical educators* (3rd. ed.). Champaign, IL: Human Kinetics.

Lieberman, L.J., Newcomer, J., McCubbin, J., & Dalrymple, N. (1997). The effects of cross age tutors on the academic learning time in physical education of children with disabilities in inclusive elementary physical education classes. *Brazilian Journal of Adapted Physical Education & Recreation, 4*, 15-32.

Orelove, F.P., Sobsey, D., Gilles, D. (Eds.). (2017). *Educating students with severe and multiple disabilities*. Baltimore, MD: Paul H. Brookes.

Peterson, D.W., & Miller, J.A. (1990). Best practices in peer-influenced learning. In A. Thomas & J. Grimes (Eds.), *Best practices in school psychology-II* (pp. 531-546). Washington, DC: National Association of School Psychologists.

Polloway, E.A., Patton, J.R., & Serna, L. (2000). *Strategies for teaching learners with special needs*. Upper Saddle River, NJ: Prentice Hall.

Chapter 6

Bechtel, P.A., Stevens, L.A., & Brett, C.E.W. (2012). Tips for dealing with behavior management issues. *Strategies: A Journal for Physical and Sport Educators, 25*(4), 30-33.

Bryan, R.R., McCubbin, J.A., & van der Mars, M.H. (2013). The ambiguous role of the paraeducator in the general physical education environment. *Adapted Physical Activity Quarterly, 30*, 164-183.

Carroll, D. (2001). Considering paraeducator training, roles, and responsibilities. *Teaching Exceptional Children, 34*(2), 60-64.

Ellis, K., Lieberman, L., & and LeRoux, D. (2009). Using differentiated instruction in physical education. *Palaestra, 24*(4), 19-23.

Giangreco, M.F., Edelman, S.W., & Broer, S.M. (2001). Respect, appreciation, and acknowledgment of paraprofessionals who support students with disabilities. *Exceptional Children, 67*(4), 485-498.

Haegele, J.A., & Kozub, F.M. (2010). A continuum of paraeducator support for utilization in adapted physical education. *TEACHING Exceptional Children Plus, 6*(5), Article 2.

Individuals with Disabilities Education Act. (2004). Public Law 108-466, sec. 602, 118.

Lee, S.H., & Haegele, J.A. (2016). Tips for effectively utilizing paraprofessional in physical education. *Journal of Physical Education, Recreation and Dance, 87*(1), 46-48.

Lieberman, L.J. (2007). *Paraeducators in physical education: A training guide to roles and responsibilities*. Champaign, IL: Human Kinetics.

Lieberman, L.J., & Houston-Wilson, C. (2018). *Strategies for inclusion: A handbook for physical educators* (3rd. ed.). Champaign, IL: Human Kinetics.

Lytle, R., Lieberman, L., & Aiello, R. (2007). Motivating paraeducators to be actively involved in physical education. *Journal of Physical Education, Recreation & Dance, 78*(4), 26-30.

Malian, I.M. (2011). Paraeducators perceptions of their roles in inclusive classrooms: A national study of paraeducators. *Electronic Journal for Inclusive Education, 2*(8).

O'Connor, J., & French, R. (1998). Paraeducators attitudes toward inclusion of students with disabilities in physical education. *Perceptual and Motor Skills, 86*, 98-98.

Physical educator's guide for working with paraprofessionals. (2013). The Presidential Youth Fitness Program, Washington, DC: US Department of Health and Human Services.

Piletic C., Davis. R., & Aschemeier, A. (2005). Paraeducators in physical education. *Journal of Physical Education, Recreation and Dance, 76*(5), 47-55.

Rouse. P. (2009). *Inclusion in physical education: Fitness, motor and social skills for students of all abilities*. Champaign, IL: Human Kinetics.

Sprick, R., Garrison, M., & Howard, L. (2005). *Para pro: Supporting the instructional process*. Eugene, OR: Pacific North West.

Twachtman-Cullen, D. (2008). *How to be a para pro: A comprehensive training manual for paraprofessionals*. Higganum, CT: Starfish Specialty Press.

Chapter 8

Cheatum, B.A., & Hammond, A.A. (2000). *Physical activities for improving children's learning and behavior: A guide to sensory motor development* (p. 132). Champaign, IL: Human Kinetics.

Couturier, L., Chepko, S., & Holt/Hale, S. (2014). *National standards & grade-level outcomes for K-12 physical education* (pp. 13, 17, 27, 30, 32, 36, 39, 43, 53, 58). Champaign, IL: Human Kinetics.

Davis, W.E., & Burton, A.W. (1991). Ecological task analysis: Translating movement behavior theory into practice. *Adapted Physical Activity Quarterly, 8*, 154-177.

Gallahue, J.D. Ozman, D.L., & Goodway, J. C. (2012). *Understanding motor development: Infants, children, adolescents, and adults* (7th ed.). New York, NY: McGraw Hill.

Hourcade, J., Pilotte, T.E., West, E., & Parette. P. (2004). A history of augmentative and alternative communication for individuals with severe and profound disabilities. *Focus on Autism and Other Developmental Disabilities, 19*(4), 235-244.

Lane, S.J., & Schaaf, R.C. (2010). Examining the neuroscience evidence for sensory-driven neuroplasticity: Implications for sensory-based occupational therapy for children and adolescents. *American Journal of Occupational Therapy, 64*, 375-390.

Special Education and Rehabilitative Services: U.S. Office of Special Education Programs. (2015, November 16). Dear colleague letter on free and appropriate public education (FAPE) that clarifies that individualized education programs (IEP) for children with disabilities must be aligned with state academic content standards for the grade in which a child is enrolled. Retrieved from www2. cd.gov/policy/speced/guid/idea/memosdcltrs/guidance-on-fape-11-17-2015.pdf

Chapter 9

Black, K., & Williamson, D.C. (2010). Inclusive game design—part 3. In A.C. Roibas, E. Stamatakis, & K. Black (Eds.), *Design for sport* (pp. 195-223). Abingdon, UK: Gower.

Block, M.E. (2016). *A teacher's guide to including students with disabilities in general physical education* (4th ed.). Baltimore, MD: Paul H. Brookes.

Boccia International Sports Federation. (2016). About boccia. Retrieved from www.bisfed.com/about-boccia

Davis, R. (2011). *Teaching disability sport*. Champaign, IL: Human Kinetics.

DePauw, K.P., & Gavron, S.J. (2005). *Disability sport* (2nd ed.). Champaign, IL: Human Kinetics.

Grant, A. (2016). Opening up the field. *Special Children, 231,* 30-32.

Hodge, S.R., Lieberman, L.J., & Murata, M.M. (2012). *Essentials of teaching adapted physical education*. Scottsdale, AZ: Holcomb Hathaway.

International Paralympic Committee. (2012). Para-table tennis: 12 facts for London 2012. Retrieved from www.paralympic.org/news/para-table-tennis-12-facts-london-2012

International Table Tennis Federation North America. (n.d.). Retrieved from http://ittfnorthamerica.com/?page_id=17

International Paralympic Committee. (2016). Sport week: History of boccia. Retrieved from www.paralympic.org/news/sport-week-history-boccia

International Wheelchair and Amputee Sports Federation. (n.d.). Retrieved from http://powerchairhockey.org/history

Kelly, L.E., & Melograno, V.J. (2004). *Developing the physical education curriculum: An achievement-based approach*. Champaign, IL: Human Kinetics.

King, G., Law, M., King, S., Rosenbaum, P., Kertoy, M.K., & Young, N.L. (2003). A conceptual model of the factors affecting the recreation and leisure participation of children with disabilities. *Physical & Occupational Therapy in Pediatrics, 23*(1), 63-90.

Kleinert, H., Miracle, S., & Sheppard-Jones, K. (2007). Including students with moderate and severe intellectual disabilities in school extracurricular and community recreation activities. *Intellectual and Developmental Disabilities, 45,* 46-55.

Lieberman, L.J., & Houston-Wilson, C. (2018). *Strategies for inclusion: Physical education for everyone*. Champaign, IL: Human Kinetics.

Little League of America. (2016). *Challenger Division*. Retrieved from www.littleleague.org/media/challenger/about.htm

Lord's Taverners. (2015). Lord's Taverners complete guide to table cricket. Retrieved from www.lordstaverners.org/a/js/third_party/tinymce/jscripts/tiny_mce/plugins/filemanager/files/11508_LT_TCGuide16_WEB.pdf

Morris, G., & Stiehl, J. (1999). *Changing kids' games* (2nd ed.). Champaign, IL: Human Kinetics.

Murphy, N.A., & Carbone, P.S. (2008). Promoting the participation of children with disabilities in sports, recreation, and physical activities. *Pediatrics, 121*(5), 1057-1061.

Paciorek, M.J. (2011). Adapted sport. In J. P. Winnick (Ed.), *Adapted physical education and sport* (5th ed., pp. 41-57). Champaign, IL: Human Kinetics.

ParaVolley. (2015). World ParaVolley medical and functional classification handbook. Retrieved from www.worldparavolley.org/wp-content/uploads/2016/10/World-ParaVolley-Classification-Handbook.pdf

ParaVolley. (2016). Sitting volleyball. Retrieved from www.worldparavolley.org/disciplines/sitting-volleyball

Ryan, J.B., Katsiyannis, A., Cadorette, D., Hodge, J., & Markham, M. (2014). Establishing adaptive sports programs for youth with moderate to severe disabilities. *Preventing School Failure, 58*(1), 32-41.

U.S. Electric Wheelchair Hockey Association. (n.d.). Retrieved from http://powerhockey.com/usa/wp-content/uploads/2014/07/NAPHA_Tournament_Rules-07-2014_rev1.pdf

U.S. Government Accountability Office. (2010). *Students with disabilities: More information and guidance could improve opportunities in physical education and athletics*. Washington, DC: Author. Retrieved from www.gao.gov/new.items/d10519.pdf

U.S. Power Soccer Association. (n.d.). Retrieved from www.powersoccerusa.org

Wilson, W.J., & Colombo-Dougovito, A.M. (2015). Inclusive and effective adapted physical education: Meeting the needs of each student. *Strategies, 28*(4), 50-52.

Chapter 10

Davis, R. (2011). *Teaching disability sport: A guide for physical educators*. Champaign, IL: Human Kinetics.

Grenier, M., & Kearns, C. (2012). The benefits of implementing disability sport into physical education: A model for success. *Journal of Physical Education Recreation and Dance, 83*(4), 24-27.

Individuals With Disabilities Education Improvement Act, H.R. 1350, Pub. L. No. P.L. 108-446 (2004).

Lieberman, L.J., & Houston-Wilson, C. (2018). *Strategies for inclusion: A handbook for physical educators* (3rd. ed.). Champaign, IL: Human Kinetics.

Northeast Passage (2016). Retrieved from http://nepassage.org/

Rapp, W. (2014). *Universal design for learning in action*. Baltimore, MD: Paul H. Brookes.

Ryan, J.B., Katsiyannis, A., Cadorette, D., Hodge, J., & Markham, M. (2014). Establishing Adaptive Sports Programs for Youth with Moderate to Severe Disabilities. *Preventing School Failure, 58*(1), 32-41. doi: 10.1080/1045988X.2012.755666

Taub, D.E., & Greer, K.R. (2000). Physical activity as a normalizing experience for school-age children with physical disabilities: Implications for legitimation of social identity and enhancement of social ties. *Journal of Sport and Social Issues, 24,* 395–414.

Chapter 11

Arnhold, R., Young, L., & Lakowski, T. (2013). Helping general physical educators and adapted physical educators address the Office of Civil Rights' Dear Colleague guidance letter: The historical and legal background leading to the Office of Civil Rights' "Dear Colleague Letter." *Journal of Physical Education, Recreation and Dance, 84*(8), 20-23.

Davis, R. (2013). Helping general physical educators and adapted physical educators address the Office of Civil Rights' Dear Colleague guidance letter. *Journal of Physical Education, Recreation and Dance, 84*(8), 19.

Individuals With Disabilities Education Improvement Act, H.R. 1350, Pub. L. No. P.L. 108-446 (2004).

Samalot-Rivera, A., & Lieberman, L.J. (2016). *Community programs.* In Aiello, R. (Ed.), *Sports, fitness and motor activities for children with disabilities: A practical approach to increased physical activity beyond the school day.* Lanham, MD: Rowman and Littlefield.

U.S. Department of Education, Office for Civil Rights. (2013, January 25). *Dear colleague letter—Extracurricular athletics for students with disabilities.* Retrieved from www2.ed.gov/about/offices/list/ocr/letters/colleague-201301-504.pdf

Chapter 12

Americans with Disabilities Act. (n.d.). Retrieved from www.ada.gov/2010_regs.htm

Archer, S. (2002). Aquatic exercise and arthritis. *Aquatic Therapy Journal, 16* (1), 29-31.

Arnhold, P., & Lepore, M. (2017). Aquatics. In Winnick, J.P. (Ed.), *Adapted physical education and sport* (5th ed.). Champaign, IL: Human Kinetics.

Binkley, H., & Schoyer, T.T. (2002). Aquatic therapy in the treatment of upper extremity injuries. *Aquatic Therapy Today, 7*(1), 49-54.

Block, M.E., & Conatser, P. (2007). Including students with disabilities in general aquatics programs. In M.E. Block (Ed.), *A teacher's guide to including students with disabilities in general physical education* (3rd ed.). Baltimore, MD: Paul H. Brookes.

Conatser, P. (2009). Conatser adapted aquatics swimming screening test (2nd ed.). Self-published. www.adaptedaquatics.org/assesment.htm

Darby, L.A., & Yaekle, B.C. (2000). Physiological responses during two types of exercise performed on land and in the water. *Journal of Sports Medicine and Physical Fitness, 40,* 303-311.

Johnson, C.C. (2005). The benefits of physical activity for youth with developmental disabilities: A systematic review. *American Journal of Health Promotion, 23*(3), 157-168.

Kelly, M., & Darrah, J. (2005). Aquatic exercise for children with cerebral palsy. *Developmental Medicine and Child Neurology, 47*(12), 838-842.

Langendorfer, S.J., & Bruya, L. (1994). *Aquatics readiness: Developing water competency in young children.* Champaign, IL: Human Kinetics.

Lepore, M., Columna, L., & Friedlander Litzner, L. (2015). *Assessments and activities for teaching swimming.* Champaign, IL: Human Kinetics.

Lepore, M., Gayle, G.W., & Stevens, S. (2007). *Adapted aquatic programming* (2nd ed.). Champaign, IL: Human Kinetics.

Patterson, C., & Grosse, S. (2013). Swimming for individuals with severe impairments: A fitness approach. *Palaestra, 27*(1): 30-35.

Pearn, J., & Franklin, R. (2013). Disability and drowning: Personal experiences, research, and practicalities of adapted aquatics. *International Journal of Aquatic Research and Education, 7,* 157-162.

Schlough, K., Nawoczenski, D., Case, L.E., Nolan, K., & Wiggleworth, J.K. (2005). The effects of aerobic exercise on endurance, strength, function, and self-perception in adolescents with spastic cerebral palsy: A report of three case studies. *Pediatric Physical Therapy, 7*(4), 234-250.

Sherrill, C. (2004). Adapted physical activity, recreation and sport: Crossdisciplinary and lifespan (6th ed). Dubuque, IA: WCB/McGraw-Hill.

Shinohara, T., Suzuki, N., Oba, M., Kawasumi, M., Kimizuka, M., & Mita, K. (2002). Effects of exercise at the AT point for children with cerebral palsy. *Hospital for Joint Diseases, 61*(1 & 2), 63-67.

USA Swimming. (n.d.). Retrieved from www.usaswimming.org/ViewMiscArticle.aspx?TabId=1755&mid=7713&ItemId=3548

Watson, R.S., Cummings, P., Quan, L., Bratton, S., & Weiss, N.S. (2001). Cervical spine injuries among submersion victims. *Journal Trauma, 51,* 658-662.

Chapter 13

Couturier, L., Chepko, S., & Holt/Hale, S. (2014). *National standards & grade-level outcomes for K-12 physical education* (pp. 13, 17, 27, 30, 32, 36, 39, 43, 53, 58). Champaign, IL: Human Kinetics.

Index

Note: Page references followed by an italicized *f* or *t* indicate information contained in figures or tables, respectively.

About the Editors

Photo courtesy of Sinthy Kounlasa.

Michelle Grenier, PhD, is an associate professor and coordinator of the health and physical education program and adapted physical education program at the University of New Hampshire. She has substantial experience working in the field of physical education and utilizing inclusive strategies for students with disabilities. She is an accomplished researcher and is editor of the text Physical Education for Students With Autism Spectrum Disorders. Dr. Grenier is internationally recognized for her work on inclusion and has presented throughout the United States. She enjoys running, cycling, swimming, and traveling the world to meet others who share her professional and personal interests.

Photo courtesy of Matt Yeoman, SUNY.

Lauren J. Lieberman, PhD, is a distinguished service professor at The College at Brockport, State University of New York. She has taught higher education since 1995 and previously taught in the Deafblind Program at Perkins School for the Blind. She is fluent in sign language and used sign as her language in earning her PhD. She infuses sign language throughout her courses.

Lieberman has written 18 books on adapted physical education and more than 118 peer-reviewed articles. She started Camp Abilities, an overnight educational sports camp for children with visual impairments. This camp is now replicated in 18 states and eight countries.

Lieberman is past chair of the Adapted Physical Activity Council (APAC). She is currently on the board of the division of recreation and sport for the Association for the Education and Rehabilitation of the Blind and Visually Impaired (AER), and she serves on the board of the United States Association of Blind Athletes (USABA). She acts as a consultant for the New York Deaf-Blind Collaborative. In her leisure time, she enjoys playing Ultimate Frisbee, biking, running, kayaking, hiking, reading, and playing the guitar.

About the Contributors

Rocco Aiello has worked for St. Mary's County Public Schools in Maryland as a coordinator of adapted physical education and corollary sports through the Department of Special Education for the past 20 years. Rocco provides educational guidance to physical education teachers and other district personnel within the 27 schools in St. Mary's County. In 2008, Rocco was named the National Teacher of the Year in Adapted Physical Education. He has authored and coauthored many book chapters and articles throughout his 30 years in education, including his first publication, *Sports, Fitness and Motor Activities for Children with Disabilities: A Comprehensive Resource Guide for Parents and Educators*. Rocco also directs and teaches children with disabilities in adapted aquatics and is the founder and executive director of Inspire Inc., an after-school and summer program for children with disabilities.

Pamela Arnhold is an assistant professor of adapted physical activity in the department of physical and health education at Slippery Rock University of Pennsylvania. For 28 years, she has taught undergraduate classes to inspire the next generations to promote active, healthy lifestyles for individuals with disabilities.

Toni Bader is a Certified Adapted Physical Educator (CAPE). She is currently developing and implementing systems and procedures to serve the adapted PE needs of over 7,300 students with special needs in the Seattle public school district. She previously taught PE for 12 years in Seattle, where she received the Symetra Hero in the Classroom award in 2008 and the SHAPE Washington Adapted PE Teacher of the Year in 2009. Toni received her bachelor's degree in adapted physical education from SUNY Cortland in 2000 and her master's in adapted physical education with a concentration in adventure education from the University of Wisconsin at La Crosse in 2001. She is currently a member of both the SHAPE Washington board and the SHAPE northwest district board.

Ken Black has worked as a practitioner in inclusive physical activity and disability sport for almost 40 years. Ken has worked independently as an advisor and consultant since 2008, supporting colleagues in schools, in the community, and in higher education. Since 2014, he has served as a senior lecturer and project advisor in inclusive sport at the University of Worcester.

Martin Block, PhD, is a professor in the department of kinesiology at the University of Virginia, where he teaches courses in adapted physical education and motor development. He is the author of over 75 peer-reviewed articles, 20 book chapters, and 5 books on adapted physical education and motor development, including *A Teachers' Guide to Including Students with Disabilities in General Physical Education* and *Developmental and Adapted Physical Activity Assessment*. Since 1988, Martin also has been a consultant with Special Olympics, Inc., where he was the primary author of the Motor Activities Training Program (MATP), a sport program for athletes with severe intellectual disabilities. Martin is the editor of the journal *Palaestra*, president of the International Federation of Adapted Physical Activity (IFAPA), and a past president of the National Consortium for Physical Education for Individuals with Disabilities (NCPEID).

Catherine Clermont has been an educator for 19 years, with 17 years in the classroom as a health and physical education teacher. In 2015, Catherine became an administrator in the special education department at the Cooperative Middle School in Stratham, New Hampshire. She obtained a bachelor's degree from Colby Sawyer College, a teaching certification in physical education from Plymouth State University, and a master's in education from Southern New Hampshire University. Catherine's accomplishments include NHIAA Athletic Director of the Year and NHAHPERD Teacher of the Year for Adapted Physical Education awards. Catherine designed and implemented the alternative physical education program at the Cooperative Middle School.

Eilleen Cuell received her master's of arts in teaching in health and physical education from the University of New Hampshire. She is currently a health and alternative physical educator at the Cooperative Middle School in Stratham, New Hampshire. Skilled in her profession, Eilleen has collaborated in creating an alternative physical education program for students of all abilities to promote lifelong fitness.

Ann Griffin is an internationally recognized expert in adapted physical education whose creativity and boundless energy inspire all of her students and the teachers she works with. She is currently a consultant in adapted physical education in Cedar Rapids, Iowa.

James Gunther has been an adapted physical education teacher with Norfolk Public Schools in Virginia since 2001. He received his master's degree from Walden University and his bachelor's degree from SUNY Cortland. James was awarded the Virginia Adapted Physical Education Teacher of the Year award (VAHPERD) in 2016.

Justin A. Haegele, PhD, is an assistant professor in the department of human movement sciences at Old Dominion University. Justin received his PhD from The Ohio State University in 2015 and his bachelor's and master's degrees from SUNY College at Brockport. He is an accomplished scholar in adapted physical education and has published numerous articles in national and international physical education and disability–related academic journals. Justin has been the recipient of several prestigious awards, including the 2015 David P. Beaver Adapted Physical Activity Young Scholar award (NCPEID) and the 2012 New York State Adapted Physical Education Teacher of the Year award (NYSAHPERD).

Sean Healy, PhD, is an assistant professor of adapted physical activity in the department of behavioral health and nutrition at the University of Delaware. He teaches a variety of undergraduate and graduate courses related to adapted physical education and inclusive recreation and is responsible for the supervision of master's thesis work. Sean's research focuses on the biopsychosocial variables influencing the health behaviors of children with disabilities and the use of remote coaching to promote health.

Cathy Houston-Wilson, PhD, has been at SUNY College at Brockport for the past 23 years, teaching classes in adapted physical education and pedagogy at both the undergraduate and graduate levels. She has also held numerous administrative positions and currently serves as chair of her department. Prior to this, Cathy worked in a residential facility for individuals with severe disabilities and also as an itinerant adapted physical education teacher. She is a frequent speaker at conferences, provides in-service training to educators, and has numerous publications to her credit. She resides in Clarendon, New York, with her husband and three children and is an avid yogi.

Mary A. Hums, PhD, is a professor of sport administration at the University of Louisville. She has worked four at Paralympic Games as well as the Para-Pan American

Games and the Olympic Games. Her research focuses on promoting opportunities for people with disabilities and also sport and human rights. Her honors include being named a North American Society for Sport Management Zeigler Lecturer and an Erasmus Mundus International Visiting Scholar.

Aija Klavina, PhD, is a professor and chief researcher at the Latvian Academy of Sport Education in Riga, Latvia. She received a PhD in education from the University of Virginia in 2007. Her research interests are collaborative teaching instructions, peer tutoring, and measures of indicators for participation in daily physical activity for children with disabilities. She is a chief of the Latvian Disabled Children and Youth Sport Federation and a board member of the Latvian Paralympic Committee. Aija has supervised more than 30 national and international project grants on topics related to adapted physical activity and inclusive education. She also has been on the board of directors of the European Federation of Adapted Physical Activities since 2014. She has published in both special education and adapted physical education journals.

David G. Lorenzi, PhD, is an associate professor in the department of kinesiology, health, and sport science at Indiana University of Pennsylvania, where he also serves as the director of the Special Needs Activity Program. David is a Certified Adapted Physical Educator (CAPE) and has taught adapted physical activity, education, and aquatics for over 20 years. During his career, he has presented and published in the areas of adapted physical activity, education, and aquatics on topics such as assessment, inclusion, and teaching strategies related to working with individuals with disabilities in physical activity settings.

Sheyla G. Martinez-Rivera currently serves as an adapted physical education professor at the University of Puerto Rico at Bayamon. With a focus on autism spectrum disorder and a passion for pretend play, gymnastics, and rhythm, Sheyla completed her graduate studies at SUNY College at Brockport. Prior to studying at SUNY College at Brockport, Sheyla played professional basketball in Puerto Rico.

Matthew Mescall is an adapted physical education and health teacher and athletic coach at the Maryland School for the Blind (MSB), where he coaches swimming, goalball, and track and field. He was nominated by his supervisors as the POSB (Principals of Schools for the Blind) 2015 Outstanding Teacher of Students Who Are Blind or Visually Impaired. Matthew has worked with the United States Association of Blind Athletes on training camps and goalball clinics nationally and internationally, including a state-sponsored trip to Russia. He is the codirector of MSB's Camp Abilities, a one-week educational sport camp for children who are blind or visually impaired, and has been a specialist at Camp Abilities Alaska. Matthew is a 2011 graduate of SUNY College at Brockport, where he was awarded the Adapted Physical Activity Council's National Most Outstanding Undergraduate of the Year.

Nancy Miller is a loving wife and mother and a devoted educator who resides on the New Hampshire seacoast. She graduated from Montclair State University with a bachelor's degree in physical education and earned a graduate certificate in adaptive physical education from the University of New Hampshire. Nancy has 27 years of teaching experience, encompassing kindergarten through 12th grade. In 2014, Nancy was awarded the New Hampshire Elementary Physical Education Teacher of the Year award from NHAHPERD. In addition to teaching at the elementary level, Nancy also enjoys coaching the elementary school's jump rope, cross country, and golf teams.

Thomas E. Moran, PhD, is an associate professor in the department of kinesiology at James Madison University. His specialty area is adapted physical education. Thomas's passion stems from his personal experiences as an individual with cerebral palsy. His scholarly work revolves around two areas: (1) addressing barriers to community-based participation for individuals with disabilities and (2) providing educators, coaches, and instructors with a systematic approach to adequately meet the needs of individuals of all abilities, including disabilities. He is the executive director of Empowerment3, the Center for Physical Activity and Wellness for Underserved Youth. A highly successful program of the center is Overcoming Barriers, a physical activity mentoring program that provides 16 programs each semester that serve more than 200 children, adolescents, and adults with disabilities in school- and community-based settings.

Debbie Phillips is a graduate of West Chester University with a degree in health, physical education, and adapted physical education. She also studied special education at Immaculata College. She has worked for the Chester County Intermediate Unit 24 in Chester County, Pennsylvania, for 15 years. She has experience in teaching elementary and middle school emotional support, and she coordinates an adapted physical education program for K-12 students at the Child and Career Development Center in Chester County. She is also a coordinator for the Special Olympics program for her school and county-wide programs.

Joy Rose is an instructional assistant at Seattle public schools.

Amaury Samalot-Rivera, PhD, was born and raised in Puerto Rico and received his bachelor's degree in secondary physical education from the University of Puerto Rico at Mayaguez. He completed his master's and doctorate degrees in sport and exercise education with a specialization in adapted physical education at Ohio State University. Currently he is an assistant professor in the physical education teaching preparation program at SUNY College at Brockport. His areas of interest and scholarship are the development of appropriate behaviors through physical education and sport, advocacy of diversity through physical education, and the transition of students with disabilities from school to the community.

Brad M. Weiner is a physical educator and an adapted physical educator in Maryland. He earned his bachelor's and master's degrees from SUNY Cortland. In 2013, Mr. Weiner was named the national adapted physical education teacher of the year. He has been the secretary and vice president for the National Consortium for Physical Education for Individuals with Disabilities (NCPEID) and the vice president and president for Maryland's Adapted Physical Education Consortium (MAPEC). He achieved national certification through Adapted Physical Education National Standards and the National Board Professional Teacher Standards, and he has certifications in administration and special education.

Morgan Wescliff is an instructional assistant at Seattle public schools.

Wesley J. Wilson is a doctoral student in the adapted physical education program at the University of Virginia. His research focuses on issues surrounding the least restrictive environment and the placement of students with disabilities, as well as the socialization of adapted physical educators. Wesley also serves as the assistant director of the Lifetime Physical Activity program in the Curry School of Education.

Eli A. Wolff is the codirector of the Royce Fellowship for Sport and Society program at Brown University and codirects the Power of Sport Lab, a platform to fuel and magnify innovation, inclusion, and social change through sport. Eli is also the mentoring coordinator at Partners for Youth with Disabilities based in Boston. He was a member of the United States Paralympic Soccer Team in the 1996 and 2004 Paralympic Games and has a master's degree in sport studies from the German Sport University of Cologne.